MW00800646

WORLD'S BEST

WORLD'S BEST

RIC CHARLESWORTH

www.riccharlesworth.com

Laura, I hope its of interest.
Thank you for inviting me to
Canada.

Ric Charlesworth.
Ottawa 2019.

RC Sports

Dedication…to all the Hockeyroos and Kookaburras who love
this game and seek to be special.

Copyright © Richard Charlesworth 2017
All rights reserved. No part of this book may be reproduced or transmitted in any form
or by any means, electronic or mechanical, including photocopying, recording or by any
information storage and retrieval system, without prior permission in writing from
the publisher.

National Library of Australia Cataloguing-in-Publication data

Creator: Charlesworth, Ric, 1952- author.
Title: World's best / Ric Charlesworth.
ISBN: 9780994641823 (paperback)
ISBN: 9780994641830 (ebook)

Subjects: Charlesworth, Ric, 1952-
Hockey coaches--Australia--Biography.
Hockey--Tournaments--Australia.
Hockey--Coaching--Australia.

Dewey Number: 796.355092

Typeset in 11/16 pt Palatino: Pickawoowoo Publishing Group
Cover design: Pickawoowoo Publishing Group

Every endeavour has been made to source the photographs and to contact the
copyright holders to obtain the necessary permission for use of photographic and quote
material used in this book. Any person or organisation that may have been inadvertently
overlooked should contact the publisher.

CONTENTS

INTRODUCTION

I grew up in perhaps one of the most isolated cities in the world, Perth Western Australia. I went to a primary school where we had a teacher who took us for hockey. We had no other schools to play against so we played fixtures against 16 and 17-year-old girls from local private schools.

Hockey was my greatest passion for as long as I can remember and I aspired to play in the Olympics – to win there and at the World Cup, our sport's biggest stages, would be amazing things to achieve.

As a player I fell short at the Olympics, losing an Olympic final and twice losing in the semi-finals. I played in the first Australian team that won the World Cup in 1986 and my life moved to other things. I had a life outside sport and a family to support.

Almost accidentally, life took a twist and I found myself back in the game working in the same place, Perth, trying to build teams that could be world's best. In my 14 years as a national coach my teams played in four World Cups and three Olympic Games. We won in Dublin, Atlanta, Utrecht, Sydney, New Delhi and The Hague. Once we fell short of the gold target. In London in 2012 we finished third (with bronze) after losing the semi-final to Germany.

So what was happening in this little node of excellence in Perth – how and why did these teams emerge to be world's best?

This book is unashamedly about being exceptional. While the title may seem presumptuous, in our sport my aim was always to set ambitious targets and stretch goals for the individuals and teams I coached. Our ambition was always to seek more, do better, to reach a level of personal and team performance that previously seemed unobtainable. My focus was less on individuals than on teams, although it is clear that great teams are replete with brilliant individuals. Coaches of great teams certainly also coach the special individuals who make up those teams.

I will outline some of the ways we went about chasing those dreams and extending ourselves. I will also outline some of the difficulties and pitfalls involved and how coaching and the quest to be world's best can go well or go wrong.

So what is exceptional? Perhaps it is encapsulated in the Jim Collins best seller *Good to Great*. Collins suggests the difference between good and great is easily measurable but not easily attained – only a few make the grade. The pathway to greatness is a considered, conscious action on the part of those who seek it. Exceptional is a performance, act, work or stance that takes one outside what we call 'normal' behaviour, outcomes or experience. It is unusual, often unorthodox and usually very difficult and challenging; it is special.

Mostly, we pass along the trajectory of our life staying comfortable, in control, not extending ourselves. Exceptional is uncomfortable, testing, difficult, often controversial and can be downright dangerous. We can look at examples outside sport. Is a whistle-blower exceptional? I would suggest the answer is often "yes".

Daniel Ellsberg brought on Watergate and helped accelerate the end of the Vietnam War. He suffered retaliation from the Nixon administration. Edward Snowden, who at the time of writing had been trapped in Russia since 2013, is a former CIA operative and whistle-blower. Chelsea Manning and Julian Assange are further examples of whistle-blowers who have forfeited their liberty to expose the truth. They have taken an exceptional route, yet hardly a comfortable one.

Had Tony Blair or John Howard had an epiphany in 2003 and realised the folly of an Iraq invasion, it would have taken them into a position of discomfort and difficulty with their greatest ally but probably would have been the right thing to do. Sir John Chilcot's recent revelations (July, 2016) outline that folly and how it unfolded.

In November 2015, in *The Australian* newspaper under the heading "Group think biggest risk to corporate growth", John Brogden, chief executive of the Australian Institute of Directors (AICD) bemoaned the fact that boards and board members often went along with strategy and decisions they didn't entirely support. At many levels it can be difficult and uncomfortable to disagree with those above you in status or power.

In sport, the quest for the exceptional is ubiquitous but the examples of exceptionality are much less obvious. Many seek 'exceptional' status; only a few attain it. Many are very good but few are exceptional and outstanding.

Lance Armstrong sought to be the world's best in cycling but lost his way. Michel Platini was an exceptional player but appears to have lost his way as an administrator amidst FIFA scandals. Questions are now being asked of Sebastian Coe as he wrestles with the practices and oversight of world athletics. Certainly former AFL Essendon coach, James Hird, sought an exceptional pathway for his club and was led astray. Perhaps the recent All Blacks are an example of a sporting team with exceptional performances. On a domestic scale the Hawthorn football team is up there. Usain Bolt, Lionel Messi, Roger Federer, Novak Djokovic, Serena Williams and LeBron James are all individuals who meet the criteria of the modern icons. Importantly, the performances of those individuals are ones with sustained and enduring legacies.

The quest to be exceptional is ubiquitous and akin to the Holy Grail in the sporting world or in most fields of endeavour. What are the elements required to be exceptional? In this book I will examine some of these elements. Skills, hard work, fine strategies and resilience are all part of it, but over and above these things is culture. I believe 'Culture trumps strategy' every time and so, unashamedly, I spend some time on this. It is a constant theme of this book and a message that underpins intrinsically resilient and consistently high performing teams.

Each individual needs to be able to deliver his or her best consistently. Together, the individuals have to work with and for one another to ensure that, regardless of some things going wrong and disappointments emerging, individuals failing or mistakes being made, the core performance is still exceptional.

I spent eight years coaching the national women's team from 1993 to 2000 and subsequently spent time in Australia, Italy, New Zealand and India writing about and working in and around sport. At the end of 2008 on returning from the subcontinent I was ready to start coaching again.

For the next six years I assumed the role of head coach of the Kookaburras (our national men's hockey team). The position was initially for the four-year Olympic cycle that characterises the normal appointment regime. After our triumphant 2010 season (the team won the World Cup, Champions Trophy and Commonwealth Games gold medal) then chief executive Mark Anderson was keen for me to extend my term, and at the time I could only see myself going for another two years after London. As time passed, and in spite of the opportunity to continue to Rio in 2016, I formed the view that for me and for the team, 2014 was an appropriate exit point – teams need to be refreshed and coaches need to be fresh.

When I stepped down in June, 2014 after our emphatic World Cup victory in The Hague, our team had clearly again confirmed our world's best status.

In the six years with the Kookaburras, we had one major slip up. Our loss to Germany in London's semi-final took us off the top of the podium for the only time in that period with the team. That London 'nadir' led to a period of intense introspection and 2013 saw the Kookaburras recovering and renewing. The mistakes of London and that period receive much attention in my chapters on the Kookaburras.

The mistakes I made, the soft spots in our culture, the vulnerabilities that were revealed in the intensity of a London semi-final are discussed. Of course no team is bulletproof. All have their own peculiar foibles, their strengths and weaknesses, and all make mistakes. The aim is to limit these and to establish mechanisms whereby the actions of one player can be covered by others and counterbalanced by teammates who are ever vigilant and alert.

The cauldron of competition at a World Championship or Olympic Games tests teams and exposes their deficiencies and can bring you down. In the semi-final or final there is no safety net – on that day you must perform.

In my time as a national coach my teams played in 21 games that were finals or semi-finals at the Olympic Games, World Cup or Champions Trophies. I could include four such games in the Commonwealth Games but these competitions did not include the absolute cream of competition (simply, the standard is lower). We did win those four games but I have not included them in the list. In those 21 games the Hockeyroos and the Kookaburras were successful 20 times. That loss was the semi-final game in London. Accordingly, the lessons from London represented critical reminders as to what was needed on such occasions.

Besides the focus on the Kookaburras and my coaching philosophy, there are a number of personal reflections on my time between coaching the Hockeyroos and the Kookaburras. During that time I worked at Fremantle Football Club and lived in Italy, New Zealand and India, where in each place the experiences were rich in learning.

Additionally, I present some of my observations about championship and some of our sport's most recent champions and the direction of sport in a corporate world. My observations of public life as an outsider to the political life of a nation come after some very turbulent years in Australian politics. Teamwork may not be in the political lexicon of the nation but perhaps it should be!

In 1994, when I was a new coach I asked Neil McLean to recommend someone who might be able to work with me on the women's team. Neil at the time was the pre-eminent practitioner in sport psychology in Western Australia and worked with Fremantle Football Club, Perth Wildcats, many professional golfers and the Kookaburras under coach Frank Murray. He suggested one of his post-graduate students, Corinne Reid, who came to the Hockeyroos fresh and without any preconceptions, limited interest in sport and no knowledge of hockey. She was training and working in clinical psychology and research.

During my time with the Hockeyroos Corinne became an integral part of my coaching team. She did not attend the 1994 World Cup (we did have some long telephone conversations!), yet she was subsequently at all our major events. Her insight, far superior to mine, as an observer of human behaviour and interpreter of team dynamics, added immeasurably to the quality of the team's evolution and eventual emergence as a truly outstanding group that became 'bulletproof' in the major events.

Hence, I have invited Corinne to contribute two chapters to this book that I believe add an outsider's view of the workings of high-performance teams. She worked with us and observed us and is ideally placed to contribute. Her two contributions are "Come to the Edge" and "The Excellence Delusion". In the first she puts herself in the role of observer and participant in an evolutionary process that she was guiding, and she observes the coaching evolution with great insight.

"The Excellence Delusion" outlines the journey of the team after our London disappointment and the transformation we tried to undertake leading into the World Cup two years later. Corinne and her assistants, Catherine Campbell and Vance Locke, undertook this process in which the demons of 2012 were confronted and discarded as we endeavoured to build a new, more resilient and challenging culture. Many times along the way we despaired at our progress yet by mid-2014 our performances suggested we had made great progress. This chapter is in my view the best writing in this book and one of the most insightful pieces of writing in coaching.

It is my view that the area of most competitive advantage in sport comes in the dimension of human behaviour. Our ability to enable individuals and teams to perform at their peak is necessary for exceptionality. Clearly, exceptionality can be stressful, difficult and uncomfortable. The emphasis on maximising our ability to cope, embrace and thrive there is at least as important as specialists in technical areas – strength and conditioning, biomechanics, rehabilitation, goal-keeping, rucking, goal kicking, etc. Nobody is more important, in my view, than a specialist in human behaviour.

Sport has progressed mightily in the past two decades. I think it was in 1997 that I was invited by Australian Cricket Coach Geoff Marsh to attend a coaching seminar at the Melbourne Cricket Ground (MCG). My brief was to 'Stir the Possum' – I was invited to challenge the orthodoxy of that environment.

I made the observation that as coach of the Hockeyroos I had a budget for our sport of about $2.5M. My support staff included; assistant coaches, specialist coaches (e.g. goal-keeping), a physiologist, a physiotherapist, a psychologist, a bio-mechanist, along with strength and conditioning expertise. Career and education personnel were also available. On the other hand, Geoff Marsh and cricket, at that stage had about $70M in annual revenue, and only three people helping him improve the players. I suggested it was time cricket became serious about improving their talent and embraced some of the practices that characterised other high-performance sports. Geoff made some inroads but it was not until the much-maligned John Buchanan came along that cricket started to seriously develop its analysis and practices to reach the level of player support and development that was possible. Viewing cricket from a distance today I imagine the environment is vastly different.

After our fall in London in 2012, Corinne's availability and return was important in the rebuilding of our damaged team. In my book *The Coach: Managing for Success,* I touched on 'mens sana in copore sana' (a healthy mind in a healthy body). In *World's Best* I outline further how critical this is. We had work to do rebuilding our damaged group after London and Corinne's return was central to that process. I firmly believe that central to outstanding team performance is mature, candid and continuous connection between the members of the team. A willingness to challenge and co-operate has to be real and open.

In Leo Tolstoy's *War and Peace* there is an interesting exchange that occurs between Prince Andrei and some soldiers before going into battle against Napoleon's forces at Borodino.

"And yet they say that war is like a game of chess?" Pierre remarked.

"Yes," replied Prince Andrei, "but with this little difference, that in chess you may think over each move as long as you please and are not limited for time, and with this difference too, that a knight is always stronger than a pawn, and two pawns are always stronger than one, while in war a battalion is sometimes stronger than a division and sometimes weaker than

a company. The relative strength of bodies of troops can never be known to anyone."

Andrei does not trust the generals and strategists in the Russian army...

"I consider that on us tomorrow's battle will depend and not on those others... Success never depends, and never will depend, on position, or equipment, or even on numbers, and least of all on position."

"But on what then?"

"On the feeling that is in me and in him," he pointed to Timokhin, *"and in each soldier.*

"...the battle is won by those who firmly resolve to win it."

Tolstoy, Leo. *War and Peace*, Chapter XXV

Tolstoy was, of course, an astute observer of human nature and understood the dynamics of human interaction and performance. This great novel endures for the quality of its philosophy as much as for the story line and plot. The parallels are obvious. Decisions on the sporting field often must be made at the blink of an eye and the relative strengths of players and teams changes all the time. It is often chaotic in the heat of the contest, and without players making good decisions, solving problems for themselves or co-operating boldly you cannot succeed. Without really committed and determined athletes the battle will be lost no matter what the strategy.

I have heard it suggested that sporting outcomes are determined like chess matches. Indeed, the media seem to be stuck in this notion of strategy and tactics provided from above. "All knowing coaches implementing strategies and plans through their athletes determine the result."

This suggestion is of course foolish, for every team has its strengths and foibles, every player can be vulnerable, fail, make mistakes or have a bad game. Every plan has an antidote and every ploy and scheme can be countered. In the end, of course, the athletes need the prerequisite skill, tactical nous and fitness to enact a strategy or game plan.

But that is never enough. The best teams contain individuals with the determination to see the task through. They never give up and they work together to achieve success. Indeed, the strength of the best teams depends on the resilience of individuals. It is only by working together that the group can succeed. The challenge is to marshal the resources of all the individuals, and when anyone falls short their teammates have to be there to help. If they feel the strength of each other it fortifies the individual and the group.

That is exceptional.

While *winning* and *performance* may be the core to this book, it is my intention also to describe how my journey continued in sport after the Olympic Games in Sydney, which at the turn of the millennium had been the centre of my focus.

After Sydney I had the opportunity to coach the Kookaburras but felt I needed a break. Hockey Australia offered me a year respite but the next World Cup was in March of 2002 and so I felt it would be unfair on the players too, not to be full-time. I declined the offer.

Subsequently, I spent time in the AFL as a consultant, with Fremantle Football Club and worked with the Australian Institute of Sport (AIS) as a mentor coach and spent time in Italy while doing some consulting in soccer and rugby and wrote my third book, *Shakespeare the Coach*.

On returning to Australia in 2004 and with the Kookaburras successful in Athens I was looking elsewhere. An opportunity to work with cricket in New Zealand proved interesting and from 2005-07 I enjoyed my New Zealand experience in another sport.

When my option to continue in New Zealand was to be considered I received two different opportunities. One was from the English Cricket Board and the other via the International Hockey Federation (FIH) to work in India. Much to the consternation of my family and after much wrangling with Indian hockey administrators I chose the subcontinental option.

Unfortunately, the experience was a difficult one, as I will outline, but what it did do was return me to the hockey environment, and on my return to Australia in 2008 I was afforded the opportunity to work with the Kookaburras. It is a great honour to be given the chance to coach one's national team, and the record of my time spent with the Kookaburras will, I hope, enable me to contextualise my coaching philosophy in the pages of a book such as this.

PART 1

KOOKABURRAS

1

V I G I L A N C E ...

As we approached the London Olympics I was acutely aware of the need to keep pushing for continual improvement. In early 2011 at our camp in Mandurah, an hour south of Perth, I set out a range of aims. I had always said Olympic medals are won in the year before. It is the quality of preparation in that year that underpins an Olympic performance. Among the list of aims set out were:

1. *The need to develop real perspective.* Winning at major events is not the normal outcome (most teams don't win). This requires an appreciation that it is possible but also a realisation that it will require exceptional performances to do it.

2. *The need to know one another better.* This I believed entailed a deeper and more informed and nuanced understanding of what made each of us tick and how we might behave under pressure.

3. *The need to align our behaviours.* I wanted us all to sign up to a list of critical behaviours, which would see us never seek to cut corners or take short cuts in our preparation. What we did in 2011 was of paramount importance. The behaviours would be generated by team discussion during the camp. It would be for the players to own and enact it.

4. *The need to keep pushing for improvement.* 2011 had to be a year in which we continued to challenge our practices and methods if we were to build on what had been achieved in the first two years.

At the time a very ill Steve Jobs was in the news and I remember including in our discussions comment about how Jobs had talked about living every day as though it was your last.

Another widely reported Jobs' quote was; *"remembering that you are going to die is the best way I know to avoid the trap of thinking you have something to lose".* It is a call to be bold and daring and embark on every day with purpose, vibrancy and curiosity – essential ingredients for learning and improving.

My message in the discussions that took place those eighteen months before London was that our aim was to be outstanding as a team. We were far from that because we needed to improve every aspect of our game to be 'bulletproof' in London. 2010 had been full of successes, winning at the World Cup, Champions Trophy and Commonwealth Games.

However, I knew by London a '2010-level performance' would not be enough... I knew it yet the great challenge of coaching is for the players to 'know and believe it too'. Hence the need for perspective as to where we actually were and how fragile our performance could be. I understood we needed to know one another better, and I was keen for a real commitment to critical behaviours and an open environment in which we could challenge our ways and practices.

Complacency and self-satisfaction can be insidious and it was what I feared most. Not that we might not be fit enough or skilled enough – that was the easy bit. The hard bit was to get your teeth into what made teams truly great. It was not sports science, technique refinement, great fitness or special tactics. Of course, that was needed. But mostly what was needed was a deep and sophisticated understanding of one another. The signatures of each team member and their likely actions and responses to the many ups and downs that were ahead of us – ups and downs that occur every day and which would surely pop up in London.

In 2011, we would have a challenging year with plenty of those ups and downs. I initiated a number of sessions on 'critical conversations' and we undertook an exercise on psychological profiling of our athletes. This provided the opportunity for them to open up about their thinking and fears and problems. While we made some progress I was a little uneasy about our readiness for London. We had most of the technical aspects under control but were we searching enough internally?

Throughout my life I have been ambitious for more. Probably I took on too much and indeed I think multitasking may be a formula for doing a lot of stuff not so well. The beauty of my time as a national coach was that it afforded me the chance to be really excellent in one area and to never die wondering about what else could have been. The feeling that life was a continual search for better leads to an urgency and rigour that underpins a daily recognition of how lucky we are to be alive and to be afforded the opportunities available to us.

A look back into the past certainly helps remind us of our good fortune. In 2009 on tour in Europe we spent time in France and Belgium where the tragedy of World War I was exposed to us. It is almost unfathomable that on one day at Fromelles more than 5000 young Australians lost their lives, were captured or maimed. It is impossible to visit these places and not recognise the folly of young lives cut short.

When one walks through Kings Park, a magnificent legacy of Perth's forefathers, you pass majestic gum trees planted along the road. In front of each tree is a plaque that remembers a fallen soldier from wars and days gone by. It is a sobering reminder of our mortality and of the fortune that we have lived beyond our teens.

So many who served did not get to have even that modest measure of life that comes from reaching one's twenties.

All of us who are healthy and have had the chance to live long and full lives ought to feel fortunate for the opportunity we have been afforded. This is especially so of those of us who were fortunate enough to grow up in Australia and who have had lives free of the violence and disruption that is the reality in many places in the world.

I have always felt very fortunate in this regard and as I feel myself hurtling towards the inevitable fate (which none of us can avoid) I sometimes ponder the messages on those plaques and what they mean for those who were left behind. It is so true that the loss and emptiness that accompanies such calamity very often shapes the lives of those left behind.

Easily my worst day was January 15, 1980, the day my father suddenly died at 63. A day, in which he went to work, came home, lay down on his bed and died of a massive heart attack. I was bereft as were the rest of the family, my mother in particular. Her death at 96, nearly 34 years later, was unhappy but expected as she had been fragile for a long time.

The death of my eldest brother a month after my mother on Christmas day 2013 really shocked me and again reinforced the reality of what limited time we have and how suddenly it can be over.

As a young resident doctor I saw quite a lot of death, and indeed from the time of first studying anatomy in the laboratory, one becomes acquainted with death but often in a detached way. At the Queen Elizabeth II Medical Centre (QE11), while working in the emergency department, one of the tasks was to certify as dead those killed in car accidents.

Regularly, you would be called down to the arrival bay where your job was to confirm the death of a young teenager who was the victim of a motorcycle or car accident. When you inquired about the circumstances of the death it was often speed or error of judgement that contributed to the fatality. Sometimes, substance abuse or alcohol were contributing factors. Given these chilling lessons I always avoided motorcycles!

In my time as a resident doctor working in the QEII medical centre I saw such pain up close, and although not directly in contact with it as family members, maybe it scratched the surface and sometimes reached deep inside.

While reading Atul Gawande's book, *The Checklist Manifesto: How to Get Things Right,* I was reminded of such a case that for nearly forty years has been in the back of my consciousness. Indeed, at a recent reunion of my graduating class – as we discussed our stories of our journeys in medicine – it seemed all of us had such cases in our memories that informed the way in which we had trained and which framed our approach to medicine and its practice. My practical career had been shorter than most but still there were defining experiences.

Gawande described a case that a fellow surgeon recalled wherein a patient arrived in the emergency department with a stab wound after an altercation at a costume party. He appeared stable and comfortable and was talking...perhaps intoxicated. He would need to go to the operating theatre to be sure the abdominal wound had not damaged his bowel. There was time to prepare him for surgery. It was not urgent.

It was only when the nurse noticed he had stopped babbling and his pulse started to race and blood pressure fell that they rapidly went into emergency mode and 'crashed' into the operating theatre. In a life and death scramble they found a belly full of blood and a puncture in the aorta lying to the left of the spinal column deep in the abdomen. The assailant's knife had passed through skin, fat, muscle, then passed the intestine to the paravertebral space. Their immediate action enabled them to stop the bleeding and fortunately the patient survived. A few more seconds could have been fatal.

Everything had been done correctly yet nobody had asked about the weapon. It turned out it had been a bayonet…the other guy at the party had been dressed as a soldier – with a bayonet! One surgeon commented that he had not seen such an injury since Vietnam. It was not what you usually saw in San Francisco. Vigilance must be the catchcry of those who want to eliminate error and seek perfection.

In medical training in the 70s, our teacher, surgeon George Pestall, set the mantra of 'eternal vigilance' for the young medical students under his tutelage, but the message was underlined in 1977 when as an intern at QEII I experienced a case that resembled that outlined by Gawande.

When I read the account I immediately recalled a young schoolboy, Luke Holland, who lost his life one evening in October, 1977. Luke's vehicle was involved in a collision with a negligent driver that evening. He arrived in the emergency department around 9pm and I was assigned to examine him. He was sitting up on a gurney and described his chest pains and we talked about school and sport. There was considerable bruising. As I recall his vital signs were stable and we determined to send him for a chest x-ray. While attending Luke I spoke with some family members by phone and indicated what had happened and his condition. My shift was coming to an end.

I last saw him as he was wheeled to the elevator to go for the x-ray. The emergency department was situated in the old Sir Charles Gairdner hospital building and the x-ray department was on the fourth floor. At the time the hospital was trying to establish its emergency credentials and was not, in my view, equipped for major trauma. Apparently, Luke had a catastrophic bleed, could not be resuscitated and died that evening. I was informed of this the next morning.

I remembered these events when I read the piece written by Gawande as there was a resonance in the presentation. However, in Luke's case it was much more personal as when examining him

I discovered he was a student in his final year at my old school Christ Church Grammar where he was the cricket team's most successful batsman and an all-round athlete and student, full of potential and enthusiasm. Many have later told me what an outstanding character and leader Luke was at the school.

The tragedy of Luke's death brought unfathomable grief to his parents and siblings and even to a school. Every such death affects all who are within range. John Donne's meditations brought forth the oft-repeated quote, "*...any man's death diminishes me, because I am involved in mankind; and therefore never send to know for whom the bell tolls; it tolls for thee*". That I still reflect in anguish at what happened that day is part of my life's learning.

I have often over the years reflected on how I, amongst others, may have failed Luke that evening. Did we miss a vital clue? Was the speed and nature of the collision taken into account? Should we have sent him to the x-ray department on the fourth floor at that time? Was he sufficiently stable?

Of course, had not a negligent driver played a part he may well have been with us today. Luke as an alert and skilled young driver would likely have had the reflexes to avoid most circumstances so was unfortunately in the wrong place at the wrong time. He was very unlucky. So fragile and serendipitous our lives can be. Yet what it did confirm in me was the message of old George Pestall that the "price of life is eternal vigilance".

Today, Luke's name is close to mine on the batting honour board in the pavilion overlooking the school oval at Mount Claremont where a plaque on the wall also remembers his life. On reading Gawande's introduction I undertook to right a wrong from that time nearly forty years ago. I was able to track down Luke's parents and share my recollection of that day while also expressing my regrets for not at least making contact with them in the days following that tragic night.

I was surprised to hear that this was the first and only time anyone from the hospital had provided any feedback to the family. At the time as a junior doctor one's seniors looked after such matters. Indeed, when I think back on those events there was never even a perfunctory debriefing of the case such was the training load and postgraduate teaching practice at that time. When I now look at the diligence with which I insist the team scrutinises sporting results it seems totally inadequate.

In *The Coach* I outlined why I thought vigilance was central to a successful coaching philosophy. It is something that accompanies life and ensures we give ourselves the best opportunity to thrive, develop and advance. A friend in the petroleum exploration and production industry used to talk of 'chronic unease', a state of continual discomfort about the risks inherent in his industry.

Perhaps the worst circumstance I think any of us can imagine is the death of a child. It reaches into our hearts and triggers emptiness and profound feelings of loss and grief. It lasts and the sorrow sinks deep into our being. Living opposite a cemetery I walk most days and read the gravestones. The messages convey heart-rending sadness. I am reminded of the words of the bard in the play *King John* when Constance laments the loss of her son Arthur. Grief might eventually go away yet few avoid the acute pain and constant reminders that accompany it.

> *"Grief fills the room up of my absent child,*
> *Lies in his bed, walks up and down with me,*
> *Puts on his pretty looks, repeats his words,*
> *Remembers me of all his gracious parts,*
> *Stuffs out his vacant garments with his form:*
> *Then have I reason to be fond of grief?"*

I pray that I might never experience such sorrow and pain, and hence I have always preached vigilance to my children in everything they are involved in. I imagine for them this may have been stifling yet I hope it is a message delivered in the context of them always being willing to try new things and take calculated risks. Yet always calculating risk.

We can all find ourselves in the wrong place at the wrong time and suffer the consequences of what is simply rotten luck. Yet, with vigilance we lessen the odds of being unlucky. Call it eternal vigilance, or as some in the mining industry call it 'chronic unease', it is prudent to be constantly looking out for that which might bring you down.

So, from the sombre we move to the sporting field. In truth I could fill the pages of this book with the stories of sporting folly contributed to by carelessness and lack of vigilance. Just as in a few moments a life can be lost, so too in a few moments the sporting contest can slip from your grasp and you are left wondering 'how' and 'what if'? For me it is a lesson for life and the bedrock coaching issue for any of us seeking exceptional performances.

The balance between risk and reward accompanies every endeavour, and when it is a grand adventure or project it is always a necessary calculation. The real discipline of elite performers is to apply the same rigour to what appear mundane and every day activities. This vigilance is not stifling as it can become automatic – a habit. In the words of Aristotle, "we are what we continually do, excellence is not an act it is a habit".

Perhaps a recent example of what I mean was viewed far and wide in Australia last year when the Brisbane Broncos led the North Queensland Cowboys with only seconds to play in the grand final of the rugby league competition. The match was decided in extra time after the North Queensland Cowboys tied the game in the last seconds of normal time.

On the last tackle in the count, with seconds to play, it looked as though the Brisbane players just relaxed a little rather than finish the game with one resounding last tackle. This allowed the ball to be kept alive and for Michael Morgan to deliver a clever pass and The Cowboys took the game to extra time. North Queensland won it with a drop goal in extra time.

A month or so later when I spoke with Wayne Bennett I could still feel the pain and frustration that accompanies such a moment. The plan and its execution had been good enough to give them victory that evening. Just moments of indecision or failure to see the game through had taken away the prize.

It reminded me of what I called 'Totti's folly' when fifteen years earlier his moment of laziness had led to Italy losing the final of the European Football Championships. Italy had the game in their grasp with only seconds to play. Francesco Totti, one of Italy's greatest players, just sauntered back to his position after a ball went past him and as he took his time the next pass to him found him offside.

The quickly taken free by France's goalkeeper found an attacker who scored the equaliser. Had Totti not been 'offside' the quick free kick would have been taken some thirty meters further from the French goal and the outcome would have been entirely different! France went on to win that game, again in extra time. These episodes are everywhere when you care to look for them.

In the Beijing Olympic Games I saw the Netherlands suffer a similar lapse in the semi-final against Germany in 2008. Scoring with three minutes to play they catastrophically allowed an equaliser because they failed to be alert and attentive to a dangerous overlapping defender with nothing to lose! Vigilance that makes you see the task right through to the end is critical. Without it there can never be world's best performances.

Atul Gawande's checklist has been part of the answer in medicine to improve the outcomes from surgery, and its applicability to other fields of endeavour is clear. It is useful in aviation, construction, investment banking and businesses of all kinds. From my perspective I believe it is indispensable in sport. Without the vigilance required, too many mistakes are made, too many short cuts taken and too many opportunities missed.

Without 'eternal vigilance' you do not get world's best performances. It should be emphasised that the vigilance of which I speak is not only unease it is also being aggressively optimistic for opportunities and to take advantage of any situation that can bring you closer to the big prize. It is vigilance for both risks and rewards.

2

BACK INTO THE FRAY

Since leaving my role with the Hockeyroos in 2000 feeling drained and in need of a break, I had always thought the men's job with the Kookaburras might be something I would like to do. I had been asked to consider taking the role back in 2000 by Linden Adamson, then CEO of the men's association (at that time the two were separate entities), but I needed a pause in coaching and went in another direction.

In 2004, after the Kookaburras success in Athens, the position was not available and so four years later while in India the possibility of a return after Beijing was on the radar. I had always had in mind a return to coaching but thinking about it and actually taking the steps to go in that direction is a different matter. Perhaps the difficulties I was facing in India helped make up my mind.

Leaving India...
Throughout the last months of my time in India in 2008, I was continually facing problems and difficulties. Following the failure of India's two teams to qualify for the Olympics in Beijing, there seemed to be a sullenness in the country and negativity about India's hockey future.

My principal frustration was the complete lack of leadership following the demise of Mr Kanwar Pal Singh Gill and K Jothikumaran and it seemed impossible to make any progress. The president and secretary of the Indian Hockey Federation had been dismissed. My position was increasingly unsustainable and financially I was bleeding as the organisation was in disarray.

I believe many of us who grew up in an era where subcontinental teams dominated hockey felt sadness at the decline in the performance of Indian and Pakistani teams over the last three decades. India last won a major championship outside Asia in 1975 in the Kuala Lumpur World Cup if one excludes the 1980 boycotted Olympics, and Pakistan's last moment of glory was in the 1994 World Cup in Sydney where they won a gripping final on penalties.

It is now more than 20 years since a subcontinental team won any major tournament even in the Pakistani inspired Champions Trophy, a tournament they inaugurated back in 1978. They won it in 1978 and 1980 but their last success was in 1994 when they beat Germany on penalties in the final. Runners-up six times in the 80s and 90s since Sydney, they have hardly figured in the main games. India's best is a third way back in 1982.

I went to India with high hopes at the end of 2007 – my remit was to assist and advise as to the things needed for India to revive the game in the country. I was supported by the International Olympic Committee (IOC) and the Federation of International Hockey (FIH) both of which needed India doing well. I was keen to work with those running the game in that capacity. Unfortunately, it was off the field that most of the difficulties manifested themselves.

While cricket dominates the sports scene in India, hockey still held a place in the minds of the nation and had enjoyed government support through the Sports Authority of India (SAI). Unfortunately, the programs were not targeted or of sufficient quality. With 2000 players in centralised programs and positions for approximately

500 professional players in company and government teams India should have been doing better.

There was a need for a great deal of work to be done focussing the resources and lifting the quality of facilities and coaching. It would be a herculean task for an efficient and focused sporting body. It was well beyond the capacity of the Indian Hockey Federation (IHF), which at the time was essentially a fiefdom run by Jothikumaran and KPS Gill. Gill is the legendary 'Super Cop' who had managed the Sikh insurgency in the Punjab so effectively in an earlier time.

Nothing could be done without these two approving it and a further complication was the workings of the SAI. In the main it was their resources that funded programs. The big shift that occurred in Indian sport after the World Cup Cricket triumph in 1983 was that cricket became privatised and hockey, the national game, remained under public sector control.

Unfortunately, a few months into 2008 Jothikumaran and Mr Gill were exposed for taking bribes in a sting operation by an Indian TV station and so the organisation (IHF) became rudderless and in the hands of SAI officials, and an 'ad hoc' Indian Olympic Committee was seemingly unable to make decisions and progress the game. Indian hockey was drifting rudderless and I had chosen to jump off.

In the middle of the year I had decided my position was not working and informed the Indians I would not be continuing. In August I made my way south from Chandigarh for the last time. Indian hockey was drifting rudderless down the Ganges towards the sea, and powerless to steer I chose to jump off and take the family home to Perth. While India was exciting and a challenge I had been defeated by the details of life there. Perhaps as a single person I would have stayed but for the family life in Chandigarh was just too hard. I was disappointed I could not make a difference.

Thankfully, now after nearly another decade and through having some stability and continued support from FIH, India is climbing up the rankings and both teams (men and women) qualified for the Rio Olympics with even a small prospect of a podium for the men!

Again a strongman is in control in Dr Narinder Batra. Their domestic league – the Hockey India League (HIL) – seems to be benefiting the country through the interactions with foreign coaches and players who inhabit the league, and the resources available through India's expanding commercial successes. I believe the local players are increasingly experiencing attitudes and practices that can only, if introduced domestically, enhance the local product.

Back home…

So it was that I returned to Australia in August, 2008. The Olympics were only weeks away and India had not qualified for the first time in living memory. I had nowhere to stay as my house in Perth was leased and for a time we lived at my mother's apartment in Cottesloe, which had recently become vacant. The boys started school and I considered what might be next.

Clearly, I was aware that Barry Dancer was finishing with the Kookaburras and there would be a process whereby different candidates would be vying for the coveted job. I felt ready for a new challenge and with the Beijing Olympics around the corner was preparing to watch our team's progression through that tournament to an anticipated semi-final showdown.

Olympics and World Cups…

The semi-final games at the Olympics or World Cup are the penultimate step on the route to the final. Every four years the chance to be Olympic or World Champion presents itself. In 2008 I was able to watch these games in Beijing. It was the perfect precursor to my return to coaching.

The big hockey tournaments run for two weeks and every game is crucial to secure a top-two position and thus a semi-final spot.

I have heard it said that some enter the tournament pacing themselves to be at their best for the finals. I am surprised at such an approach as it is so easy to find yourself outside the first two in a pool and not in the main games. Indeed that was the fate for Germany in 2000 and 2014.

Since I left the Hockeyroos that exact scenario has been evident now at three consecutive Olympics. In Athens a loss to Germany in the first game proved decisive in failing to make the semis. In Beijing and London the first games were again crucial. Even a great comeback win over Korea (5-4) eventually led to a goal difference insufficient to qualify in Beijing. Then again it was a first game loss to New Zealand in 2012 (albeit a very unlucky loss to a disputed goal) that left the goal difference between New Zealand and Australia the wrong way around.

Yes, of course, the semi-final is a crucial final step but making the semi-final in itself is necessary if one aspires to be Olympic Champion. Australia in the men's game has done this better than any other nation since the synthetic pitch era. They have made the semi-final every time in the nine times they have been at the Olympic Games since 1976. Of the others, the Netherlands have made it eight and Germany seven. Indeed, in 2000 only some freak results on the last day saw the Netherlands – the eventual champions – make the semi-finals.

I don't think the tennis player, golfer or footballer, whatever code, can really understand the Olympic cycle as they have multiple championship opportunities. Perhaps the World Cup in rugby is an equivalent in that sport. Certainly in the AFL there is a grand final every season and in soccer the World Cup (the equivalent) which seems less important than club football to many in the game. Often in the past the preparation for soccer's World Cup has been perfunctory. This seems a pity to me although I believe in recent World Cups this is less the case.

These knockout games at the four yearly event are 'hot' with possibility and importance and there is no second chance. In an hour and a half the outcome is settled. In Beijing in 2008 I was able to watch these matches more relaxed and removed than I could remember.

Hockey Australia had organised for me to go to the Olympics in Beijing to watch the competition there. My presence helped me to get up to speed with the men's scene at that elite level. It was a great opportunity and I was fortunate to share a small apartment not far from the venue with former Hockeyroos Kate Starre and Katrina Powell who were in Beijing assisting Frank Murray who was coaching the Hockeyroos.

Each day I made my way down the road (only about one kilometre) to the venue to watch matches and see the tournament unfold. My tickets were always in a different position so the routine was never the same and I went between the two fields to watch whichever match was of most interest.

The Hockeyroos did not make the semi-finals missing out on goal difference when a rampant China beat Korea 6-1 in a surprise result late in the pool matches. To miss semi-finals on goal difference is indeed a terrible experience – so close yet so far. I felt the palpable disappointment of the players as I saw them trudging out of the venue when their fate was sealed.

In the men's first semi-final, Germany and the Netherlands were in an arm-wrestle and it looked like going to extra time when the Dutch won a penalty corner with only three minutes to play. Taeke Taekema made his way to the circle to take the shot. He was the Netherlands' fearsome penalty corner specialist and leading scorer in the Olympic tournament. Germany ran bravely to block his shot but were beaten by an artifice and the Netherlands scored with a neatly executed deflection. For all intent and purposes, it was over for Germany. They were down 1-0 with three minutes to play.

All day they had made only a few opportunities yet as Germany always do they kept playing and extraordinarily Phillip Zeller appeared in the scoring circle unattended and made an equaliser with seconds left. In extra time, Germany was better but in the end it was Max Weinhold, their brilliant goalkeeper, who prevailed in the shootout when Taekema ironically failed to score from a mere seven meters.

Germany, who had looked solid but not emphatic, had made the Olympic final after being seconds from being out of the tournament. I felt for Roelant Oltmans – his return to coaching the Netherlands senior team was over – yet this group of players had been so close. The margins are often so small.

On that balmy night I made my way to my seat not sure what to expect from Australia and Spain. They had played in Rotterdam a few months earlier in the Champions Trophy final. While Australia won well at the end in Rotterdam it had been a close contest for most of the game. I had predicted these two teams to make the final in Beijing but Australia's draw with Great Britain in the final pool match saw them finish second in their pool and so they faced Spain.

Australia had a lucky start when Des Abbott deflected the ball in from an acute angle, and then after half-time led 2-0 with a great passing goal. I am always uneasy leading by two. Trailing you are at least clear about the task, whereas leading can cause unsureness about how to play. I think we became too keen on defending the lead and as Spain worked themselves back in to the game, the balance shifted until they scored the winning penalty corner with minutes to go.

The detail of the penalty corner was important. Australia lost Rob Hammond to help defend the crucial corner that Spain scored. Hammond, who was always brave and smart, was struck on the knee and had to leave the field after receiving treatment.

Liam De Young ran but to no avail as Santi Freixa scored low to Stephen Lambert's right.

Two days later Australia overwhelmed the Netherlands to take bronze and Germany prevailed over Spain 1-0 when a first-half conversion by Christopher Zeller and resolute defence was enough. Perhaps the Netherlands did not have enough to win yet they had been so close to the final game. Of the medal winners any of them had the ability to be at the top of the podium. As always the margins were slight. I returned to Australia with this message firmly in my mind.

Securing the job...and starting in 2008

After I won the coaching job a month later, one of my first acts, as coach was to visit the Australian players in Europe playing for clubs, mainly in the Netherlands. During the visit we reviewed that match and my principal concern was that we played passively after leading 2-0 after half-time. It is always difficult to have calmness and to keep playing positively in such a situation. It is one of the most important qualities one must have in elite sport. It is not about skill or technique nor fitness or tactics. It is demeanour, calmness and composure. It is a frame of mind and a belief and presence – and most importantly it is not done alone in team sport. You have others who are with you at such times. You all need to be connected to one another by the invisible bonds of knowing and understanding, and by your shared purpose.

Nothing is more important in the big game and I believed the best way to ensure your players understood and knew this was to play in as many big games and finals as one could in the years ahead.

Given the time left in 2008, we decided to gather a development group in Brisbane and looked outside our squad for players who might surprise us – players who had perhaps been overlooked and might have been late developers.

At the 2005 Junior World Cup in Rotterdam, Australia had lost in the final to Argentina yet the cohort group appeared particularly strong and by 2008 those who were in the Olympic team were on track for long careers. Were there some who might have been overlooked?

Our aim, as always, was to hit the ground running in 2009 with matches arranged for January and February. I was keen to look closely at those still in the system who might be worth considering and who might have been on the periphery.

In 2009 there would be a Junior World Cup program and it was likely that those Under-21 would get plenty of exposure. In 2008 I wanted to have the best look at those outside that group and some who maybe had not received the opportunity that every player needs to realise their potential.

I remembered the story of Danni Roche, who when I first saw her in 1994 at the National Championships was playing with Victoria. A skinny young woman, Danni had skill and an attitude.

I was told she was "not good enough". She had been in the team in 1989 and 1991, before I became coach. One day I sat down and asked her to tell the story – she had been at the Australian Institute of Sport in Perth for two years, been overseas with the team but only played a small number of minutes. She had never scored a goal and had been passed over.

I thought she offered an ability to set up play in midfield but also a knack of scoring in the attacking circle. She was included in our squad and played until a knee injury cut short her career. Her last game for Australia was the Olympic final in 1996. She is an Olympic gold medallist now!

Our development camp in late 2008 unearthed some interesting prospects and so we went into 2009 with a newish group, veterans from Beijing and before with some others worth a chance. With 2009 being a Junior World Cup year I felt we had most bases covered.

My great concern was goalkeeping. The team's two most experienced keepers who had been in Beijing were unlikely to be around. Stephen Mowlam retired and although I tried hard to convince Stephen Lambert to stay he had an expectant wife and was keen to start his own business. After some vacillation he confirmed he would not be staying in the program. Newly married and expecting their first child he and Angie made an understandable choice.

Accordingly, we would need a lot of work in this area. Nathan Burgers had played a handful of matches and from our camp in Brisbane we included George Bazeley (with only a club background) and Ross Meadows, a solid yet unspectacular keeper from Western Australia. In the long term the goalkeeping situation would take longer than ideal to fix and so we spent the next three years experimenting.

Not every story is a Danni Roche tale but perhaps one of the most pleasing was the emergence in 2009 of Glenn Turner, whose hockey evolution was not linear nor was it traditional. In the 2005 Junior World Cup, he was around but not empathic and our impression was always of one with brilliant close-in skills but without the passing and vision of a midfielder where he mostly played. Equally, he had a history of injuries and muscle strains that were of concern. He seemed to be injury prone.

Very good at indoor hockey, Turner would find his niche as a striker and after a slow start he began to emerge through the year – by the 2010 World Cup he was clearly one of the world's best strikers. Six years later he is still playing. Being located in Goulburn outside Canberra for extended periods it has been a difficult road. Most would not be able to perform but Glenn's determination and unique skill set have allowed him to survive and thrive. His record as a striker matches up well with some of our best ever.

Also from that camp came a number of others who during the next six years would play for the national team. Chris Ciriello, Ian Smyth, Simon Orchard, Daniel Hotchkis had all played for Australia, albeit only a handful of matches between them. However, over the next three years Tristan Clemons, George Bazeley, Ian Burcher, Nick Budgeon, Joel Carroll, Graeme Begbie, Matthew Butturini, Jonathon Charlesworth, Glenn Simpson, Matt Gohdes, Andrew Charter, Ross Meadows, Brent Dancer, Tim Deavin, Mark Paterson and Jason Wilson would all start for Australia in international games. Sixteen players were from a group that was mostly outside the U21 radar. The exception was Matthew Gohdes who would in 2009 be in the Junior World Cup team…he was an exciting younger player who had impressed at U18 level.

Of that group 14 would be in the Olympic squad in 2012 so the exercise was very useful in allowing the new coach to get a good idea of who was in the pipeline. Accordingly, we settled on a new squad and set about developing our plans for 2009. I hoped we would be able to play up to 40 internationals so as to have the opportunity to be ready for the big events in 2010.

The World Cup in New Delhi in March, 2010 was the target throughout 2009. It was the event on the horizon that we wanted to do well in. The bar was set high as the Kookaburras had been finalists in 2002 and 2006 only to slip at the final hurdle. On both occasions they lost to Germany in games in which they led.

I had seen both games live. In 2002 I travelled to Kuala Lumpur with my brother David and my 17-year-old son Jonathon to watch Australia. After an emphatic semi-final win over the Dutch, Australia scored first through Troy Elder (31 minutes) just before half-time but Germany replied at the stroke of half-time (35 minutes) to restore parity.

As the second half wore on an arm wrestle ensued with Germany and Australia both having their moments. In the end it was a defensive lapse that caused a turnover and allowed Oliver Domke to score the winner. Bernard Peters, the German coach who had taken over from Paul Lissek after Sydney would tell me later that he believed it was their interchange efficiency and frequency that allowed them to prevail that day in the oppressive Kuala Lumpur heat. Certainly, they interchanged more than Australia who was starting to use this tactic more and more with the arrival of Barry Dancer.

I remember Barry suggesting to me that perhaps his reluctance to use the interchange more had hurt them as the game wore on. I certainly believed that in Atlanta's heat and humidity our interchange policy in 1996 had helped us secure the gold medal. Scoring 70 per cent of our goals in the second half of the games certainly pointed to that fact. I believe most teams that went to Atlanta back then believed it would not be possible to play with high tempo in those conditions.

By 2006, I was living in New Zealand and as the World Cup came round and I had leave accrued, I found my way to Monchengladbach in the west of Germany half-way between Dusseldorf and the Dutch border.

Germany hosted the soccer World Cup and the hockey World Cup in the same year. I found accommodation in the countryside and enjoyed watching Australia progress to the final only to be shattered at the final hurdle after leading 3-1 in the second half. Making the final game in two World Cups consecutively was a tremendous effort. In KL perhaps we had not been ready and in Monchengladbach the loss of Jamie Dwyer for the final meant we lacked his composure and class that day. Perhaps that was a factor in our second half slippage.

A coaching team...

I was back in Australia at the end of 2008 and after an initial period finding my feet and establishing staffing arrangements we started to look ahead to the World Cup gazetted for Delhi in March, 2010. I had appointed Graham Reid as my senior assistant coach having had a few discussions with him during the preceding couple of years. He had started to make a name for himself in the local scene in Perth and was a little different to some others having played in the Netherlands after his years with the Kookaburras. He was in partnership in a business called Organise First, and had a perspective on the game which I believed would complement mine.

I was not sure about the other positions, which, I thought we would need, and so I was willing to wait and see what other resources might be available. One of our best decisions was to employ a young Englishman, Andy Smith, as our new operations manager. Andy was working at the Western Australian Institute of Sport (WAIS), and as a former County cricketer was very keen to absorb this new sport. During my time with the Kookaburras his efficiency and rigour in managing the program would greatly enhance our productivity as an elite operation.

We appointed Jason Duff to look after our Junior World Cup team, which, would be competing in the middle of 2009. Jason, an IT boffin who had played for the Kookaburras in the Sydney Olympics, would combine his coaching with his role as video analyst. He was particularly keen to progress his coaching. The JWC team that had been developed under the guidance of Mark Hager gave Jason a stimulating task for the next nine months.

The future role for the junior team and my second assistant were also on my mind so I had a discussion with Paul Gaudoin, who at the time was teaching at Aquinas College. Paul had been captain of the Kookaburras in 2004 when he was unable to go to Athens due to a severe knee injury. The timing had been heartbreaking and his career finished with two bronze Olympic medals rather than a golden finale. Paul was coaching Western Australia and his decision would be whether to leave teaching for coaching. Committed to the school for 2009 I hoped Paul might be willing to take the chance in 2010.

Every team requires very good strength and conditioning leadership and this was provided in the form of Ted Polglaze who had previously worked at WAIS under Steve Lawrence when I was with the Hockeyroos. Unfortunately, Ted became ill with lymphoma in the ensuing years and this greatly diminished our resources in this area. As team psychologist I retained Neil Mclean who had worked with Barry Dancer and gave us useful continuity when a lot of changes were being initiated.

Both of Barry's assistants, Colin Batch and Mark Hager, would move on to coach national teams in Europe and New Zealand with much success. As much as anything my reason for not employing both was that I could not offer either a promotion once I had appointed Graham Reid and I believed both needed a new challenge with their own team in the future. The decisions I made to let both of these coaches go were difficult as both had been loyal and able assistants to Barry Dancer.

Colin is presently coach of New Zealand's men's team after a stint with Belgium as head coach in London. Mark has distinguished himself with the NZ women's team taking them to London and Rio. Their performance in London was outstanding where they finished 4[th,] a best ever result for the NZ women. Indeed, they failed against eventual Olympic Champions the Netherlands in the semi-final only on penalties after a tied result at full-time. Unfortunately for Mark the story was repeated in Rio.

The Colonel...Paul Lissek...an outlier

There was one more part to the jigsaw I was contemplating. I had my eyes on a former German coach, Paul Lissek, who became nicknamed 'the Colonel' after his likeness to Hogan's Heroes character Colonel Klink! I have always believed that as much as possible we should challenge our beliefs and rigorously test our way of playing. Who better to assist in this process than someone from outside who was experienced and from a totally different way of thinking? For some time I had entertained the possibility of asking if he would consider such a role.

Paul Lissek had taken Germany to a gold medal in Barcelona in 1992 after many successful years with the German U21 team. During his 10 years as national coach Germany had always been contenders. They won eight medals (4 gold, 3 silver and 1 bronze) at the Champions Trophy, three times were European Champions and won bronze at the 1998 World Cup on top of the 1992 gold. Their worst finishes were twice fourth, and fifth at Sydney. His record was exceptional and I believed even at 62 he was as passionate as ever. Hockey had "dominated my life from early years till today" he said in his communication to me.

Paul had lost his head-coach role with Germany after Sydney, and after a stint in Malaysia as head coach he was still in that country working in junior development. He was as passionate as ever and I suspected would be keen for a job with another 'big' team that could contend for major championships. His name was raised whenever people discussed coaching in India and I had the opportunity to raise the issue with him when we talked at various competitions. At Ipoh, in 2008, while he was assisting in Malaysia I mentioned that I felt he would be someone I would like to have involved if I eventually got a job in India or Australia.

Whenever we did talk his enthusiasm for the game was palpable and he needed no encouragement to start drawing plays and training ideas to debate and share. He was totally into the game and as a single man who had been living outside Germany for some years he was available. He was mobile and interested. My problem would be to convince Andy Smith that we could afford it!

Paul would prove to be a valuable member of our team and one who introduced many new ways of looking at hockey. He was essentially a driver of standards with his teams, and someone with such a depth of experience is difficult to find available and engaged.

The coaching situation allowed him access to all we were doing and I always felt he was totally committed to our team. All the way through to London he would be with us.

While he was on another part of the coaching spectrum to me, his insights ignited new ideas and challenged our way of thinking about both defence and attack. Paul had in fact played against me when he represented Germany back in 1975 in Kuala Lumpur where I remember us playing out a tough draw on soggy grass fields in the Malaysian capital. In mid-July, 2009 Paul joined us in Perth and he was part of our program from then on.

By the beginning of 2009 we were due to start playing competitions with a visit by the Netherlands under their new coach Michel van den Heuvel. My first game as coach came after only a few days with the squad where we stayed in Fremantle and played four matches against Holland under their new regime.

The first two were in the South West of WA. In Busselton we were outplayed losing 4-2 and of course the new coach's ideas came under scrutiny. We were better in Bunbury a day or so later and in Perth emphatically dealt with the Netherlands 6-1. That result led to a final game in which our opponents were very defensive (we drew 1-1) and perhaps this week was the catalyst for a period where the Dutch played quite conservatively against us over the next 15 months. Van den Heuvel, a respected and successful club coach, would lose his job after finishing third in New Delhi at the World Cup. Third was not good enough for the ambitious Dutch. I was very surprised when I heard of the change for in my view the Netherlands team of 2010 had performed to their level to finish third.

The year was full of activity because after the Dutch departed in January we hosted Belgium in February in Canberra. The Europeans sweltered in the heat but after a surprising draw were comfortably defeated. The draw was clear evidence that we were a work in progress.

Late in May we made our way to France where we played at the Racing club in Paris and experienced tough local competition before spending a day visiting the battlefields of World War I in France and Belgium on our way to Hamburg. The sobering experience of our visits to Villers-Bretonneux and the famous service at Menin Gate in Ypres took up time but were important reminders of the young Australian experience of earlier generations.

In Hamburg we played two friendly matches against Germany. In spite of creating many opportunities we were twice beaten by a goal by our more efficient opponents with their determined defenders and brilliant goalkeeper. We had been invited to the Hamburg Masters and as the weekend approached played against the Netherlands and England before meeting Germany again in the final on Sunday, June 7. Our 6-2 demolition of the German team was emphatic and I believed the start of building belief that we would be able to play our pressing game effectively against all opposition.

After two matches in England we returned home via Singapore where our Junior World Cup team lost a semi-final thriller to Germany in extra time. We finished the winter playing Malaysia and Canada in Australia and winning the Oceania competition in Invercargill in August. New Zealand had generously arranged to play in Invercargill for their advantage and in August the weather was truly difficult. This victory ensured our qualification for the World Cup in Delhi in 2010. October saw us in Malaysia playing more matches and introducing more debutant players. Indeed, in 2009 fourteen players made their debuts for Australia. That is the most in any year since records have been available.

The big test of our progress would be the Champions Trophy to be held in Melbourne in the last week of November and early December. I believed it would help indicate whether we were truly progressing and ready for a March World Cup in Delhi. In November we played against Spain in Perth and after an emphatic win proceeded to lose the next day. We were still shaky!

A week later in Melbourne we defeated Korea, the Netherlands and England before being out-scored by Germany in game four. The message was clear to me – we still did not have it all together. The next match against Spain was tight until we broke away in the second half and so we found ourselves meeting Germany in the final on December 6.

I believed we could win but still there were holes in our game and Germany were well equipped to take advantage of our soft spots. By half-time we were trailing 1-3 – we had let ourselves down with defensive lapses but I felt we were making penetrations and could recover. We scored four unanswered goals to win. An early second-half corner conversion saw De Young netting a rebound, followed by Luke Doerner scoring twice from penalty corners and a superb finish in the last moments by Fergus Kavanagh, which made for a convincing second half.

The recovery after half-time was pleasing yet the lapses early on told a story. We were making enough chances and goals but needed to have a more resilient defence. Defensive rigour had never been Australia's strong point. I resolved that we would need to become the best defensive team in the world to ensure we were able to win the big tournaments.

After a short Christmas break we played Korea in Hobart at the end of January and a couple of games against NZ in mid-February. NZ were on their way to Delhi, and the World Cup was only a couple of weeks away. In Hobart we played Kieran Govers for the first time. Kieran had impressed at the junior World Cup but he had had long-standing problems with his hips and this was not a good sign in a teenager. In 2007 he had surgery for a labral tear and impingement and after meeting him after the Junior World Cup it was resolved to have further surgery.

I saw him as a potential Olympian in London but felt without further intervention his career might not go anywhere. So it was pleasing that by January he was able to make his debut, and such was his versatility that we punted on him for the World Cup. Undoubtedly it was his penalty corner flinging that recommended him to us and gave us a backstop for Luke Doerner. It was a risk but at the time Chris Ciriello was not performing and options like Matthew Butturini were off the pace.

I believed, supported by medical opinion, that Kieran might be lucky if he was to make the London Olympics. It is a great credit to him that at the time of writing he has played 116 internationals with 57 goals and he played in Delhi, London and The Hague (two World Cups and an Olympics). Sadly, repeated hamstring injuries ruled him out of contention for Rio. In my view it is only his tremendous diligence in preparing and rehabilitating himself that allowed him to play this long and with such distinction. Given the misfortune of his hip morphology his career at the elite level is a testimony to his character and courage. In The Hague in 2014 where I last saw him play up close, he scored a couple of the best goals you will ever see.

World Cup 2010
The National Hockey stadium in New Delhi sits only a few hundred metres from India Gate, a 42m high war memorial that bestrides the Rajpath on the eastern edge of the ceremonial axis. It evokes the architectural style of the triumphal arches seen in Paris and Rome. Designed by Sir Edwin Lutyens, it is central to Indian ceremonial activity on the big days of remembrance and celebration.

It is always a busy place yet on the morning of March 13, 2010 after a mid-morning training session at the stadium we stopped our minibus and alighted to have our photo taken in front of the famous monument. The commanding arch towered above us as we stood in its shadow. That evening we would return to the stadium to play the World Cup final against Germany.

Such training sessions have no purpose besides allowing the players help pass the time of day. Sitting around all day waiting for a match can be draining. Indeed being hotel-bound (as we were in Delhi for security reasons) can be very debilitating. After two weeks in which we had been confined to our hotel, getting out and going training had utility for our mindset if not for honing our skills.

Ten hours later the players would be mounting the podium having secured a memorable World Cup victory against our most difficult opponent in a cauldron of noise and chaos. Such games are always great challenges and great tests and usually there are moments of high drama.

Germany had secured a final berth by virtue of a comfortable victory over England (4-1) in the semi-final – the same team that had upset us on the first day! They had been undefeated through the competition although they did draw with Korea and the Netherlands. Our tournament had been distinctly uncomfortable for the coaching staff and players alike, as after losing on the first day we had left ourselves little margin for error.

Against England we had failed to take chances and we had leaked soft opportunities. It reminded me of a World Cup opener 16 years earlier in Dublin when the Hockeyroos had slipped up on the first day to Russia. I hoped at the time our tournament would parallel that outcome eventually. That early loss meant that we had to win every match in the sequence that followed: India (5-2), Spain (2-0) South Africa (10-0) and Pakistan (2-1). And so we found ourselves playing the Netherlands in the semi-final. The game was eventually decided 2-1 after we led 2-0 till a late consolation goal to the Netherlands. Dutch supporters were critical of their team's negative tactics that day and I believe this led to the demise of Michel van den Heuvel after the tournament.

So it was that evening that our bus weaved its way through the early evening traffic on the ten-minute drive to the National stadium close by India Gate where we had stopped for our photograph that morning. For the third time in nine months we would meet Germany in a tournament final. The first in Hamburg had been a small local match on their home soil. Next, in December, 2009 we met in Melbourne for the Champions Trophy final but this was the biggest game; the World Cup final in the centre of Delhi. It was hockey's spiritual home in a country that had dominated the game for nearly half a century.

The game started well for us with Eddie Ockenden scoring from close range after six minutes. It was a set play from a free hit near the circle. We had visited Bunbury in the south-west of Western Australia before the tournament for a training weekend. One morning there we spent much time practising the short pass and change of direction to enter the circle. On this occasion the move was not perfect but it spilt off Max Muller's stick and Eddie swooped on the ball and tucked it under the hapless keeper.

After this start we threatened to dominate the game with further opportunities but failed to cash in. While the brilliant Weinhold was missing in goal for Germany, his replacement, Tim Jessulat, made a couple of brilliant reflex saves. One off a Doerner penalty corner was simply outstanding and so we led by only the solitary goal at half-time. Germany did not threaten our goal except for a wide corner shot, but this lead was unlikely to be enough.

Germany played better in the second half and from four penalty corners equalised and awakened the crowd to a nail biting final 12 minutes. Before the game I was most worried about our penalty corner defence and so it proved our Achilles heel as we succumbed. Fortunately, we only succumbed once. Germany played a clever 'ninety degree' pass to Moritz Furste from Jan Marco Montag and our runner was beaten. Furste's shot went central as Nathan Burgers dived to his right. The actual corner from which they scored came from a needless penalty when Mark Knowles was judged to have pushed the ball away rather than leaving it alone. It was a reflex action as the whistle blew and hardly deserving of the sanction. These things can decide such matches.

With 15 minutes remaining an arm wrestle ensued. Germany won another questionable corner and our first runner blocked the shot. A well-won penalty corner was our next good chance. The umpire missed the German foot but Des Abbott was quick to appeal for the video. The slick work of manager David Hatt and Graham Reid ensured that Doerner was on the field. The Germans protested Doerner's arrival on the field in vain and he scored low to Jessulat's right.

We led into the last 10 minutes but Germany made another penalty corner and again the pass left deceived us to give them a goal chance. This time Burgers made the body save down the centre and minutes later we could have settled the game through Butturini whose shot hit the post. Germany persisted but did not make another chance.

As the game ebbed away time seemed stretched as it always does in such situations but as Grant Schubert raised the ball above his head and the buzzer sounded we were World Champions again, some 26 years after we had won for the first time in London in 1986 when I had been playing. Always difficult to beat, Germany had been a formidable force and while I was delighted, I knew we needed to improve considerably through the next years leading into London.

In the tournament there had been many pleasing performances with Simon Orchard and Ockenden coming of age at international level. Dwyer was at his peak, Abbott and Turner were so dangerous up front, while surprisingly Schubert played well without scoring. Doerner, a tough defender, was the leading scorer from corners, and Knowles, Kavanagh, Begbie and Kiel Brown proved difficult to pass as the competition evolved. In midfield Butturini emerged to play well having replaced an unlucky Brent Livermore in a tough selection choice. Two of our experienced seniors in Hammond and De Young were solid throughout and made significant contributions with Hammond's combative approach really important to our group. Junior World Cup players Govers and Matthew Swann had their first taste of a big competition. I was still concerned about our custodians yet in the final Nathan saved when required. George Bazeley who had played in the Champions trophy final three months earlier was not used in the final.

Many parts of our game were not solidified yet. Three months later we would win the Champions Trophy undefeated in Monchengladbach beating England in the final and then in October we won against India in Delhi to take out the Commonwealth Games gold. It had turned out to be a very successful year. Better than I had felt possible when we first played in Hobart at the start of the year.

A month or so after the World Cup the coaches all got together and we spent a day deciding what we needed to stop doing, start doing and continue doing. It was to be a partial blueprint for the years leading up to London. A principle aim was to become the best defence in the world by conceding the least opportunities to our opponents. It is not so well understood by the hockey community in general but Australia already had the best defence. We had least goals against in every competition but the perception was still of an attacking unit. I believed, however that it was nowhere near as good as I thought it could be.

Every aspect of our performance was assessed and more than anything else that – and our finishing efficiency – were the main aims. London I hoped would be the measure of our progress and 2010 ended with plans for 2011 and keenness to take more steps that would make us stronger.

3

N A D I R   I N   L O N D O N

Sometimes you can see victory or defeat coming from the distance, you feel their inevitability and you cannot do much about it. During my playing career I had both experiences at different times and on many occasions. I remember losing 7-1 to Pakistan in January, 1980 in Karachi and feeling helpless to do anything to change it – we were so totally out-scored that day. We weren't out-played just out-scored; there is a difference. We were 0-4 after 45 minutes and nothing was working. We had our chances yet every time Pakistan entered the scoring zone they scored! Then, two days later against the Netherlands after being 2-2 at the break we were leading 6-2 with ten minutes left. The result was also inevitable...this time in our favour. Those moments of utter certainty were moments to savour. In the international game they do not come that often.

More often than not, however, the contest is tight and that 'imposter' (defeat) can easily sneak up on you and surprise you with its capriciousness. You would think that after a lifetime in sport one would be prepared for this, ready to absorb and understand it yet my experience is one of not being able to breathe deeply and be fatalistic. For as long as the contest continues there is always hope and the chance of redemption. So many times a late moment of brilliance or team play has snatched victory from a draw or defeat. Often this tight game holds you in its thrall right up until the final whistle and then suddenly one must deal with the outcome. Either the letdown, confusion and devastation is there, or the pure elation and adrenaline buzz surrounds you.

On August 9, 2012 in such a game, I experienced the pain of having a game snatched away. Then at the end, a minute or two of inevitability with a loss looming, the Kookaburras fell short in the critical semi-final in London. As the final moments ebbed away on that warm afternoon, I again experienced something of that hopelessness and desolation.

We did not play as I would have liked that day and there were a range of contributing factors, which I will outline later. The game was there to win; we had a good enough team to win if we played well, yet we fell short that afternoon. Over my 14 years coaching the national women and men that was the only time we did not win a big match at a major tournament. When I think about it soberly perhaps it had to happen one day, yet that does not make it any easier nor does it erase the guilt I feel for the mistakes I made in the lead up to that day.

In the first minute of the game we had a great chance. Turner was right in front and as the ball came he was pushed in the back by his German marker who cleverly fell also as the ball passed by. In the first minute you are reluctant to use your referral, as the pictures may not accurately show the incident. We let it pass without referring to the third umpire. We scored first after 22 minutes when Turner's shot was blocked and Govers powerfully drove home the rebound.

In the first half, both teams were understandably cautious and both had two penalty corners. The first against us was defended soundly, but on the second corner against us, we made a wrong call.

It was an inexplicable error, which probably cost us mightily, as from a relatively weak shot Germany scored and restored parity. Sitting on the bench next to Fergus Kavanagh I could see we set up incorrectly but you are powerless to do anything. The corner had resulted from sloppy play and such signs are not good. Our attacking corners resulted in powerful shots (if not ideally directed). Germany's Max Weinhold, in goal, saved well on both occasions.

At half time it was 1-1. There is much at stake in such a game. It is better to just focus on 'task' but it is hard to do. No need to panic but we were not playing so well and seemed a little anxious. We decided to start one-on-one in the second half in order to make us more assertive and 'take the game on'. That was the central message at half-time. It seemed we needed to ignite ourselves. It was a hot day and perhaps because we were playing in the afternoon for the first time we seemed strangely off balance.

After half-time we started better. We scored again after another barrage of shots from close range. More reason for belief, yet again we seemed unwilling to press home our advantage with more enterprise. Again, from my position on the bench I felt we became conservative and risk-averse at a time when we should have been assertive and positive. My constant message that day was to 'take the game on'. We had not done that yet sometimes there is some action, which can ignite and motivate. Clearly my entreaties weren't doing it!

Instead of taking on our opponents and forcing them to turn and chase us we played the ball to the other end and set up to defend. It was not our characteristic approach and something we had always tried to avoid. After the game many of the players complained that they felt tired and drained. It was a warm day and we were playing for the first time in the afternoon but I think the issue was more mental than physical.

There was a point in the second half when I felt we could have taken over. Germany were tired too, and two German players had an altercation mid-pitch when Martin Haner blasted the ball into Tobias Hauke's foot. Christopher Zeller had just been sent off for disputing a decision and his brother Phillip was on his haunches looking exhausted... So Germany was a man down, a goal down, and showing signs of wear. It was a time to assert ourselves. In sport you need to seize such moments.

A minute or two later two of our best players, Jamie Dwyer and Simon Orchard, disconnected with one another and the resultant turnover caught us sneaking forward. Germany equalised when Hauke fed to Matthius Witthaus and his modest shot caught Nathan Burgers advancing rather than balanced. Germany suddenly had some oxygen and we needed to respond.

Glenn Turner was complaining of a sore calf muscle and our vitality at the front seemed diminished by his limitation. It is sure this limited our ability to counterattack. Any diminution of your team has that effect. The goal to Germany lifted them but I hoped it would strengthen our resolve. Such moments and disappointments can always occur in the ebb and flow of the match.

Some people suggest the signs were there when Germany had a goal disallowed earlier in the second half when the ball was played above the head. At the time I believed it was a clear breach of the rule and gave it scant consideration. However, it was a piece of play where we were indecisive in our response and that worries any coach.

From one's experience in the game you know that sometimes there are games that go like this and the team seems 'out of sorts'. We have all experienced this. Usually, someone lifts his or her game (and often the team) out of that state. I kept hoping we had the resources to do so for we needed a spark. I wondered if we could find that spark?

Games at the big tournaments are regularly up and down affairs and you expect you will go through the yo-yo ride. It would really test us now as we had twice relinquished a lead. Germany's strength has always been their ability to just stay on task and keep testing an opponent. It was now an arm wrestle and both teams had opportunities. It is often small details that bring you down and that can cause you the next problem.

Minutes later, Mathew Butturini failed to close down Moritz Furste on the half line, Tim Deavin over compensated in covering the 'hot line' to the goal and as a consequence Furste found Christopher Zeller with Liam De Young behind inside the circle. He found a foot, the umpire missed it, but Zeller was certain and it was clear on the video replay – corner!

Germany converted in a way we had discussed in the lead up that very morning by slipping the ball left to Timo Wess. The defensive running method of the first half, which we felt would assist defence against this corner, was not employed! Eleven minutes to play and we needed to lift. I felt we did lift and indeed made a couple of good penetrations without a real chance.

It then got much worse when Germany broke away as we pressed forward. The cross from a break down the left was perfect; Mark Knowles dived despairingly and Florian Fuchs (chased by Ockenden) dived also and deflected into an empty goal when Nathan Burgers misjudged the ball and was stranded in no-man's land. Only seven minutes remained and there was so much to do. In that time of desperation we made two very good chances but Weinhold saved well on both occasions. We removed our GK and tried to breach the difference but the time ebbed away and in just a few minutes the game had slipped from us and we were shattered as the final whistle blew.

Afterwards, we felt only devastation and disappointment. The central focus of our quest had, in a few minutes, been wrenched away. We were, as the New Zealanders like to say, GUTTED. When I had accepted the job I had always known that it was the two games at the end of the Olympics that would be the measure of my tenure. This is the Olympic challenge that our sport always faces and we had fallen short that afternoon.

The victors that afternoon would go on to win the final in an arm wrestle with Netherlands. The hero that evening would be a relatively unknown and unsung German player Jan Philipp Rabente who would score twice for the winners. The second goal that sealed the result in the 66th minute would likely have been disallowed had the Netherlands players or bench had the presence of mind to appeal as Rabente scored after passing across behind the goal before the final tip in. I feel confident the German players would have protested had the boot been on the other foot!

Afterwards you do not know what to say, where to look, you wonder whether life can ever return to normal. In the quest to win an Olympic title everything else has been put aside and now somehow you must go on without the prize ahead. I think, in the change room, I said something about how we needed to salvage something from the wreckage. A bronze medal match would be played in two days. Accordingly, we had to stick to our recovery routine and go on. I wonder if anyone was listening? We were numbed by the enormity and finality of our loss. To the great credit of the staff and players we played pretty well two days later to secure the bronze medal against Great Britain.

Our families waited patiently to see us and seemed as flat as we were. There was a hug of comfort and many tears. Oscar and Hugo were as crushed as I was – so young, 12 and 10, and so used to watching the Kookaburras win. They were bewildered. I, of course, had seen and experienced it all before but it did not make it any better or any easier except I knew eventually it would pass.

Four years earlier in Beijing I had watched the players meet families after that fateful loss to Spain. As I had made my way out of the stadium that evening I had felt their pain at a distance, removed from the reality but able to reflect on experiences I had had as a player many years before. This time I was right in the middle of it and it was not pleasant.

Now, 40 years after losing the Olympic final in Montreal, I can still feel some of the emotion that I experienced that day and in the days that followed. In 1978, 1982, 1984 and 1988 I was a player in teams that lost in semi-finals at World Cups and Olympic games. Each game was different, each loss devastating in its own way. A couple were dead unlucky, and we played well enough to have won in 1978 and 1984. In one we lost on a penalty shootout. That was 1982 and it is the worst way to go out. In 1988 and in the 1976 Olympic final we played poorly but still could have 'jagged' it even right up to the end.

What all of these playing experiences had done for me was to cause me to look at what we lacked, how we might improve, what was necessary to win on the crucial days when there was no second chance. The recurring message was excellent preparation, more preparation, better preparation, thorough preparation, so that the chances of things going wrong were less and the ability to deal with the unexpected was possible.

That is why I think this is one of the most important chapters of this book and also so difficult to write as it is about our failure to achieve our aim. It takes in what happened that day and the considerations that followed. The review, evaluation and examination of our preparation and performance in London would take months and be a catalyst for what was an altogether much better experience in The Hague two years hence.

If you are truly going to examine the performance at the Olympics then the review must be forensic and challenge all the elements of the program. Unfortunately, it is hard to have this sort of scrutiny when things are going well. Usually it takes a disaster to go there. For the Kookaburras, with our high expectations, the bronze medal was the catalyst that led to that necessary introspection.

Informally, of course, the review started within minutes of the game ending. It would continue well into 2013 and its conclusions would bring about many adjustments and changes to what was in essence a very good program – a program which nevertheless needed to be renewed and refreshed to enable us to be World Champions again in 2014 in The Hague.

My immediate response was usual for me. I wanted to watch the game and review the critical events that shaped it. I knew that statistically we had not been as dominant as we had wanted to be and I knew that some of the factors that had been out of our control had not helped. Also, of course, we needed to look at ourselves and examine our preparation and our conduct in and before the tournament.

When we looked back over the months leading into the Olympics, there were, as always, elements that did not go as well as we had hoped.

It started with the release of the Olympic program which was the most unbalanced I had ever seen. Initially, we were gazetted to play three games at 8.30 in the morning! In a tournament, this entails waking at 5am to begin preparations and denies the chance to develop a routine, which is so important as the competition builds to the critical matches. Indeed, the semi-final match was our first afternoon game of the tournament!

At every Olympics the schedule of early matches has always been shared between the teams equally and this extreme departure from fairness was an appalling outcome. There was no consultation and we made the most strenuous objections and eventually received two 8.30 starts and two 10.45 starts with a 7pm game against the hosts (GB) in the middle. I believed this schedule was a factor in our dullness on semi-final day but of course only one of the factors. Our opponent that day, Germany had its earliest game at 1.35pm without even one morning game in the two weeks!

The rationale for the program, as such things so often are these days, was that it suited the southern hemisphere TV scheduling. This was foolish because the cameras at that time in the morning were looking directly into the sun (they are set up for afternoon matches) and so the pictures at that time were hopeless. In truth there was no rationale. It was just unbalanced and unfair and served no media purpose. Our early games did not appear on Australian television.

For our preparation matches we had started in February, 2012 playing Argentina and the Netherlands in Perth. We seemed on track winning all five games with the group progressing nicely towards its fitness and strength goals. Unfortunately, in March China and Japan did not provide the competition we would have liked. An Olympics in the northern hemisphere never affords access to European teams at that time of year, and so it was we looked to Asia.

Nevertheless, as we prepared to go to Europe for the test event on the Olympic pitch in May I was quite happy with where we were physically and technically. During the previous year I had introduced a program on crucial conversations because I believed we did not always get the candour we should have exhibited. I was not convinced about our preparedness for what London might bring and whether we had the resilience we would need. I hoped the test event would tease out some of those just coasting. I was not worried about the result as much as how it might be a catalyst for sharpening us and showing real toughness under pressure.

Unfortunately, on the first day against India Graeme Begbie collapsed on the pitch with a second ACL injury that would effectively finish his international career. It was a cruel blow for someone who had had such a positive impact on our team in 2009 and 2010. Begbie impressed at the National championships early in 2009 and later that season made his debut. In 2010 he played very well at the World Cup in New Delhi but by the Champions Trophy in Germany in 2010 he was starting to experience knee pain.

Begbie was a remarkable tale as he had damaged his ACL as a junior and been advised not to have a repair. Without an ACL he played and competed until the wear and tear became too much leading to increasing pain and swelling. He was advised to have a reconstruction. In 2012, having recovered from that reconstruction, Graeme was making his return in the test event when disaster struck and he injured his other knee! As with many such injuries it occurred in a relatively benign situation without any great speed or force involved.

The loss of Begbie was a setback for he had a competitiveness and calmness about him that is rare. Even when I watch him play now four years later in club hockey this remains part of his DNA and in spite of his physical limits he is very effective. However, in the midst of Olympic preparation, we had a squad of 30 and so one moves on, but many of us felt deeply for this young man and his lost Olympic dream. Additionally, I thought we would miss what he brought in terms of a calm, steady, thoughtful, tough and resourceful defender.

Also, central to my thinking was the management of Des Abbott, our brilliant centre forward who suffered from deteriorating mobility as a result of long-standing damage to the articular cartilage in his knee. The diminished range of motion in his ankle on the same leg also impacted on his mobility and all along Des was only a 50:50 chance of making it.

Des' program was appropriately modified and while Des travelled to London in May we did not plan to play him there. He would be used sparingly in the lead up to give him the best chance of being able to contribute in August. He would require a cortisone injection in the lead up to the Olympic tournament and we hoped he would respond positively as he had done in the past.

In London during the test event we lost to Germany in our first match in a game where we did not play that well. The round game saw us lead and then lose concentration after a fortunate early goal. Germany scored twice from our errors rather than any brilliance on their part and the analysis behind the score revealed a very close encounter. I believed we would be chastened and expected the final to be another matter.

Perhaps also I underestimated the determination of our opponent to do well in that tournament. When Germany started playing before the GB team was back on the field in their clash I thought it was just bad manners…perhaps it reflected another approach, as there was a ruthlessness smouldering inside their team. Two days later we got a flavour of that when leading by a goal and quite dominant we were awarded a penalty stroke. Simon Orchard duly converted but in an extraordinary turn of events the Germans went to the umpire and appealed the decision claiming that Orchard had illegally dragged the ball. I was gobsmacked when the goal was overruled!

Apparently, they had seen Orchard score in an earlier game and decided to challenge if he scored a stroke – indeed had spoken to the umpires before the game indicating their reason. It was not something I would even have contemplated but it did reveal a hard edge to their approach at the test event.

Instead of leading 2-0 we faltered, and as the game unfolded so did our team. After complete dominance we were behind 1-2 at half-time, a situation German coach Markus Weise described as a 'miracle' in the post-match interview. An early converted corner to Germany in the second half further unsettled us and in the end we lost by three. It was the largest margin against Germany during my coaching tenure. Our loss reflected there was much to do and our European tour would further test us as we moved to Belgium and then on to Mannheim where we would meet Germany again. So we licked our wounds and moved on to Antwerp.

The days in Belgium were spent repairing our group both mentally and physically and getting ready for another crack at Germany. Belgium was busy with their preparations and so our two games against them were a little anticlimactic and I was disappointed their clubs did not release some of the Belgium players. We won 8-2 and 5-1 but were flattered by these scores. In Mannheim nine days after losing to Germany in London we beat them 3-0 and then 2-1 on the next day.

I remember thinking that these results were indeed very good, as the two German umpires did not do us any favours at all! The defensive effort was much better and I felt the chastening experience in London had ensured we were really ready to play. Des Abbott and Jamie Dwyer, who we rested in London, played in these games and although still looking limited Des played his role as an attacking target. I was worried that he was not able to press and chase but still felt hopeful about his chances.

On our return to Australia at the end of May I still believed we were on track. I was not disappointed with the losses in the tournament as I believed we would benefit from the wake-up message that went along with those earlier results. In June we played against the talented Koreans and won three times with one draw. These were our last games before the selection of the team and that process was not something I was looking forward to.

The selection of the Olympic team for London in 2012 was perhaps the most difficult ever during my coaching life. There were many reasons for this, not the least of which was the fact that we had built a deep squad of about 30 and only 16 would make it. The Olympic

Games allows for teams of 16 players whereas teams of 18 play in all other major hockey events.

There were many other things to complicate matters. As always there are players suffering injuries, which constantly require scrutiny. These are dynamic situations requiring judgement and prognostication as to the playing ability of the team members. Equally, blending personalities, covering possible contingencies (flexibility is needed) and the relevant form and trajectory of all players is factored in.

Generally, a dozen are fairly solid but the rest of the places are subject to flux and change throughout the lead up. It was no different in 2012 and as we usually did we asked the players for their selections. Who did they want alongside them in the Olympic cauldron?

The year 2012 had all of these elements plus the fact that my son, Jonathon, was a contender. Having your son in the team is not a problem if he is one of the first selected but in Jonathon's case he was a borderline contender. For any coach this is a difficult and complicating factor. I believed Jonathon, as a disciplined and clear thinking defensive midfielder, would be in contention in some circumstances in that line but he would need to perform in the lead up.

In our squad we had perhaps four or five athletes in that category. They were ready to fill a spot if required depending on other contingencies and selections but they were as yet unproven in high competition. Your squad always contains such players and they often surprise and play a crucial role in lifting training tone. They never take short cuts because they know they cannot afford to.

Unfortunately for Jonathon he suffered a calf injury to slow down his preparation and then in April-May, a day or so before the Olympic test event in London, he experienced severe pain in his hip while climbing out of a low chair. He was unable to play and his prospects of earning a place diminished dramatically. Following an injection in London, two weeks later he played solidly in Mannheim where we defeated Germany twice on their home turf but he had lost a lot of his momentum.

In a hockey team there are also various specialists who are an essential ingredient. An obvious one is the goalkeeper and here again the question was whether to take one or two? An injured goalkeeper could be replaced during the tournament if you took only one in your group of sixteen. However, should a problem occur early in a crucial game it could be critical and no replacement was possible. A field player may have to play there!

Most teams (ourselves included) went into London with only one goalkeeper in our first 16 and with a reserve outside. A calculated risk but one most of us were willing to take. Goal keeping was not our strongest suit and while we had worked hard to rectify this in the years before London it was an area of softness in our group. After Beijing, Mowlam and Lambert our best two keepers, both retired as I outlined earlier. Nathan Burgers, the team number three, assumed a position in the team with George Bazeley, Ross Meadows, Andrew Charter and Tristan Clemons. All would play during the lead up years to London.

I considered the possibility of taking two goalkeepers in the 16 but rejected it for the extra field player option. My reasoning was that you were only likely to make a change in the tournament if there was injury or one goalkeeper had a really poor performance. In the first case, you could replace for the next game and in the latter case, you might find out too late to do anything anyway. This would prove to be a most prescient view.

Earlier in 2012 we had settled on a 2; 3; 2; 3; GK formation (there are 11 on field and the rest interchange.) This was the set-up which the majority of the players felt comfortable with. The big question about this way of setting up is that the central defenders need to be clear about who is free and who is marking. When miscommunications occur they can be catastrophic. Accordingly, we went about selecting for London. After the test event I had three or four big headaches. Goal keeping still worried me – Luke Doerner's form had been poor and he was not as good on corners as he had been. Abbott's injury, which left him 'proppy', and the hand injury sustained by Rob Hammond in the test event – along with his repeated leg injuries – were all matters of concern.

There is of course no opportunity to ever know what else you might have done, what might have worked better, what players would thrive and those that might freeze in the big competition. During the past three years we had played in every final in every tournament and shown ourselves to be able to perform under pressure. I hoped that would be sufficient. Even if we had a bad day there would be a critical mass of leaders to endure. That is what every coach hopes for.

In the end we took Nathan Burgers who was solid till the semi-final, a game in which he was not at his best. Nathan had the best reflexes and was solid until that match but as I was all too aware with no second keeper such a day can be fatal. Andrew Charter who would play so well two years later at the World Cup was close and indeed had played very well the previous year when given opportunity. He was a ready replacement outside the Olympic Village.

The decision to leave out Doerner was devilishly difficult. He had been crucial for us with his corners for the past three years but was waning in that art all year and his field play had diminished. Always a slow turner he relied on his strength and bodywork to block and the game's speed was catching up on him. We would of course miss his toughness, bravery in the defensive circle and his experience on the corners. Unfortunately, at the test event he had given away more than he could score.

We punted on Abbott but as the next few weeks went by had to make a very hard call on his soundness for the rigours of an Olympic tournament. Hammond's hand injury and inconsistent fitness led to him being overlooked in a very strong midfield. In defence we had speed, great tackling and mobility and, I believed, we had the most creative midfield. At the front Turner complimented Kieran Govers and Gohdes and a form player who initially missed out in Russell Ford. Ford was very close, and when Des Abbott was replaced took his Olympic chance after being so close four years earlier for Beijing. I was confident it was a team that could win but it was not our best team. Abbott, Begbie and Hammond would have made that team had they been fully fit.

Perhaps my worst day in the lead up to the Olympics came on the day we made the final decision on Des Abbott. I had watched him closely at training and in games and he was struggling to show the agility and fitness that could compliment his tremendous skill and timing. Des is a big guy and in a crowded scoring circle was able to take and hold positions of strength. He could beat a defender with his quick hands but he was struggling to then break free and get a shot. He was limited in his ability to chase and press because of his mobility.

I took footage of Des in club games, in trial games and of course in all our matches, and it was clear that he was not at the level of two years earlier. We had been hopeful that the administered cortisone would free him up but some weeks before London I came to the conclusion that I was not willing to go into the tournament with Des limping from the first game. I met Des and his Dad in Peter Steele's office and we talked through our thinking and the decision. Des and his father David were naturally very upset and in any such situation there is no easy way to pass on the decision.

There was nothing we could do to give him more time. Time had been his enemy and we had no more solutions that might be able to make a difference. I left Pete's office emotionally drained and flattened by the enormity of the disappointment that Des was feeling.

In 1986 at the World Cup in London, I had some of my greatest moments in the game in the Indian summer days of October. Our national team was unbeaten (one draw with Germany). We scored 31 goals and had seven against in seven matches. While we did not play so emphatically in the final, our 2-1 victory over the hosts was enough. A team that had stumbled in Los Angeles had made amends. Twenty-six years later in the London Olympics I was to experience my greatest disappointment as a coach in the same city.

The Olympic Games are never an easy event in our sport, whereas at a World Cup or even Champions Trophy (annual or biennial) hockey is the focus and the full support team and players are comfortable. This is not possible where enough space is seldom available. Players and a few support staff live in cramped accommodation while others can only access venues and the village intermittently. It is a wholly unsatisfactory arrangement. Meeting rooms are difficult and those who stay outside and visit daily have nowhere to go to do their work. A desk is rare.

So the biggest event, held every four years sees compromise necessary and distraction heightened in the village environment. At least in Sydney I had my own donga with a desk and bathroom. In London, Graeme Reid, my assistant coach, and I were very close to one another; two single beds, two wardrobes in about 10 square metres.

You don't expect to be comfortable, it is always stressful at such competitions, yet in London the schedule of two early starts interrupted by a night game, then two more early games and an afternoon semi-final did not allow for any routine to our Olympic tournament and exacerbated the discomfort of the living arrangements.

In our pool I expected Spain and England to be our biggest contenders. Spain had played a brilliant Champions Trophy in November 2011 when we played a difficult game to win 1-0 in the final. We scored a controversial goal with only minutes to go. I believed they were the most difficult team for us and England as hosts would of course be likely to play above themselves at home.

Spain (as can happen at such an event) unravelled on the first two days. They suffered a surprise draw with Pakistan and then lost to us 0-5. During those games their two best players were seriously injured and with the departure of Pol Amat and Santi Friexa their chances slipped away badly, although even on the last day they were still semi-final contenders when playing Great Britain. Our play in the early games was crisp and clinical and though hardly challenged, our defence solid. We had accounted for South Africa (6-0) and Spain (5-0).

Next day, against Argentina (always difficult) we again played well leading 2-0 at half-time. The second half started well and we continued to make chances and penetrate but failed to capitalise when what I call 'the elements of the game' conspired against us. Poor umpiring and perhaps an overconfident feeling cost us as the game threw up surprises. We played in an own goal and Argentina equalised against the run of play, to our great disappointment. While our chances continued we found ourselves accepting a draw. With the next game looming you look at it, then accept the perfunctory analysis and move on.

Leading Great Britain 3-0 two days later and again sliding to 3-3 draw represented a minor crisis and left the commentators questioning our form, our pedigree and musing as to how this could happen. Unfortunately, at the Olympics those who report are often ill versed in hockey knowledge. Draws happen a lot... the extraordinary thing about our two draws is that we conceded five goals. Three of which were 'own goals'. This represented an unusual cluster of bad luck. 'Own goals' are a one in fifty-game occurrence and to concede three in two consecutive games was indeed very rare.

These results meant we had to at least draw with Pakistan to secure a place in the semi-finals. So two days later we again woke up early and proceeded to wallop Pakistan 7-0. We had played strongly in the early morning and come away convincing winners, thereby finishing on top of our pool. Accordingly, we would meet Germany who was runner-up in the other pool in a match to be played mid-afternoon two days hence. It was a distance ahead but the time would skip by as we prepared for the most important match we would play in since we met Germany in the World Cup final more than two years before.

That evening we went to watch Germany play New Zealand in their meaningless final game for they had already qualified for the semi-finals six days earlier by virtue of three wins (twice by a solitary goal against Korea and Belgium) Trailing 2-5 shortly after half-time that evening they salvaged a draw at 5-5. They were not impressive but I think we all knew that the team we were due to meet would be wholly different.

So it was that we prepared for Germany and in a few fateful minutes it slipped away as I described at the beginning of this chapter. I was not prepared for the hollowness and the disappointment and came home to a period of desolation. I spent a few days in York 100km east of Perth where I planted my olive trees and tried to understand the things that we had failed to prepare for that had brought us undone. The answer is never one thing; it is always multifactorial and I understood that is sometimes what happens. You miss things and they do catch up with you…unfortunately for us Germany had, on that day, seized on our errors with devastating effect. We made too many errors.

In the month after our return from London I wrote via email to Markus Weise, my coaching opponent that day. I congratulated him on the performance of his team and of course indicated that we would be up for the challenges ahead against his team. He wrote back thanking me and making the observation that for him such disappointments had been the catalyst for renewed determination and building even better teams. I did not know whether it could be done but I did want to rectify the damage that we had suffered and was acutely aware the Kookaburras were hurting.

The feedback from the players, some direct to me, and some via the Australian Sports Commission anonymous survey, which was collected annually, told the story. My rating had dropped and I was communicating less openly and making more mistakes!! When you have a squad of 30 and only 16 make the final cut it is not surprising that there are many who blame you for missing out, or bias, or poor planning. I have always been aware of this…it is the stuff every coach must face.

My reflections matured over the following weeks but were still not greatly different to what I had thought as I had made my way across the Olympic Park back to the village where people would know what had happened and be uneasy in your presence. You would have to face up to the disapproving silences and sombre journeys in the lift.

We had slipped up at some crucial moments, made too many errors, seemed to lose our assertiveness when it was most needed and had been less connected when we needed to be tight. Our penalty corner defence (best in the tournament until that day) had been poor and our leaders had not been able to change the tone of the game.

By year's end we had made a number of changes and I hoped we were heading to a better place. I had discussions with Kathleen Partridge in London at an offsite gathering and asked her if she was interested in working with our goalkeepers. She agreed. In my view she was the best goal keeping coach in the country and I believed she would bring the rigour to our goal keeping program that I had wanted to change at the end of 2011. I had run into resistance in Hockey Australia. I would not accept compromise this time. It was my biggest regret that I had not been able to affect this change a year earlier. It was my biggest mistake in the Olympic lead up.

Kathleen, when appointed would become the first female to my knowledge to join the coaching staff of a male national team. In the next two years she would work with Andrew Charter, Tyler Lovell, Tristan Clemons and Leon Hayward to elevate the quality of our goal keeping group. By the time we got to the World Cup in 2014 we had assured and confident custodians and much of the credit for this was Kathleen's.

Neil Mclean, our long serving psychologist would move on, and I managed to secure Corinne Reid who had worked with me and the Hockeyroos. Corinne was at Murdoch University as an associate professor in the Psychology Department and in charge of research programs and clinical direction. She was very busy but agreed to find the time as well as bring two of her graduate students to embellish the approach. During the next 20 months they set about refreshing and rejuvenating our group in a way that added to the technical and tactical advancement that I hoped we were making.

The work of Corinne, Catherine Campbell and Vance Locke would shake up our athletes and enliven our connectedness in a way that was both challenging and disruptive...it was risky but it was needed and some of the assumptions that I had previously held about leadership and team dynamics were at the heart of the task.

I hoped we would get much better at understanding one another, challenging one another and at being able to connect better anticipating risks and problems rather than reacting to them.

Brendyn Appleby arrived in the program to replace Ted Polglaze, our physiologist, whose illness had slowed him down. Ted was keen to embark on further study while working less. A new face always creates excitement in the gym and Brendyn's methods brought freshness there. Meanwhile Ellen Hawes our outstanding physiotherapist would provide continuity. At times she and Brendyn would lock horns…good to keep everyone on their toes!

Whatever else happened in the next two years I was determined to make sure we fully understood that our quest was for exceptionality not more of the same. I believed in order to go there we needed to be uncomfortable in that journey. My experience of the fantastic elation and satisfaction that comes when teams perform at exceptional levels told me that such performances only came about because of exceptional co-operation and a willingness to go into uncomfortable places and be exposed to rigorous challenge.

4

FINISHING WITH THE
KOOKABURRAS

June 15th, 2014.

Sixteen tense minutes remain to be played in the World Cup final when Chris Ciriello scores his third goal from the circle edge to give us a 5-1 lead. It is still too early to celebrate but certainly a score that fills one with confidence. Graham Reid and I had a quick moment in which we acknowledged the situation. In the Commonwealth Games final four years earlier in 2010 we only felt secure at 5-0!

To lose from this score would make this the worst day ever, yet in ten more minutes it would feel like a best ever day!! We were always reluctant to celebrate as the last stanza had to be played out.

At thirteen minutes left Liam De Young gathered another superb overhead from Knowles but his shot went wide of the far post. Knowles is in my view the world's best at throwing these penetrating balls, and throughout the tournament had done so with telling effect. It is wonderful when your principal defender can be so offensively dangerous.

Still with thirteen minutes the feisty Hammond got a temporary suspension and so we were a player down. Eleven minutes and Jacob Whetton's turnover led to a penalty corner for the Netherlands. Thankfully, Hayward's running and Charter in goals thwarted their repeated attempts. Jeremy Hayward our youngest and newest Kookaburra had perfected this brave and necessary art of blocking corner shots.

At eight minutes we again repelled a Dutch moment in our defensive circle and at six minutes Jamie Dwyer finished the game with a trademark goal. At 6-1 in the World Cup Final with still half a dozen minutes to play we were well able to call ourselves 'World's Best'.

I had thought that should we win it was the best way for me to finish my coaching career and had determined to do so. Such days are always memorable for their sense of achievement and the relief that goes with them. A score like this one was extraordinary. I remember in 2003 as I watched the final of the rugby World Cup in Sydney the game was decided by a drop goal scored by Johnny Wilkinson when the scores were tied in extra time.

Straight after that game Coach Clive Woodward was interviewed and observed that it had been a perfect performance and had all gone according to plan. I was bemused as I always had the aim of annihilating the opposition rather than an extra time cliffhanger! Indeed for me the near perfect result was 6-1 in the World Cup final!

While we had started solidly and I felt we were handling the ball well, the first good chances to score were made by the Netherlands. Mark Knowles, our captain and named later that day as player of the tournament, made a 'school boy' error to allow the Dutch a penalty corner. Andrew Charter and our defensive group twice thwarted Mink Van der Weerden, their mercurial penalty corner taker. That felt like on open punch that missed the mark; penalty corner defence is more than the goalkeeper (although he is 60 per cent of it), and in Jeremy Hayward, Rob Hammond and Tim Deavin we were well equipped to pressure the shot. In Kieran Govers we had a brave and able postman.

The combination of defenders ably co-ordinated by Paul Gaudoin, assistant coach for the past year, had a reliable and organised quality about them. Early in the game they committed and combined to thwart what I expected to be the Netherlands greatest threat.

Of course, the goal that gave the stadium voice and the Dutch extra belief came as a surprise. It seems such goals always do. Jeroen Herzberger cleverly slipped past Hammond and made the scoring area as Simon Orchard and Eddie Ockenden closed him down. His tomahawk shot was perfect, missing the lunges of Simon and Ed and placed a few centimetres inside the post. Charter had no chance. It was a brilliantly executed skill – perhaps unstoppable. We trailed 1-0, as indeed the Hockeyroos had done 16 years earlier in Utrecht in another World Cup final. On that occasion I was still finding my seat on the bench when the Netherlands scored in the first seconds of the game in another full stadium with a crowd dressed in orange and screaming for Holland.

Going down early in the game gives time for recovery and focuses everyone. An early goal against is never good but it can have the effect of giving definition to a team's task. We had been in the game and had chances but now we needed to redouble our efforts and keep making chances.

Our first goal was a result of this sustained pressure. A clever free hit between Knowles, Matthew Swann and Matt Gohdes brought the brilliant Dutch goalkeeper Jaap Stockmann into play and Simon Orchard won a penalty corner from the rebound. Enter Chris Ciriello, maligned for his perceived failure to score consistently in London, his shot was low, to the left and with a little luck Stockmann toed it past the double post defence. It crashed into the boards at the back of the goal making that sound hockey players love to hear.

We believed Ciriello had the power and placement to beat Stockmann to his right and the start was truly confirming. We had much more corner depth than two years before and Ciriello, always enigmatic, was having a consistent year. With an Anglo Indian mother and Italian father he was truly representative of multicultural Australia. Skilled and a sure ball handler and creative passer he offered a unique skill set. We just had to be sure he was vigilant in his defensive endeavours.

Now the game was alive and the crowd hushed in anticipation of the contest ahead; 15 minutes left to play in the first half and the scores were level 1-1. What followed during the next forty minutes was quite unexpected but also extremely satisfying…in some ways a coach's dream.

Four minutes later it was Herzberger who failed to shadow Govers as that player scored with a shot equally as telling as the Dutch first goal. Govers shot was rasping and seemingly was in the net before Stockmann moved. Govers, the consummate professional in all his preparation, was rewarded.

For the next ten minutes we continued to attack and two more penalty corners and other chances were thwarted. We went to the break without being rewarded. The Netherlands, early leaders, seemed to be just hanging on but half-time can often allow a team to regroup.

I was just as anxious as I had been at the start of the game. Indeed, leading it almost seemed there was more to lose. My life in sport had been replete with examples of upsets and turnarounds. Whenever it seemed a game was under control I knew how quickly things could change. My apprehensions fuelled my vigilance and were a driver of my quest for thoroughness.

Earlier in the day as the players filed past the World Cup trophy prior to the national anthems, I had noticed their intense focus while a number of the Dutch players felt inclined to touch the prize.

Our players seemed immersed in the moment and the task that lay ahead. There were some good signs in the first half and the statistics indicated we had controlled possession and chances.

We spent half-time reaffirming our plans and reminding ourselves of what was needed. Relentless pressure on the opposition all over the field, calmness when we have the ball, willingness to all be involved whenever the chance to penetrate appeared and clarity around every set-play situation.

Only minutes into the second half Orchard's brilliant approach provided Turner with a chance to finish with his reflexes from close range. Simon Orchard is a rare talent with the speed and skill to make goals out of nothing much. At the edge of the scoring circle he lifted the ball and accelerated, the tackle was clumsy and as the ball fell free he passed across the scoring area where Turner, ever aware, shot with the reverse. The shot was saved but the vigilant Turner finished before a despairing Wouter Jolie and Stockmann.

Then twelve minutes into the half Ciriello made it 4-1, beating Stockmann again. We had dominated the half and never allowed our opponents an opportunity. Eight years earlier a second half two-goal lead had been forfeited in a World Cup final but this seemed unlikely as we were playing really purposefully. It was becoming emphatic yet the last period of the game needed to be played…as it turned out we played it well.

Eight months earlier…

2013 had finished very badly for me. It was one of the toughest periods of my life to date. On November 24 as I drove to watch Oscar's cricket match I received a call from my oldest brother, John, telling me our mother had passed away. It was a Sunday and although Mum at 96 had been suffering dementia for some years it was still a stunning shock. It did not get any better as the year ebbed away. On the late afternoon of Christmas Day John's wife, Helen, called to tell me of John's sudden death to a heart attack that afternoon. In a month the family I had grown up with was reduced to three – half were left. My father had died suddenly more than three decades earlier. David, Judy and myself – the youngest three remained.

During the year since London, we had spent much time during which our team culture was questioned and examined. The fallout from our London disappointment was all around and my sense of having let down the team was ever present. The London result at times hovered over the team like a dark cloud and seemed to darken the mood of the place. At the end of 2012 we had retained the Champions Trophy in Melbourne when Kieran Gover's extra-time strike had broken the deadlock with the Netherlands. Five Champions Trophies in succession should have confirmed our quality but the Olympic loss loomed larger.

Still, during 2013 we had games to play, a team to rejuvenate and refresh and a World Cup for which we needed to qualify. On a personal note, I faced hip replacement surgery scheduled for March and October. This would allow me to be ready for the World League finals, scheduled for December 2013. These games would be the last big competition before the World Cup in June 2014. At that stage my contract was due to cease in August 2014 after the Commonwealth Games in Glasgow. I felt 70 per cent sure I would finish then, although the gate to Rio had not been closed.

In March 2013, in the Azlan Shah Tournament in Ipoh, we defeated Malaysia 3-2 in a noisy final before a sell-out crowd. After playing four matches against South Korea in May we met the Netherlands and Belgium in warm-up games before the World League Semi-Finals in Rotterdam in June.

The World League Semi-Final was part of the qualification apparatus for the 2014 World Cup and a semi-final place (top four) would almost be sufficient for us to confirm our place in the World Cup. On beating India 5-1 in the quarterfinal my relief was palpable.

Three days later we accounted for the Netherlands 4-3 in the semi-final. In the final we lost to Belgium in a penalty shoot-out after tying 2-2 at full time.

The International Hockey Federation (FIH) had instituted the 'penalty shootout' immediately at the end of full time. I much preferred the 15 minute extra time with 'Golden Goal' as I believed hockey ought to decide such encounters, with the penalty shootout only involved after 15 minutes of extra time was exhausted. It was clear to me that FIH wanted more upsets and less predictability in the outcomes of their competitions and this was one of the measures that would bring about those outcomes.

Anyway, experience with shootouts can always be useful and that particular shootout went for nine turns before we faltered. It was tied after the first five! Orchard and Trent Mitton both succeeded twice in the pressure of the shootout…not an easy thing to do. The attackers did well but Andrew Charter in goal would need some work, as after a good start he was a little too passive. Interestingly, Belgium used their reserve GK Jeremy Gucassoff rather than their first choice for the field, Vincent Vanash. Clearly, in this specialised area Gucassoff was more proficient in the shootout.

Our performance in Europe had been reasonably solid and we had learnt more about our opponents. We defeated the Netherlands three times and played two draws and a loss with Belgium. Belgium were continuing to improve and as their very successful crop of juniors were moving into senior ranks the belief of the team was growing. Since we first played them in my time in February 2009 in the heat of Canberra they had progressed rapidly. It was a testimony to their work in developing the game countywide. I knew at the World Cup they would be serious contenders.

New Zealand, Spain and India and Ireland all had moments of real quality but one wondered whether they could sustain that quality for extended periods.

The packed calendar for the year later led to the World League finals being moved to January and so it was I departed Australia on Tuesday, January 7 for Delhi, after my brother's funeral on the 6th. The team were already ensconced in their hotel when I arrived, and from the 10th to the 18th we performed a little erratically with good wins against Belgium, Argentina and India but twice succumbed to the Netherlands and were unlucky in the bronze medal game against England when a bizarre umpiring interpretation denied us the chance of a shootout on the final whistle.

It was not an emphatic performance yet privately I was feeling better as we returned home. Just about everything that could go wrong had done so and we had left a number of first choice players out, as we endeavoured to manage the load for the Hockey India League (HIL) in which a majority of our players were involved. I was very glad I had decided to stay away from coaching in the HIL as that would have complicated the very hectic year in prospect. In the end there would be eight players in the World Cup team who were not in India in January. This was an indication that we were not at full strength as the focus was firmly on The Hague.

Additionally, some very soft goals had been scored against us, which I believed were unlikely to happen with our first choice goalkeeper. No matter what one's team does on the field one or two clangers by the goalkeeper can amount to a sufficient reason for failure.

During the first months of 2014 the players were either resting in a 'no hockey' phase or playing for their HIL teams in India. Our great challenge once they all returned at the end of February would be to galvanise the group in the few months ahead leading into the World Cup. We did not have many international matches planned but I felt that given the HIL commitment it was about right.

Coaches always worry about getting the right amount of games leading into competition but I felt in this case less was better. When invited by Germany to go to a competition in Europe a week earlier than we intended we decided against being away the extra week. One always has to remember that the main games of the competition are at the end of a period away and another week living out of suitcases can be too much. I believed on balance the extra week away was the greater risk to being fresh on June 15.

During the lead up to the World Cup in 2014 we played again at the Azlan Shah tournament winning convincingly against the hosts 8-3. Too many goals against, but Ciriello's four goals in the final indicated he was still improving. Jeremy Hayward was coming into contention with his corners developing, and so with Kieran Govers and Glenn Simpson we had four plausible corner options. After London one of our aims had been to develop more corner options and it was a credit to the work of recent retiree Luke Doerner who was making his mark working with both the women and the men.

Around Easter, matches against NZ were sharp and competitive, and with lead-up games ahead in England in late May we were becoming ready. Technically, we had made a good deal of progress since London. Kathleen Partridge had done wonderful work with our goalkeepers. She was proving that gender was no barrier. She had their respect and attention due largely to her tough uncompromising manner and the rigour of her approach. She had coached Hockeyroo goalkeeper Toni Cronk to the best ever performance in a tournament in London where she conceded only twice in that competition.

In Andrew Charter, Tyler Lovell, George Bazeley and Tristan Clemons we had greater depth and quality and our penalty corner defence had improved. Our attacking corners were better thanks to Luke Doerner and our flexibility around the field was continuing to develop…we had options across the lines and flexibility is critical in such tournaments over two weeks.

Of course we had our problems. There are always problems and injuries are the worst of these. After appearing to re-injure his hamstring for a third time we were at the point of ruling out Jamie Dwyer from contention. The initial report from the radiologist when re-examined however, was not so clear and with his strength being measured as undiminished we kept his availability alive. I remember my call to our doctor Pete Steele on the morning we were going to meet with Jamie. I asked him to look again and be sure. In cross-referencing all the data thankfully we got it right. Jamie arrived pretty gloomy that morning but left with hope.

Our fitness was at a high level as Brendyn Appleby, new to our group, had added extra thoroughness and a different approach to our strength and conditioning program. In the lead up to London the illness suffered by our fitness expert Ted Polglaze had made us less than perfect in this area.

However, the real shift in our group had occurred in the culture of our players. After London I had been keen for a change in this area and the inclusion of Corinne Reid and two of her graduate students, Catherine Campbell and Vance Locke, had greatly improved the resources available in this area. Neil Mclean had been a trusted and diligent colleague and had worked for over a decade with Barry Dancer and then myself. He had been for some time the pre-eminent sports psychologist around. However, I wanted a new pair of eyes and a new approach to the team dynamics and believed Corinne might be able to provide that.

Corinne had been in on my long coaching journey since my early days with the Hockeyroos. From her time as a graduate student from UWA, she had been a critical friend and advisor through my time with the Hockeyroos and subsequently as a good friend who knew me well and was willing to bring her considerable skills to our program. I asked her to spend some time observing the workings of the Kookaburras and gave her unfettered access to the group. She had a weekly session with the group and along with her graduate students was involved in all our preparation and competition during 2013. Critically, she had the charter to also reflect on London and the pall I felt it cast over our efforts to progress.

Corinne, never one to pull her punches, identified a range of weaknesses and set about implementing shifts and a catharsis that we hoped would make a difference. We needed a rebuild in leadership, coaching method and tone, communication and most importantly honesty. All teams grow and evolve, and from time to time need to be reminded of their vulnerability. They need constant vigilance to achieve special outcomes.

The Kookaburras were no different and, just as the London semi-final had revealed soft spots in our team, it also afforded us the experience that might be sufficient to push for more. We were committed to 'seeking greatness' and in order to do that we had to better know ourselves and discover more about one another.

We had thought we were in a good place but our slip-up revealed differently. Our ability to challenge one another as players and coaches hadn't been good enough and to get to a better place would require tough messages. Corinne's challenge was to see if she could help us become truly able to live up to a standard which allowed everyone to hold one another to account. A truly 'team first' culture was the aim.

I believe a quote from one of our senior players, Rob Hammond, in 2014 gives a view of what we were facing. It identifies the issue. I believe Corinne uses this quote elsewhere in the book when writing about the transformative process. I am happy for it to appear twice as it underlines our journey. *"The hardest step for me was...to first understand that our culture was not resilient, not 'team first'. It was 'closed minded' (and therefore lacked the honesty that would become the backbone of our identity). Yeah we were 'good' as a team, but by no means were we truly great when we set out on this challenge."*

Under Corinne's oversight everyone in the group would be challenged to grow themselves and the team without fear or favour – with the ultimate goal of making our team think and act in a way in which 'team first' was lived and breathed by all every minute. It meant understanding and dealing with discontent. It is important not to hide from it or ignore it. It meant we all needed to have the courage to speak up. It meant we needed to define the borders of the group and work with each person whether we agreed or didn't. In the end, some of our most perplexed and difficult resistors became allies.

It also meant that eventually we took a path to a different leadership structure to my preferred option, which was to share the role. At least that was what we believed would work best until we could develop further depth in that area. The continual nurturing of new leaders is essential in any co-operative venture. In competitive team sport it is one of the most critical activities and must be continuous and ongoing.

Corinne was never confident that we would achieve all we wanted by The Hague but we certainly went a long way towards our goal by the time we arrived there in June. Certainly, you can never get everything perfect and the time always comes when you must settle for your line up and then manage the problems that come along. You hope most ardently that all the preparation will be reflected in the cohesiveness and skill execution under the pressure of competition.

Seeking Greatness

To share a flavour of what we had been trying to do I have included an excerpt from an email from Corinne we all shared after our last Tuesday meeting at which we had discussed our various signatures and how we might together manage the difficult weeks ahead.

"Last Tuesday we talked about what memories you want to take away from your World Cup experience and how we are going to create these

memories now – how each choice that we make from here is a new foundation stone for those memories.

"We talked about being conscious in the choices we make to do this tour differently – to live our vision of 'seeking greatness'.

"We talked about how to know the difference between our 'stressed self' and our 'best self' and how to recognise when we (and others) move between these two different parts of our signature. It has been great to hear from a number of you that this conversation has led you to do this week differently in the lead-up to departure. Your coaches have also noticed that a number of you have been more fully 'present' at training this week – that people have started to overcome the niggles and jitters of last week and focus in on task at hand despite the stress – moving from your 'stressed self' to your 'best self'. Many of you have also engaged more actively with the off-field team in planning the tour, thinking about rooming etc. All good signs of consciousness in preparation – a fabulous start.

"The task now is to keep walking consciously toward The Hague, to keep track of your own groundedness and the groundedness of your teammates. What is entirely predictable is that each day will present new challenges, both expected and unexpected, familiar and unfamiliar. Moreover, that these challenges will happen at a time when we are more stressed than usual, when there is 'hot cognition' that affects our thinking, and when small issues can feel like big issues very quickly (remember when we talked about social contagion?)

"Our readiness for the World Cup will be in large part measured by how we respond to those challenges as individuals and as a team. What was clear last Tuesday night is that we are ready to do this differently – that we ARE doing it differently. As a team we are much further along in knowing our own signatures and the signatures of our teammates. We are much further along in understanding how to 'take it down a notch' or 'take it up a notch' when we veer toward our stress signatures and how to help our teammates do the same. We are much further along in our ability to have (and be open to) critical conversations with one another and in our

*willingness to do so – to leave nothing to chance, or to fate, or to wearing the 'right' coloured underwear (!!), but to **create** our own destiny through commitment to our new way of being and our way of playing. After 18 months of 'Tuesday nights' we are ready.*

"Make the most of the coming days..."

The email continued for a few more lines espousing the need to 'leave no opportunity for regrets'. It encapsulates the work of many months in building a much more 'bulletproof' team; a team that might be able to dominate the opposition.

In the end we came to the toughest of days when we selected our team. The World Cup allows for eighteen players including two goalkeepers. Now our squad was deep and there were few injured. Before London, injuries interfered with the selection of Abbott, Begbie and Hammond but there were no notable losses this time. At this stage Jamie Dwyer's scare had not knocked him out of contention. Indeed, as it turned out later the injuries would come in the last few days before competition started. Even with eighteen and two travelling reserves (insurance against late problems that might arise in the Netherlands) some very deserving players would miss out.

Selection day was tough and it was quite late in the afternoon that I made it home. I remember it as a Saturday and the team was to be ratified by our CEO by the afternoon of Sunday. Then, after the players had been informed, the press release would occur on Tuesday. This schedule allowed us the evening to contemplate our selections and confirm them Sunday morning so our operations manager could get the process completed for action during the next week.

Whenever you finalise a team on such a day for one of the big events in the calendar there are inevitable doubts and uncertainty that play on your mind. These concerns are always there and the final selections always involve considerations of balance and flexibility. This was no different and indeed the selection process, which is by nature collegial, always contains one or two very close calls. I was uneasy that night when I lay down to sleep. I felt like perhaps we needed to think again. It was a view I had raised at the table before we rose to leave.

Two years earlier Luke Doerner had questioned our judgement when we omitted him before London. The concern is sometimes the bias of selective abstraction where you see what you want to see or omit bits that inconveniently do not fit into the picture that you may have in your mind. In selections I believe you need always to be aware of your preconceptions and biases. We all have them. That is one reason why I like the idea of an independent selector from outside the coaching group where 'group think' can easily sneak into considerations.

In the morning I awoke with it still front of mind. Carmen, my wife, wasn't able to advise but heard all the arguments. For the only time I can recollect in my time as a national coach I rang my fellow coaches and expressed the view that we should reconsider. After a couple of phone calls it was agreed and we made a change to the team that we had agreed the day before. Only the small group involved that day will ever know what the change was but one player went in and another went out. So we had eighteen for the World Cup plus two substitutes in Matt Gohdes and Tim Deavin who would accompany us right up until the competition began. It would, as fate would decide, change again in the final days and hours before our team had to be submitted in The Hague.

After our lead-up matches against England where we played pretty well at Bisham Abbey, we made our way to The Hague by bus! A neat idea but it was a very long journey and probably not ideal. Our accommodation at a beachfront hotel was, however, very good and away from distractions. The water provided an easy release of tension and ideal recovery place in the chilly waters of the North Sea after matches.

Scheveningen is a beachside suburb in The Hague. It has a long sandy beach, an esplanade, a pier and lighthouse. It is popular for water sports and it is a busy place during summer. The name Scheveningen was used as a shibboleth during World War II to identify German spies. German and Dutch native speakers pronounce the initial 'sch' differently. English speakers just get lost in the guttural 'ghhs' that proper pronunciation entails.

So during the 2014 World Cup in the Dutch city that is the seat of government, we stayed at a hotel in Scheveningen and trained at the nearby Klein Switzerland Club. The club had suffered the ignominy of demotion from the Dutch first division in recent years but still boasted excellent facilities. I had played there in the October of 1980 when we delivered the Dutch a 6-2 drubbing on a tour paid for by Malcolm Fraser's Government to compensate for the folly of the Olympic boycott. I hoped that perhaps we could repeat that result 34 years later if we were to meet the Dutch!

The Kyocera Stadium in The Hague is a large bowl that stands out as you approach it rather like my dog's food bowl that sits in the corner of our living room. It is the home of ADO Den Haag, the city's major football club. It was the venue for the 2014 World Cup tournament for men's and women's hockey, a celebration of hockey that only the Dutch could enact. The club's colours are green and gold and when we visited the venue I secretly thought this was a good omen. We were at home in the Netherlands with these colours! The ADO stands for 'Alles Doot Oefening', translated as 'everything through practice'. For me that too was a good fit for my philosophy.

We played at that stadium against Argentina in a practice match a few days after arriving in The Hague, and were challenged by them in the first half before a solid win in the second half. It was a good grounding result. We trained at the Klein Switzerland Club, which was convenient, and we were close to ready with just a match against Germany due for the final days. Unfortunately for Glenn Simpson a blow to the foot in England had not settled and the fracture diagnosis confirmed in Holland ruled him out in those last days.

Glenn had been close to selection for London and over my period with the team developed into a worthy first choice. The Hague was to be his first selection for one of the 'big' tournaments and he was cut down so devastatingly after being so close. A hip injury would later intervene to limit his Rio ambitions. His wife, Perry, and his family were in Holland for the competition. It was truly heartbreaking news for him and his family.

Then against Germany in our last practice match Russell Ford came off the field complaining of calf pain and in the hours before we submitted our team an MRI revealed a calf injury that would rule 'Rusty' out. Again Russell's parents had got on a plane leaving Australia two hours before and they arrived in Holland to the devastating news of their son's misfortune. Russell's story was indeed one of last minute selection disappointment, inclusion and injury. In 2006 he was a late inclusion in the World Cup team, he missed the 2008 Olympics, he flew to Delhi in 2010 as an emergency but returned home when not required. He replaced Des Abbott in 2012 for London and then in 2014 when selected for The Hague was withdrawn because of an injury hours before the tournament team was submitted.

Both Matt Gohdes and Tim Deavin were included. We were very grateful to have had them there and available as emergencies. For Victorians Simpson and Ford it was shattering as both had played some of their best ever hockey to gain selection and such last moment exits are indeed heart breaking. The picture of them leaving the team hotel filled me with sadness. Both were deserving of a grander fate than to watch from the sidelines.

While concerned about the losses I was at least assured by the form of Matt Gohdes and Tim Deavin who had both taken up their chance as travelling reserves with gusto and would be able to fit in seamlessly. Their progression through the tournament confirmed this. We moved Rob Hammond forward into the midfield. Deavin as a defender suited our balance well. Gohdes, starting to fulfil his great potential, would play forward as a direct swap for Ford. At such times the depth of the program is tested and I was glad we had worked so hard to build this depth.

As defending champions we found ourselves playing the first game of the competition against Malaysia in the Kyocera Stadium. Early on that first day it was pleasantly only half-full and we struggled against our near neighbours who knew us well. It was only after about 20 minutes that the deadlock was broken when Turner converted from an 'against the play' breakaway after a quick and accurate pass from Kavanagh. The first game of any competition is often a tense affair and this first 20 minutes was no exception as we played nervously, and Malaysia, with dangerous counterattack potential, tested us.

Against the Spanish early goals settled us and we were convincing winners with Deavin scoring in the second minute and then climbing the fence! His antics drew criticism from teammates and coaches. It served as a reminder not to get ahead of yourself. When a player from another team fell menacingly and hurt himself doing a similar thing Deavo was suitably chastened.

Belgium was our most difficult opponent and after leading by three early in the second half we were again a little untidy. Belgium played with purpose and strength and confirmed their form of a year earlier when we had met them in World League matches in Rotterdam. Eddie Ockenden's goal at the beginning of the half was brilliant when he ghosted into the circle on the right and hit a low rocketing back hander, or tomma!

Nearly assured of a final place we scored in the first minute against England through Ghodes' brilliant strike but my highlight came six seconds before half time when Knowles launched a speculative high ball into the English circle and the sleeping keeper was caught napping and Govers guided the ball from above his head into the goal. This was a ringing endorsement of the rule allowing such aerial play.

For a coach such moments are pure vindication as the previous game I had berated our players when they stopped playing with seconds left on the clock. I have always believed that you can score in the first and last seconds of any game and your duty is to search for such opportunities. 0-4 at half time England was done! Eventually they would lose 0-5 but the effect of that goal was to snuff out any ambition they may have still had.

I believed Belgium would get past England after playing them both during the rounds. However, surprisingly England beat Belgium two days later to progress to the semi-finals. At the elite level there is never an easy final and the last round game between Belgium and England was effectively a quarterfinal.

In that vital game at the end of the round, a very determined England team thwarted Belgium. Interestingly, England advanced with a negative goal difference of eight for and nine against whereas Belgium had seventeen for and twelve against. I was not surprised when Belgium defeated Germany in the play off for fifth place. They, along with Germany, were the teams that would have expected much more in The Hague.

And so we were in another crucial semi-final. Whoever you meet in such a match is going to be in form, and in the case of Argentina they had made the semi-finals on the back of defeating Germany in the round game and had pushed the Netherlands also. Their penalty corners were excellent and Gonzalo Peillat would be the tournament's leading scorer. We would need to defend these situations well. Additionally, a compact defence underpinned them while their dangerous forwards were capable of creating trouble against any team. Our pre-tournament practice match and recent struggles with Argentina meant we respected their pedigree.

One of the most pleasing aspects of the tournament so far was that our penalty corner conversion and defence had been amongst the best in the tournament. Between them, Ciriello, Hayward and Govers would score twelve times over the competition from penalty corners and so we had a range of threats available and the advantage of unpredictability with our double battery at the top of the circle. Luke Doerner oversaw feedback to each of them during the competition from his home in Tasmania…the wonders of modern communication!

Our defence of these situations was also excellent, and indeed only one penalty corner was scored against us in the seven matches. This was late in the semi-final where captain Mark Knowles wisely suggested we could run a 'safe' line against Peillat as the match was already won. Our penalty corner defence had received much attention after London when some crucial slip-ups were so costly. As important as anything was the work of Paul Gaudoin in this area and our decision to have a special extra meeting to ensure we were on top of the details. This 'checklist' mentality is essential.

The semi-final game was one that you dream about as we scored early again when Govers fired in the perfect PC after four minutes, and then at twenty minutes Hayward, hardly used until then, fired at the postman to make it 2-0. Hayward's preferred shot was to that side, unlike Ciriello and Govers. As he had not been seen he had less respect from our opponents who rushed at the senior flickers. Jeremy scored twice that day along with Ciriello and Whetton and we were in the main game at the end of the tournament as was always our aim.

England fought gamely against the Netherlands but van der Weerden decided it before half time and the Dutch were content to hold on winning 1-0. In 1998, with the Hockeyroos, we had met Holland in a World Cup final in their home country so the Kookaburras would do so too. I knew the stadium would be coloured orange and the opposition motivated beyond what one would find anywhere else. So often, a buoyant home team wins such tournaments.

On my return to the hotel I was excited and yet apprehensive… the job was not complete and a big win in the semi-final can often be the worst lead in to a final. I got on my bike and went for a long ride as the evening took over from the twilight. We would train the next day and be interested observers of the fate of the Hockeyroos who were also pitted against Holland in a World Cup final.

The World Cup final in The Hague on June 15, 2014 is a day that I shall always remember fondly. The morning went quickly as meetings and preparations for our ultimate game filled in the time. There is not much special to say on such a day as most of the work has been done: prepare for the 'what ifs'; emphasise some core details and be calm and clear. Two short meetings to ensure attacking and defensive corners are ready – these crucial set plays that require details and clarity followed the final team meeting – a life in the game taught me that.

Four years earlier in Delhi I had not been so calm. I had only been the men's coach for fifteen months and still parts of our game were not solid. "Are we ready?" was in my mind back then. Our penalty corner defence had me very much concerned back then. Four years later in The Hague, indeed even in London before our disappointing semi-final, I felt more comfortable about our preparation.

The journey to the ground on the evening of June 15 was, as all such journeys are, sombre, full of tension and resolve. Along the way we passed the local prison, which is the home of those detained by the International Criminal Court domiciled in The Hague. Slobodan Milosevic died there in 2006 a few weeks before the verdict was due after his four-year trial. As we passed the walls each day I tried to imagine the life inside such a place, but not on this day...the game ahead was all.

We had prepared as well as possible, played with increasing quality as the tournament progressed, overcome Argentina in the semi-final and would meet the hosts on the last day. The previous day, while at training, we heard sketchy reports about the women's final when the Hockeyroos fell short on the final day against their nemesis. They lost 0-2. In the women's game, the Netherlands' record over the decade since Athens had been pretty emphatic.

In Atlanta in 1996 with the Hockeyroos, on the day before the Olympic final, we made our way to our training venue in the afternoon and were there during the men's semi-final – Australia versus Spain. We tried to concentrate on one last training session but inevitably we were distracted by news of the men's match – they fell short and on this occasion as we went about our work at Klein Switzerland Club the news was also not good.

The Hockeyroos' quest had bravely fallen short yet they had done much under the stewardship of Adam Commens since London and their progress was rewarded with a silver medal with ten other nations in their wake.

I remember little about our arrival at the Kyocera Stadium and in a blur of activity we were soon into the game and its wonderful outcome. When I reflect on our play that day I remember the brilliant way Ockenden outplayed the best Dutchman Robbert Kemperman, I remember Knowles playing like Franz Beckenbauer at the back, I remember a whole team single-minded in purpose yet collectively connected.

Orchard made a goal, won corners and chased when there was danger; Turner and Govers scored, won corners and were ever dangerous; Ciriello finished as planned; Kavanagh and Swann were relentless tackling and intercepting everything, Gohdes and Whetton were terrier-like and always a threat yet defended, often deep in defence; Dwyer, De Young and Hammond, our veterans, ran like younger men and calmed the team with their assurance and skill. Deavin and Hayward were uncompromising and never beaten; tough guy Aran Zalewski was combative filling the middle with his presence. Charter played a faultless game in goal and in the last minutes Tyler Lovell even had an opportunity to show his stuff with a brilliant save. Every player contributed and at the end they were all elated.

In Appendix No.5 you can see my notes for that day reproduced… not much special about them. You can see our planned corners on the right of the page and my reminder to self to 'B CALM' at the top.

Interestingly, after an initial flurry when the Netherlands won a penalty corner and then scored from the field until their next corner about an hour later their goal opportunity total (GOT) score was about five or six. It was the quality of our defence that was special that day. The Netherlands had little penetration and momentum throughout most of the game.

As a player I had been part of Australia's first World Cup win in London in 1986 and now 28 years later we had secured the trophy for the third time. It was something I had never thought possible back in the 1980s but I had now coached four teams to World Cup victories and this one in Holland had been the most emphatic. The relief and release of emotion was great and the elation special. The players would celebrate and after the press conference I caught up with my daughter Libby who had made her way from London for the weekend. It was a much happier scene than in London 2012.

I remember going into the change room to find Chris Ciriello sitting on a bench with his hand on the World Cup just staring ahead in a dream state. He was startled when I made a noise. The players were invited on stage at the large hall out the back of the venue and sang and danced and then came the return bus trip to our hotel. Staff greeted us and then you were in the solitude of your room and just alone with your thoughts for maybe half an hour.

It was determined that we would go to one of the beachside bars where the supporters and friends would make sure this night was a memorable one. There were some speeches, much drinking, lots of noise and backslapping and everything was fine…it always is when you win.

I told Cam Vale, our CEO, and Trish Heberle our high performance manager that I felt it was the right time to finish for me. I was drained of all energy and believed it was time for others to take over. I know it messed up their plans as succession was due eight weeks later after the Commonwealth Games but for me this was right and for the team and my successors it was time for them to start. Between us we determined to leave any announcement until our return to Perth. I was happy to wind down as the team prepared for Glasgow and my last week at work would be the week in which the team departed for Scotland.

Over the next month and a half our Commonwealth Games team, which we had selected before going to the World Cup, emerged and found their place. Senior players De Young and Hammond retired and a new chapter began for others going to Glasgow. Those two had been outstanding players for well over a decade. They had played in an era where Australia had won Olympic gold and bronze and World Cup silver and gold and everything else in between. They were not just recipients of this great era. They were clearly very much central agents in that era. Skilled players, gifted athletes and great competitors each in their own way, they left the sport triumphant World Champions.

We had selected the Commonwealth Games team with a view to only include those we believed would be still playing in Rio and so there were some disappointed players. Thankfully, all that would soon be someone else's problem. The meetings regarding selection went ahead and the team for Glasgow prepared with fervour and enthusiasm as the event drew closer.

I was sad but also glad as I wound up this chapter of my life, which started with my appointment in October 2008. We had all got together for the first time in January 2009 to play the Netherlands in Busselton and it finished against the same team at their home in The Hague with such a wonderful result in the final of the World Cup.

PART 2

COACHING

5

"AUSTRALIA IS WEAK ON TACTICS..."

In July 2010, as we prepared for the Champions Trophy in Monchengladbach in the south-west of Germany, a piece appeared in the news attributed to Jason Lee, the coach of the English team. The reigning European Champions and a team that surprised us earlier in the year at the World Cup, England would eventually meet us in the final on August 8.

In an interview about the teams Jason suggested that while Australia had a gifted team they were tactically weaker than the other teams and therefore vulnerable. It was true that I was not a tactical zealot believing that players were best served by an approach that was proactive rather than reactive. We had a way of playing that I thought was capable of allowing us to handle every situation and so adherence to it would bring success. On any particular day we might have some specific ploys that fitted the nature and idiosyncrasies of our opponent but essentially we played our game.

Because our game was inherently attacking I believed we did not need to do too much different when chasing the game (being behind). And when in front, I believed it was often a mistake to become defensive as teams lost purpose and tended to keep losing the ball rather than getting to the other end where the game could be 'finished' with another goal. In *The Coach*, I devoted a whole chapter to this approach where I outlined that you should *never defend a lead.*

I was of course clear about the need for us all to understand and know what we were trying to do. Essentially, we were being more fluid and flexible and players had licence to interchange across and within their lines and go wherever they thought they could exploit the opposition's deficiencies and vulnerabilities. I firmly believe you can never be out of position if your team has the ball...just always be aware you may lose it! Sometimes it must have looked like chaos and sometimes it was; yet we were learning more about how to do it.

The piece that was attributed to Jason, incensed my assistant Graham Reid and indeed was something of a surprise to us all, yet on consideration, it did cause us to examine our modus operandi and I have always believed such introspection is only good. Graham and myself were joined by Paul Gaudoin in 2010, and we were all different in our emphasis on tactical matters.

Paul was probably the most interventionist of the three with Graeme next then myself as the least prescriptive about these matters. My approach fits with my view, long held, that the players are not 'chess pieces' on the field to be directed from outside. I believed them to be more autonomous instinctive entities who needed to co-operate effectively with one another and continuously calculate risk and reward for themselves.

There is not one way of coaching that is superior or best. Indeed nuance, context and practicality all influence the way in which coaches decide to deploy their resources in any situation. During my time with the Hockeyroos, I sat in the middle of a tactical continuum with Bob Haigh the least tactical and Frank Murray a tactical zealot.

Tactics or Strategy?

In Alistair Campbell's book *Winners* there is an interesting discussion about the difference between tactics and strategy. For Alistair, strategy is the driving plan and tactics are directed at a certain moment. Jose Mourinho, on the other hand, had the view that tactics are the model and the principles you use, and strategy – being strategic – was when you do something for a particular reason against a particular opponent to be effective. These strategic moves can be both assertive and reactive. Assertive actions often just reinforce your way of doing things. Reactive actions can be quite disruptive to your way. I am cautious about reacting too much to an opponent.

Of course there are occasions when it is necessary to adjust to a tactic used by another team. In the World Cup game against Spain in New Delhi in 2010 we were being outplayed by overhead balls down our left side in defence and needed to spend a few minutes at half-time putting in place an antidote. Such situations are quite rare when your players are flexible and able to adjust for themselves but sometimes in the hurly burly of competition this is not possible or does not happen and intervention is required.

In the end it does not matter to me, although my critical reaction to the discussion was to see things according to Campbell. Of course, the argument is only a semantic one as to what you call these things. Rather than have a strategy I like to think of a 'way of playing' as a model for how we as a team go about playing the game.

It is within this context that we then apply particular tactics in any particular situation and take advantage of our opponents' vulnerabilities. Very often the vulnerabilities of the opposition may also be the reason for their success so this requires an ability to deal with complexity and paradox. Whatever else you may want to do, it is also critical that whatever 'way of playing' and tactics are pursued these things must be owned by the players. They must be committed to and believe in them for the team to be really, really effective.

In *The Coach* in a chapter titled 'So you Want to Be a Coach' I outline the five qualities I believe every coach must have and develop in order to undertake the role. Being knowledgeable, eager to learn, flexible towards change, consistent and always honest in all interactions with players and staff are the required qualities.

I believe in order to succeed at the highest level these things are pertinent but it is perhaps now valuable to expand on what this means. I will outline many of the things that are in the arsenal of a coach who is aiming to take any team to the pinnacle.

Central to this is the role of the coach as leader. This, I believe, entails two essential elements. Firstly, real definition about how you want your team to be, how it should play and why it should play that way. Secondly, coaches must have the capacity to convince others to follow and buy in. Persuasion is the essential element for any coach, new or old. There is no one way to do this for it is an art and requires conviction, finesse, a willingness to set the tone yourself and exemplify what is required. Agility and finesse are essential as one tries to find ways to take the whole team on what can be a difficult and confronting journey into unknown territory.

A Way of Playing the Game

Accordingly, I thought it might be valuable to outline conceptually what I have always tried to do with teams I coached. A set of guidelines that can direct and lead us in the direction that challenges and extends.

Part of this is my personal inclination. Partly, it comes from my vast experience in the game in particular and sport in general. Partly, it is what I believe is rational and effective and pragmatic.

Yet also it goes with my sense of justice and fairness, which, from my earliest days, was a principle underlined by my father as to how one ought to try to live a good life. The list will no doubt seem contradictory and paradoxical at times, however I hope there is an internal consistency in the approach, which will become evident as the reader moves through it.

In the end, I believe this is the route to take if one seeks to reach one's potential at the highest level for the longest time. It is a formula for aspiring to be 'world's best'.

1. Take up the great challenge of the endeavour... I have always believed in having the highest ambition. In the 1970s when I was beginning as an elite athlete in cricket and hockey I remember reading *Psycho-Cybernetics* which was perhaps the first book espousing psychology's importance in sport. The central thesis of the book written by Maxwell Maltz was that we are like guided missiles in our lives and we usually end up where we aim. You don't win the gold medal by aiming at being a semi-finalist...you better have really challenging goals that take you to the top and to the limits of what is possible.

In hockey the great challenge is to score goals, but as the players all become better defenders and the goalkeeper has all new equipment – so he is completely fearless – the task gets harder all the time. Teams defend with every player and scoring is becoming ever more difficult. It is, however, the dream of every player to score and it was always my view that success required a huge emphasis on this aspect.

The great puzzle to be unlocked was how to score. Accordingly, much time and energy was devoted to this aspect of the game. Defending and feeling able to resist opponents was vital too but the exciting and creative challenge was to score. It was the thing that 'dreams were made of' to paraphrase Prospero from *The Tempest*. Every kid who plays sports where a goal is the measure of the score and difference between teams imagines himself or herself kicking or hitting a goal. I hear children commentating aloud what they are imagining in their minds.

At every training session and in almost every drill we undertook at practice there was the scoring of a goal as the logical end point.

2. Never compromise on quality... Quality must be your guiding principle in all you do. No short cuts and no slick and easy solutions...beware the seduction of easy! Every coach who shapes any team should endeavour to always emphasise the need for quality in every aspect of training and preparation. Your task is to be the guide to what real quality is and guard against those things that dilute it in games and on the training track.

The coach's encouragement and redirection can constantly assure quality is valued. The video camera provides support and assistant coaches must always be vigilant too. Accordingly, all coaching staff are continually reinforcing the need for the highest standards.

Later in the book in the chapter on "Comfort the Troubled..." I talk about the team value that demands we never cheat. While the morality and correctness of such an approach makes sense, the additional pragmatic gain from such an approach is that it means we must focus on quality and never take a short cut.

3. Continually test your limits and always be willing to go further. I have always believed the records of the past ought to be the goals for the present group. A good exercise is to ask yourself the question: *"What might seem impossible or unlikely but if we did it would it make a big difference?"* I believe you should challenge yourself by asking this question on a regular basis. It is often surprising how such an approach can stimulate a new angle, a new idea and interesting experimentation.

There are always new skills and techniques and tactics being developed and trialled constantly. If you are open to utilise and experiment with these things then you provide an example of openness and discovery, which can ensure your group is always progressive.

Often change occurs as a response to changes in the rules and regulations of the game, while sometimes it is the experimentation of the players that reveals new ideas. Equally, there are teams and players all over the world who are doing things differently. If you are serious about changing and growing then you will be examining what is happening in other places and other sports.

In the NBA in 1979 the three-point line was introduced. In that season only three per cent of shots were three pointers. Over three decades that number grew to 22 per cent and didn't change that much. It seems stability had been reached. Given that basketballers are almost equally efficient from 23 feet as 24 feet yet the reward is 50 per cent better it had to make sense to take more long shots. We may well now wonder why it took so long for this strategy to unfold but unfold it has. The Golden State Warriors stellar season has seen them outstanding in the regular season. Their slip up in the play-off finals after leading 3-1 is another story! However, their successes have been due significantly to their three-point approach...one which changed the thinking in the game. In baseball the 'money-ball' story is yet another example of changing the paradigm whereby the criteria for selecting talent that may have been time honoured has been shown to be superseded by data analysis.

Another essential element of testing your limits is the requirement to be bold and a willingness to take risks. Invariably, it is the youthful tyros who are most willing to embrace this and so you 'ignore youth at your peril'. Experience, an often overrated commodity, is more about how quickly one learns rather than how many games one has played!

4. Be smart... What's happening elsewhere, how can we go further? Who can help us and where should we look for new and better ways to do things? I have always been an unashamed bower bird always looking for ideas to collect and, where appropriate, to include in our game.

With the Hockeyroos we set up a group within the team that was charged with looking at other sports and other circumstances where there might have been a parallel that would be useful to us.

I watched a great deal of Australian Rules football because here was a game more like our game than any other in the world. Practically unlimited interchange, no offside (so players are ahead of the ball and 360 degree vision is needed), 'play on' from any situation and at the pointy end of the ground, where you try to score, it is crowded. Of course the ball moves much faster in hockey and the field is smaller but many of the aspects mentioned are quite unique to those games and tactically there are many similarities. The hockey coach has much to learn from Australian football. There was a time when I watched a lot of soccer but the removal of offside changed much.

Additionally, hockey now 'plays on' from any breach and so flows continuously. Soccer is staccato as the stoppages and free kicks are all set plays these days and so have much less relevance to our game.

5. Diligence is essential. Nobody gets good at anything without rigorous application…lots of practice. Anders Ericsson's "ten thousand hours" has validity in my view as long as it is accompanied by quality feedback and continuous searching to extend one's skills and do things that are new and more challenging. Outstanding performers in sport become so because of their work ethic, which enables them to polish what are often God given gifts.

There is much more required in a complex integrated team game. There is a need to be able to involve all members and develop the discipline to pay attention to the detail necessary for the skills to be the difference. This means avoiding omissions and the negligence that so often can bring down teams who get lazy or over-confident and complacent.

In the final of the 2002 World Cup in soccer the goalkeeper of the tournament was Oliver Kahn, captain of the team and at the top of his game, yet it was a fumbled save by this brilliant player that allowed Ronaldo to tap in the decisive goal while the German defenders watched flat footed. A rule for our team was that you always had to 'run in case' as this allowed the unexpected to be dealt with.

Recently watching the European Championships round of sixteen game between Italy and Spain I saw a similar goal scored by Giorgio Chiellini when another brilliant goalkeeper in David de Gea of Spain blocked a ball and the Italian got to the spillage first!

The need for diligence can never be understated. Any goal scored against our team is usually the result of four or five consecutive errors. Had any one of those errors not occurred the scoring opportunity would have been averted.

This is the place for Atul Gawande's 'checklist'. The indispensable tool that is essential in flying planes safely, performing surgery, building skyscrapers or indeed ensuring that things aren't overlooked on the sporting field. Conscious attention to checklists ensures the buy-in and engagement of all, and the discipline required to limit avoidable errors that do not necessarily relate to your skills but might be due to inattention or distraction which manifest themselves often when the pressure is great.

Devil in the detail... In any match there are many, many moments, which if they were handled differently would change the course of the game. Little incidents that lead to different outcomes depending on what those involved are able to do. Sometimes, it is the decision of the umpire that leads to a shift in the game; sometimes it is a simple piece of skill or a skill error that makes a difference as outlined above.

It is critical that every athlete understands that his or her actions must be of quality in every incident to ensure they give your team the best chance of success. In a low scoring game such as soccer or hockey these actions will be crucial in close matches.

In our crucial semi-final in London just before we mishandled and allowed our opponent back into the game the umpire missed a ball blatantly kicked by Phillip Zeller. Simon Orchard raised his hand but just got on with it when the ball went into our scoring circle... moments later Germany scored due to our error. It would have been quite different had the umpire seen the kick and awarded a free and the ball had gone to the other end of the field.

These 'sliding door' moments are the stuff of competitive team sports adjudicated by fallible umpires and with fallible players. It can be frustrating and it rankles yet determination to get every single incident right is the only answer. Vigilance and attention to the details are essential. You cannot ensure the umpire gets it right every time but you must endeavour to look after your piece of play. At least then you control the things you can control.

6. Never cheat... We know what is fair and claiming something you didn't earn can lead to a slippery slope of seeking a short cut or taking something that isn't deserved. During my time with the Hockeyroos and the Kookaburras there was always healthy debate about this approach, which was often a point of disagreement and dispute. What the argument did tease out was the importance of setting really high standards for ourselves. Standards that required us to be exceptional and which differentiated us from others. Not everyone in the team was convinced this strategy made sense as most of our opponents were pleased to take any opportunity, when it was presented. I hoped we set for ourselves a higher standard.

In 2014 on the way to the World Cup we played against England at Bisham Abbey in a practice match a few days after we arrived. Such matches were always difficult as we had travelled far and were still finding our feet. We started reasonably but after about 15 minutes the English were gifted a goal when the umpire failed to recognise a direct pass into the scoring circle, which ought to have been disallowed. Our players stopped playing as the English player scored. I was most surprised when the opposition claimed the goal.

For our team it was a blessing, as it required us to work harder and wake up from our slumber. The game was close deep into the second half. It was exactly the sort of struggle that we needed in preparation for the World Cup. As we walked across the field after the match I knew we had England's measure given they could not overcome us courtesy of their fortuitous start and our jet-lagged state that day.

When Australia scored in the final of the World League tournament in June of 2015 against Belgium in Antwerp with three minutes to play in the last quarter and at 0-0, there was initially celebration. However, Kieran Govers immediately indicated to the umpire that the ball had hit an Australian foot. It was not a goal!

The English commentator's response was to say, "that is an extraordinary display of sportsmanship at that level of competition". The incident was televised on Foxtel – the same evening Nick Kyrgios went off the rails at Wimbledon and Australian sportsmanship received a roasting. For the next week the news media were happy to cover the aberrant behaviour of Kyrgios.

The sportsmanship displayed by Govers on Foxtel that evening never received recognition or coverage in the Australian media. It is a great pity the sports journalists of this country are not interested in such actions but rather focus on the ranting, spoilt and petulant!

For the Kookaburras though it is an important principle that underpins real quality…that you set standards for yourselves that overreach those of other teams and cultures.

7. Humility. I was always aware that what we did was not the most important thing in the world. Indeed when one considers the actual value of our endeavour it is hard to see it as anything other than a somewhat self-indulgent activity pursued by a very fortunate group who were very lucky to have the opportunity to do so. Yes, we sought to be the world's best at this game while the vast majority of those on the planet were in the grip of a daily crisis fighting for survival. We were damned lucky and indeed some of the motivation to become exceptional came from an awareness of our appreciation of that good fortune.

Equally, humility underpins a position in which you know you are fallible and that something less than your best ought not to be contemplated. In his book, Atul Gawande not only sees the checklist as being a valuable tool to ensure diligence and team involvement, indeed, he underlines it as an indication of perspective and humility. Humility is a characteristic of most of the best performers.

8. Build resilience by always finding ways to make training harder than the game and by seeking out the most difficult opponents. Excellence is never easy and to be outstanding we must go through difficult times. Often we hear that this or that champion 'makes it look easy'. This never means that it is easy only that they are so proficient that their performance appears effortless.

Deliver honest and challenging feedback and never, ever give up in any contest. The best athletes know that in seconds one can change the momentum and course of a contest. They have seen it happen, experienced it and believe their actions will make a difference as long as they stay in the contest. At training it is vital to put your athletes in situations where defeat or loss is a constant consideration...the best will fight their way out of this situation or go down giving their all.

9. Team first. The measure of everything that occurs in a team should be 'is it in the best interests of the team'? This is the question that you should ask when assessing the actions of the group. Is this for the good/benefit of the team? Is the effect of this good for the team? Does it help the team? Many in your program may wish to introduce new ideas and new challenges and when evaluating the effectiveness of these moves the framework utilised should be 'is this in the interests' of the individuals and the team. I have found this one of the most effective ways of evaluating the efficacy of team practices and individual actions.

10. Everyday. The process of improvement is iterative and what you do every day is the pathway to being special. The pursuit of defined goals leading to incremental progress is the pathway to mastery. Continuous improvement, regular feedback and constantly stretching one's targets can get you there.

I hope I have established a philosophical foundation of our game. But where does this lead us when it comes to the practical application of playing the game on the field? How do these guidelines inform a way of playing a continuous invasion game in which scoring is difficult with a limited and crowded scoring zone and a big goalkeeper filling the net while wrapped in high density foam that renders him/her fearless against almost any shot.

Of course coaches spend much time on assisting players improve their skills and techniques in order to make them reliable exponents of the game. Unless one can consistently execute the technical aspects of the game you are in trouble. However, once that is a given, then it is the higher order details that ensure you are in the contest.

And so from that conceptual base comes the most simplified kernel of the game...there are four elements:

1. **GET IT**...WIN THE BALL by PRESSURING the OPPONENT

2. **KEEP IT** (POSSESSION) AND GET **PENETRATION** so as to... CREATE SCORING CHANCES

3. **CREATE SCORING CHANCES**...SHOOT to SCORE or IF YOU LOSE POSSESSION...

4. **GET IT BACK** (FORCE ERRORS through pressure) and then start again

Around that superstructure sit the elements that make up a 'way of playing', which for me contains the things that bring success – regardless of whatever line up or tactical approach one might wish to utilise on any given day! These are the basic tenets of my way of playing.

1. Possession is important but must be in balance with penetration. Remember that possession passes can be forward passes (indeed the best possession passes go forward!) not just backwards and sideways. Along with this goes the mantra that as soon as you get the ball always 'look long'...you may not decide to pass long but at least you should look there first.

Equally, whenever addressing the ball to start the play from the sideline or any free hit we want to look long and consider the most dangerous and penetrating options first. Such assertive searching for the forward option can indeed make the lateral options more available and interesting. All of this means variety in how you play.

While I have always liked sweeping passing movements and wonderful dribbling and stick skills I have always been pragmatic enough to know that a straight line is the shortest distance between two points. If that route is available use it or at least threaten to use it to open up other ways to penetrate.

2. Build a defence first and have a way of defending that you feel confident will deny the opponent any easy chances to score. This way your focus can always be on scoring if you are confident your default method is solid. I want my team to start defending immediately every time the ball is lost and as high up the field as possible. Wherever you are on the field deny time and space to the opponent. This entails aggressive and assertive pressing whenever the opposition wins the ball and is looking to penetrate your area.

Wherever we lose the ball we want to fight and apply pressure immediately to win it back. I never want our opponents to be comfortable with the ball and have too much time to contemplate the options available.

The big change that occurred in hockey and how defences operate came at the end of 1996 when FIH in their wisdom decided to remove the offside rule from the statutes. The effect of this was supposed to make the game more attacking with more goals being scored. Offside exists in almost every similar game. In basketball it is time in the keyway; in soccer there must be two defenders (one is often the goalkeeper) between the goal and the farthest forward player in the attacking half; and in rugby it occurs in rucks and mauls where there is an imaginary offside line. Also, forward passes aren't allowed with the hands, and when kicking, players cannot be forward of the ball and then endeavour to get it.

It is a way of having space in the scoring area and it was not a change I was sure about at the time. Indeed, in my lifetime in hockey there had been many changes to the rule and how it was applied and each had led to an initial goal scoring spree and then an adjustment by defences to close space and gaps. As predicted scoring went up but the predictable response was that everyone started defending with all eleven players and scoring was strangled.

It was an inadvertent rule change that crept into hockey that saved us from a really dull game! During the late nineties the Argentineans started to experiment with using the 'edge' of the stick to hit on the reverse. Had this not happened defences would have ruled and scoring would have been much more difficult.

The "tomma" shot with the edge allowed attackers to use either side of the body and thus made defending more difficult. Almost 50 per cent of goals are now scored in this way. Every defence now deploys all players to defend when they lose the ball and the lack of an offside rule does make it very crowded back there. I watch a lot of AFL because it is one of the few games where there is no offside and so players are ahead of the ball...hurling and Gaelic football also fit here.

Because of this I favour a pressing defence in our attacking half, as it does not allow opponents to fire balls into our danger zones so easily. If one plays the game in the defensive half your opponent is going to be able to deliver balls into the scoring area too easily. I am always keen for the advantage line to be well up the field where we harass and pressure so as not to afford them that opportunity. Of course, being able to defend close to goal must also be instituted and trained, as it is inevitable the opponent will get there sometimes!

3. Be unpredictable and as much as possible have many ways to challenge and win the ball and penetrate and score. To be unpredictable you need players to be flexible and multi-skilled in their play, so they can defend and attack and are comfortable on both sides of the field and have licence to go where they can cause or quell danger. In the end the aim is always to deceive or outsmart one's opponent and so they are caught off guard or overreact in one area leaving them vulnerable elsewhere. If done well this deception creates hesitation and doubt and indecisive play...and thus it causes errors.

Of course the paradox in all this is that while we want to deceive our opponents and be difficult to read, players on your own team need to be able to read one another and this can be increasingly difficult. It is why much more energy and time must go into knowing and understanding one another. In a complex integrated team game in which the opposition are constantly trying to destroy your work and build something for themselves, perhaps one of the most important abilities is to read one another and be able to understand and anticipate where the game and action is heading.

4. Get the set plays right. This important part of the game can make an enormous difference. About 40-50 per cent of the goals scored in hockey come from corner situations and so training and preparing to defend the corners and score corners is critical. The place of the checklist here is obvious.

The specialist roles involved in these plays require continuous attention and polishing. I was never satisfied that we had every option covered and we tried to broaden our personnel in these areas so there were more possibilities and we could be more unpredictable in these plays.

There are many other situations where play restarts or is close to the goal and so near danger. From every angle on the pitch a player needs to understand the possibilities and what might work to ensure maximal advantage.

5. Practice making goals. This is not about making goals (as in constructing a set of goals!). It relates to the great romance of the game and the aim of the game, which is to score goals. Whatever your orientation in the game we all know that without scoring you cannot win. There is an adrenaline rush whenever one scores even when the final touch may be the most banal and simple event such as a final tip in.

Almost every drill and training situation we did in my years with the national teams (both men and women) had, as the end point, for the attacking team a goal shot or goal chance, and the crafting of those opportunities is in my view the most exciting and challenging part of the game. My aim as a coach was always to encourage the desire of hockey players to score, and indeed my belief was that every player on the field except the GK ought to, from time to time if sufficiently adventurous, find themselves taking a shot at goal.

This is not really radical nowadays but in earlier times…in the 90s with the Hockeyroos it was quite a big shift. In many sports this trend is evident. Goals increasingly come from everywhere and via as many routes as possible…it's all part of being unpredictable.

In the AFL in the fifteen-year period from 1970 to 1985 the leading goal kicker scored over a hundred goals in a season eight times.

Between 1985 and 2000 it was twelve times. Since 2000 it has only been achieved twice in 16 years. Heroic, single person goal-kicking feats are a thing of the past as tactics change and more players are afforded the opportunity to go forward when appropriate. One great scorer is too predictable and too easily foiled

6. Try new stuff. Without willingness to experiment and search for better ways to do things any advantage that a team earns and builds can quickly evaporate. I have always believed that the best teams are continually evolving and being renewed and refreshed. This involves discovering new talent, seeking new ways to do things and refining methods and ideas continuously. There is always pressure to produce results that can guarantee funding, memberships and sponsorship but again it is only success in the big events that really confirms the team's position and status.

Equally, the best players are constantly seeking to try new things and add to their repertoire. As a coach your most important source of innovation comes from players who are exploring the edges of the game. The tomahawk's emergence was an example of this as have been the recent emergence of lifts, which were pioneered by 'jinks' in the 80s.

In *The Coach* I made the point that the Hockeyroos had a much better record in the big events than in the games they played day in and day out during the lead up to these events. I opined that this was because during this time we were experimenting and refining our plans. Indeed this is borne out by the statistics, which show that the Hockeyroos and Kookaburras had almost identical winning percentages to one another, 78 per cent, whereas in the big events against the best opposition the percentage was higher! For the Hockeyroos it was 81.6 per cent and for the Kookaburras 86.7 per cent.

Whatever else was happening FIH always kept us busy dealing with its latest rule changes. Interchange, offside, auto play from free hits, penalty corner interpretations, changes to the high ball and how to play it and the throwing of overheads all required a response and creative solutions. FIH provided much fertile ground for us to grow our strategy and tactics.

7. Share the load... Everyone has a role and without very good co-operation and understanding between teammates it is very difficult to succeed in team sports as everyone's fortunes are interrelated.

I was lucky in 1993 when I took over the Hockeyroos because around that time the rules changed so that teams were allowed unlimited interchange between the bench and players on the field. We embraced the change and indeed eventually it was important in making a much deeper squad for our team as the years went by.

In every game we played 16 players with no 'bench sitters'. Now the international game allows for 18. Whereas in the 90s there was resistance to resting on the bench, now it is seen as a necessary opportunity to refresh and recharge and for coaches an opportunity to redirect or advise.

So there it is in a nutshell; not rocket science, nothing particularly novel or radical other than a willingness to keep searching for better ways to do things. Certainly, it was not a reactive tactical approach to our opponents but a firm belief in our method, a conceptual understanding of how and why and a willingness to share the load and together to endure. I thought by the middle of 2010 we were on our way. We were still not cohesive enough and still needed more polish and we were far from being as open with one another as we needed. That would take more time but the framework was in place.

Accordingly, we marched onto the field in Monchengladbach on August 8 to meet England in the final of the Champions Trophy. We were convincing winners that day – 4-0 when we broke free in the second half. We may have been "weak on tactics" when we played Jason's team that day but whatever it was we did it sure did work! When we overcame the Indians in New Delhi a few months later at the Commonwealth Games we had concluded a very successful year.

So one may ask; how does this broad conceptual framework manifest itself as you go forward? In the lead up to the World Cup in The Hague in 2014 we developed a sheet which outlined the technical and conceptual bits that I believed essential as we went into that year with a World Cup and Commonwealth Games. The elements of that sheet which appears in the Appendix 6 go to applying **pressure**; being **calm**; playing with **speed** and **toughness**; being **flexible**; ensuring we were **active without the ball**; being **efficient in the scoring zone** and always being **assertive.**

There are important tactics and strategy, which underpin how we seek to succeed. No matter how complex or simple they may be it is never possible to put them into practice without the players being able to reproduce their technical skills under pressure and being able to co-operate effectively at the same time. Hence there is a dilemma for all coaches. Where do you place most emphasis? Is it fitness, technical skill, tactics, team cohesion or urgency, intensity and competitiveness? The answer is easy to say but harder to do... you need to do it all, and strategy or tactics – whatever you call it – is only part of the picture.

6

"COMFORT THE TROUBLED AND TROUBLE THE COMFORTABLE"

"Comfort the Troubled and Trouble the Comfortable"
Dietrich Bonhoeffer, 20th Century Martyr 1906-45

Over the period of my life as a coach I have variously used this little aphorism, which is quite a good description of my general approach to coaching. I have never pretended it was my saying, as I believe I picked it up somewhere in the 1990s as I grew as a coach. It was originally accredited to Dietrich Bonhoeffer, a German Lutheran pastor who resisted the Nazis. It sounds like it has a place in Christian theology and sentiment. Another of his aphorisms perhaps strikes a chord with modern day climate-change advocates who assert: "The ultimate test of a moral society is the kind of world that it leaves to its children."

The task of the coach is to assist athletes to realise their potential and to do that in a way in which, while challenged and stretched, they are not harmed. The coach seeks to create an environment in which personal growth is accompanied by physical development, new skill acquisition, tactical and 'game sense' learning, competitive resilience and the ability to co-operate and participate in a team environment.

Even the coach of an individual athlete must focus on these later elements for it is rare that such athletes do not have training partners and work in squads in which they must co-operate and share as they learn and develop. Indeed their very opposition is one of the crucial parts of the equation that influence change and provide challenge. The team-sport athlete must, of course, pay much more attention to these team requirements.

Along the way the course of learning ebbs and flows and there are moments of exhilaration and exasperation. There are times when we progress and times of regression; there are achievements and disappointments.

Team coaches have this experience with each individual as well as experiencing the circumstances where the group goes either up or down...these journeys are the very backbone and fibre of coaching. The pathway to building a team of developing individuals is replete with tales of individual heartache and struggle and of the discovery of what it means to be in a group with a shared goal and direction.

The process of changing old habits or redefining and establishing new habits is the stuff of the daily coaching task. We create situations, challenge and cajole so that adaptation occurs. The adaptation that is wrought is physical, technical, tactical and mental. The process is iterative, interactive and incremental, and one hopes, sustainable.

Coaches constantly measure and test in competitive training and game situations. In the end the ultimate exam is to be able to perform at the highest level against the best opposition. That cauldron of competition for the Kookaburras and the Hockeyroos was the World Cup, Olympic Games, and Champions Trophy in which the best teams from the world were our opponents.

Forced adaptation occurs where the athletes are seeking to perform at the edge of their ability where they might often fail.

Skill acquisition experts often refer to the "challenge point" at which we might often fail but which represents progress and learning as we master the ways to move past such points. Equally, in order to master any activity much time and energy is required to get there. In *The Coach* I also challenged the existing fascination that many sports watchers and commentators have with 'flair'. My proposition was that 'flair'-exceptional episodes of brilliance is really 'superior practiced skill'.

Ericsson...ten thousand hours

It was in 1993 that Anders Ericsson wrote his seminal work about the role of practice in mastery of skill (The Role of Deliberate Practice in the Acquisition of Expert Performance). The example used was of violinists. In particular it was noted the very best of them averaged 10,000 hours to reach that point of mastery. Others were indeed very good and some less able and the defining criteria for the development of their talent was the quantity and quality of their practice.

Recently, Malcolm Gladwell popularised this idea in his excellent book *Outliers,* and a debate ensued regarding the role of natural talent in the achievement of expertise. Mathew Syed took up the case in his book *Bounce* and others have disputed the thesis. To me it has always appeared clear that both are required to be outstanding – whether one is trying to solve mathematical problems, play the violin or chess, or kick or throw a ball.

Obviously, some activities such as running fast require some innate gifts but these gifts will never be realised without deliberate and challenging practice – many, many hours of it. Equally, if you practise only the same things without trying to do increasingly difficult things, then you only get better at what you can already do. The best coaches continually lift the bar and challenge. Great players do the same; they challenge themselves and willingly go where their skills are tested and they may fail. They are never afraid of the challenge points.

When I see exceptional skills exhibited or displayed, or exceptional team performances, I believe I am seeing superior practiced skill or methods. These things are not just a coincidence of serendipity but also the result of many, many hours of practice, play, experience and challenges – challenges that may have defeated us in the past but that can be overcome and are manageable.

Ambition...we usually end up where we aim.
In order to go there the team, individual, leader and coach must subscribe to the highest ambition. Without high ambition little is achieved. I referred earlier to the book *Psycho-Cybernetics*, perhaps one of the earliest tomes on sports psychology. Written by Maxwell Maltz, a plastic surgeon by training who believed self-affirmation and mental visualisation were important in determining the satisfaction experienced by his surgical patients.

The central thesis of the book, which sold more than four million copies, was that we are like guided missiles in our lives. "We usually end up where we aim." In order to achieve greatly one needs high ambition. You don't win a medal at the Olympics if you are happy only to qualify or are just happy to be there. You don't win the grand final if you are just happy to be in the finals.

Over my 14 years as head coach of the national teams in the men's and women's game I have never met an athlete who was in the program who knew how good they could be. They invariably did not know what the borders of their talent might be and most arrive with ambitions that will not totally explore their talent. I believe one of my greatest achievements in coaching has been to stretch and extend the vision and ambition of our athletes and training program.

During my brief time with New Zealand Cricket between 2005-07, I felt one of the major differences I observed between the New

Zealand cricketers and those in Australia was that some Kiwi players (not all) believed they had made it when they played for New Zealand. I believe most of those selected for Australia see their selection as a conduit to becoming one of the best players in the world. It is difficult to see why this might be and certainly an emerging Kane Williamson or Tim Southee was never short of ambition. One speculates that it comes from a deep-seated experience of the challenges across the ditch. Certainly such modest ambition was not found in New Zealand rugby!

I remember one day I decided to challenge the Blackcaps as to the quality of our batting program. I wrote on the board an Australian batting line-up and next to it the New Zealand line-up. The Australian line up was Katich, Langer, Hussey, Martin, Gilchrist, Marsh or something of that order...I could have added Rogers or Voges or another Hussey. Whatever it was there were five or six Australians with an average of more that 40. I think only Stephen Fleming from NZ had an average above 40.

I asked which was the better line-up and they responded, predictably, that it was Australia! Their defensive accompaniment was that Australia had 22 million people and NZ had only four million. My response was that this was not the Australian batting line-up but that of Western Australia with a population of two million! I think I made the point that it was not necessarily the numbers that mattered but the quality of your program and the degree of your ambition!

No compromise

My belief has always been that the quest to be outstanding is a daily, continuous challenge that we embark on and that can be obsessive and all encompassing. As coach one needs to push, prompt, drive, challenge, test and require with the same energy and enthusiasm that is expected from the athletes. Without that drive, determination and single-mindedness, corners will be cut and compromises will ensue. The result will be a dilution of quality and diminishing standards.

In the late 90s as we approached the Sydney Olympics, I had the good fortune to have contact with Herb Elliott who I had greatly admired since the age of eight. I read about and watched newsreels of his 1960 Rome Olympics gold medal in the 1500 metres. Here was a young West Australian from Aquinas College who was world champion and world record holder. Herb Elliott provided advice and support for the athletes and coaches and one quote sat well with me.

"The champion understands that small compromises, small compromises that are evident only to them, are not small compromises at all; they are a decision to concede on championship and slip back to the rest of the field."

The best athletes drive themselves and can accomplish greatly but even someone with Elliott's drive needed the eccentric Percy Cerutty to guide, challenge, push and cajole.

The constant challenge for the leader is to provide comfort and support for some while for others the need is for disruption and challenge. This essential paradox is the space every coach inhabits on a daily, hourly basis. The art and craft of coaching requires you to get the assessments right about what is most appropriate at any point in time.

The finesse of the coach, the art of coaching revolves around this paradox and how one manages individuals, groups and indeed staff so as to enable elite performance. This journey is inevitably rocky and replete with stresses, conflicts, disappointments and mistakes.

In their seminal paper, "The Work of Leadership", Ronald Heifetz and Donald Laurie alluded to the view that followers want comfort, stability and solutions from their leaders. They described that as *"babysitting"* and argued forcefully that real leaders ask hard questions and knock people out of their comfort zones. They then spend their energy and time managing the resultant distress.

In such an environment there is a need for candour and honesty and one should never expect friendship to be part of the relationship with one's coach.

Mutual respect is important in the relationship for it to be productive but it is seldom an easy or familiar interaction. Sometimes after the job is done and people have moved on, friendship can develop but to be truly objective and challenging it is rarely part of the deal.

There is an ever-present tension because the coach needs to be empathetic and supportive while at the same time needing to extend and push individuals beyond what is comfortable and easy. In business theory there is discussion about complex adaptive systems and the need to move away from what is close to agreement and close to certainty in order to explore new solutions and to open up to discovering better ways of doing things.

What business describes as "best practice" often is close to agreement and certainty yet in a new world of disruption and rapidly advancing technology that is a formula for stagnation and obsolescence. Equally, individuals in sport and teams, just like businesses, constantly need to be seeking better ways to do things and better solutions if they are to avoid becoming obsolete.

Crucial conversations

Coaches try to understand the circumstances of every one of their charges. They are constantly seeking help in their quest to find how they might assist each athlete realise their potential. In order to do this effectively it is incumbent on them to never avoid the difficult conversations that inevitably arise. I think there are three elements to such conversations. They are *important* to both parties, there is often a *disagreement* and there is *emotion* involved.

Along the pathway to being outstanding there are usually moments where the opportunity arrives to send a message to the team or an individual, and whenever these moments arrive a good coach will take them. Sometimes it occurs as you walk off the training pitch and something from the session requires explanation or reinforcement. Sometimes, the day after a particular performance, as you wait at the airport, the opportunity is there to challenge or expose a moment from the game. Perhaps you want to ask why in the heat of battle something occurred? Ideally, the players would come to the coach but egos being what they are this does not occur enough, and so coaches find themselves initiating such opportunities.

In the end the best coaches hope to occupy a place where they have the respect of the players for their knowledge and where they are also seen as having the players' best interests at heart. Then, I believe the athlete is most likely to receive feedback with an open mind and process it effectively. Our natural response to criticism is often 'fight or flight', and yet this primal response is hardly the best way to achieve a learning framework.

In their very good book titled *Crucial Conversations*, the authors (Kerry Patterson, Joseph Grenny, Ron McMillan and Al Switzer) talk about someone receiving really blistering feedback and instead of fighting or withdrawing they allow it to influence them. Usually they do this because they respect the person delivering the feedback and believe this person has their best interests at heart.

I like to think I had some capacity to engage in such conversations effectively as a coach, because without being able or willing to do so coaches will struggle to communicate effectively to a whole range of athletes. At some stage it will be necessary for all of them. Selection, injury, slips in form, personal crisis, team tactics and personnel are all catalysts for such conversations and in my time I had some very difficult ones.

Losing an Olympic Dream

Perhaps the most difficult was the one I had to have with Des Abbott about a month before the London Olympics as I outlined earlier in the book. As it became obvious that Des would not be able to reach his level in London I consulted with others and scrutinized his performance. I wanted to take him but was wrestling with the consequences of such a choice. When the planned cortisone injections did not improve his mobility a decision time loomed.

I have always been reluctant to go into the Games with an injured player (I had seen this mistake made too often), and any attempt to replace Des during the competition on injury grounds would be difficult given his history. The meeting we arranged with Des and his father Dave was one of the most difficult of my coaching life as we discussed the judgement we had made and listened to the contrary views. Des had a great record of playing 'on one leg' and genuinely felt he would be able to contribute, and so in the end I was left with a very unhappy player whose great ambition was taken away so cruelly.

I did what I thought was right for the team as I believed his diminished mobility would remove Des' capacity to intimidate opponents and he would be too easily covered. While this was evident at elite level, at club level Des was still able to score. I believed at international level he would be unable to get away with what worked against club players.

I remember going home completely drained and dismayed as, with all such decisions, there is always a lingering doubt and you empathise with someone who is shattered by the consequences of your decision. There is never a way of knowing whether you have made the correct decision as nobody ever gets to see what might have happened – but of course there are many speculators out there with an opinion.

The reality of the coaching task is being required to make such decisions on a regular basis. In 1994, one of our team's vice-captains, Liane Tooth, was ruled out of the Dublin World Cup the day before we left due to a hamstring injury. A 19-year-old, Kate Allen, took her place in the team. Kate went on to perform admirably during the tournament.

On our return from the tournament I met with Liane to discuss her future. I told her that at 34 I believed she might struggle to make the 1996 Olympics given her recent trajectory. She was unsure what she wanted and we decided to have a few days to consider what her future might look like. Such decisions need to be taken only after thorough consideration.

When we met a few days later Liane was quite clear that she loved playing and she would like to do everything possible to go to Atlanta, then two years away. Liane was a great team player, highly skilled and a hard working and fastidious trainer so I was happy to have her in the squad as she was a thorough team player. I indicated that if she was playing well enough there would be a place for her in the team two years hence.

Two years later Liane made the Atlanta team and went on to play a terrific tournament and secured her second Olympic gold medal. An open and honest sharing of my position allowed us all to clarify the situation and as is often the case her determination to give her all to the task allowed her to reach that brilliant milestone. It was of course the fact that she was such a good influence in the group and set such high standards for herself and thereby influenced the group that made it possible for us to allow her the opportunity.

One of my regrets when I left the Kookaburras was that the lead-up to the Commonwealth Games was so soon after the World Cup and timing necessitated the selection of the Commonwealth Games team before we went to the World Cup. Accordingly, the decision was made to select a team from those we determined would most likely be contenders for Rio in 2016. I believed strongly that the team would need significant renewal for it to be at its best in Rio and this selection was the first step in that direction.

This decision was a collective judgement made with an eye on the future and an understanding that some of the senior players would feel aggrieved. I decided, while in The Hague, to leave the coaching role immediately and so was not going to the Commonwealth Games. The meetings that followed the selection announcement would be an opportunity to deal with this fallout. Two of the senior players in Liam De Young and Rob Hammond announced their retirements and both made contact.

However, Jamie Dwyer did not, as was customary, arrange a post-selection meeting in which his situation might have been able to be discussed. Sometimes that is the way it turns out and to this day I believe it was remiss of him not to do so. It would have allowed the situation to be clarified and I would have given him a direct outline of my thinking as indeed I had done with Liane many years earlier.

Jamie did not have a very good year in 2014 and his injuries and form were all factors in our deliberation. Elsewhere in the book (Finishing with the Kookaburras) I outline how close we went to ruling Jamie out in the weeks before the tournament and ironically, it was my request for the evidence to be reviewed that handed him a lifeline!

Peer pressure/interaction

For many the critical coach-player relationship is the main unit of currency in the team environment when it comes to the team's direction and individual coaching. Of course this means all the coaching staff not only the head coach as there are many and varied inputs into the coaching mix.

I believe, however, there is another dimension given too little attention. It is the dynamic that is the interaction between one player and another. The vibrancy of these intra-player relationships are central to having team members who learn from one another and understand how each other might act under pressure and in any particular situation.

I am often asked about the difference between coaching men and women after having worked with both national teams. For me one of the major differences is that I believe that women are more likely to be open about these relationships and interactions whereas male players tend to be more egotistical and less likely to share and question one another. Accordingly, these things require more effort with a group of men than women in order to improve the peer relationships and interactions.

As is outlined elsewhere in the book (Nadir in London), after our disappointment in London action in this area was a critical part of rebuilding the group's dynamics.

In my own experience as a player I had not been as good as I could have been in this area. When in later life I look back on how I was in my youth and at my self-centredness and indifference to such matters, I am horrified by my younger self! In 1984 as captain of the team going to Los Angeles I was roomed with Jim Irvine, one of our most significant players in the 70s and early 80s.

Jim had an Achilles tendon injury, which lingered and then became persistent as the Olympics loomed closer. It threatened his place in the Olympic team, and for about ten days the team travelled together and played in Vancouver before going to LA. During that time I was Jim's roommate.

I don't think we ever had more than a cursory conversation on the injury during those ten days. I was not confident Jim would make it and expressed that view to the staff but I ought to have had more direct discussion with Jim about the matter. At least I ought to have had an honest discussion about Jim's position and prospects, his injury and the likely effect on the team if he wasn't able to perform. In the end I believe the staff made a poor decision to include him in the team and the implications of the decision manifested themselves later when we played a semi-final against Pakistan.

In that game Jim was included to play and accordingly David Bell was omitted because of concern over his hamstring soundness. We were reluctant to go into the game with two players under a cloud. There were no interchangeable substitutions in those days and only two substitutions allowed in total. I believe we made the wrong call on that occasion but it was the presence of a partially fit Jim in the group that influenced our choice.

After our disappointment in London and on the way to renovating our culture we moved to increase and improve the amount of interaction within our group so that our culture would be able to sustain itself in a continuing way. It is critical to any team that besides all the skill and physical prowess there be a connectedness and collegial environment that both supports and challenges.

I have for some time been impressed by the work of Mimi Silbert whose program at the Delancey Street Foundation established and built a residential education community for people massively disadvantaged by generational poverty and with multiple social problems. In their book *The Influencer, The Power to Change Anything,* Patterson, Grenny, David Maxfield and McMillan describe the astonishing success of the programs in which those in the program act as mentors and supporters for one another.

Here, some of the most hardened and disadvantaged participants play a pivotal role in creating an environment of behavioural change in those new to the program by their ability to exemplify and call out unwanted and unproductive habits and actions. The code of the street for many of those in generational poverty and with multiple social problems it seems is, *"only look after yourself and don't rat on anyone else".*

At Delancey the plan was to try to reverse these two unhelpful behaviours. If you could do that they believed you could change everything. The program required everyone to be responsible for someone else's success and for everyone to confront everyone else whenever they violated this code. Effectively, they are all involved with each other in changing their lives. All being givers and receivers and functioning like an extended family.

The message for those who coach and aspire to make change and develop talent and co-operation in their charges is that peer influence is an indispensable source of influence and change. You ignore it at your peril and if utilised effectively you will find that efficacy to be hugely beneficial. This does not mean peers are mere supporters and cheerleaders for their mates. It means they, like coaches, challenge attitudes and behaviours that cut across the team goals and standards and hold one another to account in the interests of the team and its shared values.

The shared goal of everyone associated with a team that aspires to achieve outstanding results is to collectively work for that purpose, and it is only by *troubling the comfortable and comforting the troubled* that we operate in an environment that might take you there... to the place where the exceptional performance is aspired to and expected and it is not easy to get there or comfortable to stay there.

7

N U M B E R S   M A T T E R

Charles Percy Snow studied chemistry and physics in Leicester before getting a scholarship to Cambridge where he completed a PhD in physics (spectroscopy). The scientist was also a novelist and married to a writer. He held a number of important civil service positions during the Second World War and up until 1960. He was knighted in 1957. In 1959, CP Snow spoke famously in his Rede lecture at Cambridge about "The Two Cultures".

Essentially, he described the literary intellectuals and the scientists of his time as being poles apart. "Between the two a gulf of mutual incomprehension – sometimes, particularly among the young – hostility and dislike, but most of all a lack of understanding." Interesting when you consider that both these groups ought to be filled with curiosity and wonder as they work in their various fields of endeavour. Snow, who operated in both places, argued strongly for the closing of this gap and doing so with urgency.

The same type of dichotomy exists in almost all areas of endeavour. Surgeons and physicians often seem poles apart; engineers and lawyers spend their undergraduate years wrestling for campus supremacy; architects and builders find many reasons to disagree and the list goes on. In sport, the battle between those who are controlling and those who cede more power to the players is one schism but perhaps one of the newest areas of division is between the sports scientists and the instinctive and pragmatic coach. Of course, ideally, they co-operate but in many franchises the tension between the analytical boffins and coaching artists abounds.

This is a debate that asks whether coaching is more art than science. Over the past decades I have heard the question posed often: Is coaching more art than science? The answer, of course, is that to do the job well coaches need to embrace both cultures. You have to be able, in this modern era, to be on top of the science involved with sports physiology, medicine, strength and conditioning, sports analysis, biomechanics, psychology and human behaviour and skill acquisition.

There is finesse required to deal with the nuances of managing people and effectively getting them to realise their potential and engage in the processes of team and personal development. There is room for instinct, experience and the critical ingredient of empathy but also the numbers matter and you need be conversant with what they mean and how you develop and interpret them.

Sporting contests are raw drama. The media speculates, the pundits predict. Many are bemused and don't care while fans talk in bars and brag and pontificate. Every fan thinks they are an expert but what is really happening? How do you know, and what information tells you where your team fits? Is it on track? What parts of your game need attention and how are coaches going to diagnose any problems with accuracy and overcome the deficiencies?

Teams in competitive team sport are dynamic, evolving and organic organisations and the result is built on a lot of interactions, and many incidents. Many small contributions collectively are the things, which make up any team's performance and these contributions in sum make up the difference between teams.

In *The Coach* in a chapter called "Always Look Behind the Result" I outlined where we were with the Hockeyroos back in 2000. How we measured performance way back then. We were without the resources to measure, in real time, performance with any degree of precision in a complicated, complex integrated team activity. Every individual's interactions and contributions were identified, noted and collated. Therefore, some objective measure of their individual performance was available but still this was far from perfect as a measurement of their contribution without having the ball was so difficult. How do you watch what is happening when the players do not have the ball? When they are preparing for it to arrive, timing their intervention, their leads and their tackles, and running to cover in defence or create an attacking opportunity?

This capacity is a long way away and presently outside our resources and even, I suspect, those of the most elite and wealthy involved in continuous invasion games like AFL or soccer. Some 'slower' games (more time-outs) like gridiron or games with less players like basketball or with more stoppages (rugby) may have answers or be able to be analysed play by play. However, hockey's fluency, like AFL or soccer, make this difficult as the game ebbs and flows and continuously requires contributions around the ball to be backed up by contributions away from the ball.

'Prozone', the elite analysis system used in the English Premier League allows for some of this analysis, yet the use of this data in game time is very challenging for a coach. Managers still sit on the touchline and 'watch the game' and follow their instincts and experience. The input from others with specialist, clearly defined and often very narrow roles, also allows them to tinker and adjust as best fits the team's performance on the day. This is not an exact science and indeed the contribution of the coach is perhaps worth a few per cent when it comes down to it. The 'master stroke' where a substitution is made and the new player scores sometimes happens but often it was a planned formulaic move anyway.

With digital analysis our ability to quickly and in real-time get statistics on individual contests and players may sometimes help. Sometimes, the physical load on players can be measured and loads adjusted, and sometimes deciding which of the pre-planned moves to make is determined by the coaches' instinct and play reading skill. Generally, the benefit of the real-time stats is to confirm or help solidify our impressions. Sometimes they may in fact indicate that our impressions may not be so accurate!

So how do coaches form their view about what is happening in a game? I had my moments of success and times I didn't get it right. Every coach is continually searching for ways to improve this. In some sports the coach is 'high and dry' as in rugby and others on the sideline (soccer or basketball). In our game we had a choice and indeed I preferred to be on the bench close to the action while an assistant took the bird's eye view. A case can be made for either viewing option. In hockey we generally do both things with someone in each role and connected by wireless communication.

In the 2010 World Cup, however, after some tension between the tournament director and myself, I found myself up high in the grandstand on the day of the final and in radio contact with my assistant coach, Graham Reid, on the bench. During the last 20 minutes of that game with the score level we had some moments!

I was lucky that 'Poss' (Reid) and manager David Hatt were calm and thorough as their interactions with the technical official were crucial. Their actions insured Luke Doerner being allowed onto the pitch in a critical moment. Indeed, had Germany conceded the obvious penalty corner, rather than going to a video replay in the hope that the pictures would be inconclusive they could have changed their day!

Des Abbott had cleverly wrong-footed a German defender to earn a penalty. The referee missed this action and so the video umpire was called in to adjudicate. The German player must have known he was at fault. Had he admitted his error then Doerner on the sideline would not have been able to enter the field! However, as the decision was being adjudicated Doerner was allowed to enter the pitch, as had been the practice throughout the competition. He subsequently scored the resulting penalty! An interesting reflection on how one ought to deal with video referral.

While the detail of the individuals absorbs many of us, and we like to read the numbers on some screen, the head coach is looking at the big picture. He is constantly trying to measure progress and put the team in context. Of course each individual contribution tallied together makes up the total picture for the team and not every contribution is as important as another. The big picture assessment entails a grasp of the details and sometimes minutia as well as a global perspective as to what the major trends and solutions may be. It's the stuff of *Thinking Fast and Slow* by Daniel Kahneman in which the author outlines the value and appropriate circumstances to utilise the various approaches available for making good decisions.

Every team has key performance indicators (KPIs), which are measured every time they play. These are critical statistics, which they believe are the keys to playing well. I once asked five times best and fairest for Fitzroy and premiership winning AFL coach Paul Roos what was his most important statistic. Interestingly, he said, "missed tackles". When one looks at the point of breakaways and beginning of many counterattacks I can see why he chose that statistic as being crucial for his team and the way they played.

I have earlier pointed out that in a strange way our game of hockey has become more like AFL football than any other game in the world. Unlimited interchange, no offside so players are ahead of the ball, play on from every situation and at the pointy end where you score it is crowded. These are significant similarities and although it takes much longer to get the ball from one end to the other (usually three or more kicks) and there is much more physicality in Australian football, many of the strategies utilised are similar.

Champion data provide footy coaches with myriad statistics but what do these numbers tell you about your team? For some teams the statistics mean different things. For example, making tackles is important but getting the most tackles may mean that you are doing that because the other team has the ball more than your team. That is probably not a good thing! However, if you want to score and win then getting good possessions 'inside 50' is critical and a larger number than your opponent is important. Naturally, the quality of those scoring chances is critical but all things being equal the more the better.

For some time now I have held the view that a team's percentage was one of the best indicators of a team's relative merit. Certainly I think in the AFL this is one of the readily available statistics that tracks progress and quality. In 2015 the following chart identifies the relative points and percentages of the teams in the AFL season of 22 games.

While Fremantle finished top on points you can see their percentage was only marginally better than the sixth ranked team, the Bulldogs. Clearly West Coast and Hawthorn (both just behind Fremantle on points) were the dominant teams over the season. I was not surprised when they played in the grand final. I believe when the numbers are so emphatic as they were in this case over a long season they are indicative of quality and merit and the finals series vindicated that interpretation. Likewise in 2016, while Hawthorn are still at the top of the table their percentage this year ought be a reason to think they are not playing at last year's level. I would not be backing them this year on those numbers!

The criticism of Fremantle was that they did not have sufficient penetration to kick winning scores, and in the finals while they defended well this let them down. I should not be misunderstood here for I believe every team needs to build a defence first, but without the capacity to hurt the opposition defending in and of itself is not enough. It can work in a low scoring game like hockey, or soccer in particular, but no so much when scoring is higher.

Australian Football League (AFL)		
	Pts	%
Fremantle FC	68	118.7
West Coast Eagles	66	148.2
Hawthorne FC	64	158.4
Sydney FC	64	127.1
Richmond FC	60	123.1
Western Bulldogs	56	115.1

Coaches search for objectivity. The debate as to whether coaching is 'art or science' will rage endlessly and in some ways is quite pointless as the best coaches must utilise and display affinity with both. However, I have great faith in the numbers as I believe when the data are significantly large they are a good indicator of quality.

Quite recently I had cause while trying to select players from other nations for my chapter on 'Champions' to correspond with Markus Weise, my opponent as Germany's coach while I was with the Kookaburras. Markus has coached both the German men and women to gold medals. I was asking him about his German women's team in 2004 and in particular his goalkeeper in that tournament, Louisa Walter.

His little tale of her selection is a reminder of the need for objectivity. It also goes to a really reasoned approach to understanding the elements outside pure technical ability that are so crucial in selecting the right people.

"I would clearly include goalie Louisa Walter to your short list, as she contributed really a lot to our 2004 victory in Athens, not only as a first-class goalie but also due to her first-class personality and mentality. Being a more calm and introvert person I was clearly in danger of overlooking her in the process of nominating the best players. I still pat myself on my shoulder sometimes for having had another deep think and having put in the effort of studying hundreds of video scenes of the three goalies to establish an 'objective' evaluation of the girls. All of a sudden I had a clear number 1, 2 and 3 even though prior to that analysis I thought it wouldn't matter a lot whom I choose from three very good goalies. Sometimes our brain plays tricks and we only see what we want to see..." Marcus Weise, June 2016

"Sometimes our brain plays tricks and we only see what we want to see..." In my experience as a coach the error of **'selective abstraction or confirmation bias'** are ways of thinking which we must be vigilant to avoid. The need for objectivity is central to the selection process just as in the introduction I am reminded that 'group think' is another perilous folly.

The question arises; in any individual game how can the numbers be used to interpret and analyse what is going on, what is happening? Every coach wants a way of measuring that can help reinforce and adjust the gut feel and instinctive assessments that are made in real-time as the game unfolds before their eyes. "First you have to watch the game", was the message Dockers coach Ross Lyon gave a TV journalist when questioned about this last year. I wholeheartedly agree with this but what numbers can assist you? The answer is you need to find what are the best measures you can establish to objectively assist in assessing performance for the team and individuals. What are the measures you need to put in place to play well individually and as a team? This is necessary because you have to look behind the score.

My search throughout the 90s and until I finished formal coaching in 2014 was for more and better objective data whereby one could measure performance and compare players, assess team performance and measure competence. Finding the best measure of what we were trying to achieve was for me a constant search and something we always aimed to improve.

In *The Coach*, I talked about our winning percentage during my eight years with the Hockeyroos and about my search for an analysis tool to objectify performance. Goal shots for and against were an easily accessible tool. During the late 90s as digital analysis was being born in our game and statistics started gaining a place in the coaching lexicon, we used to do match statistics manually after the game. We coaches would sit in front of the video and call each event; tackle, possession pass, interception, possession pass, penetration run. Every event for every player was recorded and often debated.

Athletes started attending these sessions and indeed 'debate' the calls, and the utility of these sessions increased as they morphed into coaching and learning opportunities. Practically the whole team would be present sometimes and these occasions proved very beneficial for individual and team learning. The statistics gave us a picture of each player's game as incidents were assigned positive or negative value and in the end the quotient reflected the efficiency and or the value of each player.

The scores needed to be finessed to allow for strikers to be encouraged to take the right risks. Defenders were by nature risk averse but some needed to go forward when appropriate and take calculated risks. The midfielders again had a slightly different profile. We learnt a lot about our game from these numbers but collecting them was time consuming and difficult when in the cauldron of a two-week tournament.

With digital analysis becoming available more and more after Sydney I found that by 2009 when I started with the Kookaburras much more data was available. Columns and categories of events were measured and each piece of information could have attached video footage that players and coaches could observe and so review much more effectively.

The Invisible Game...

Players are able to observe all their interactions with the ball, and 'on-ball' activity is readily accessible as games were videoed live. Unfortunately, this analysis still falls short of ideal as for about 97 per cent of the time on the field the player is without the ball. Movement, action, positioning when 'off the ball' is crucial to effective performance and there are many ways we can 'know' what is happening but we need to look for it. The problem for the coach is that the ball tends to be a magnet for the observer's eyes. It takes time to also learn to look at the action 'off the ball'.

Cameras at different angles, multiple cameras, GPS co-ordinates, laser analysis and various analytical algorithms allow for disclosure of this sort of information and assist coaches in being able to influence this part of the game – the INVISIBLE game. Increasingly, we are working on developing our skill and the players' ability to understand and interpret this invisible game.

As I outline elsewhere in the chapter "The More Things Change" in this book, video has allowed us a view of the game in a way that was only a dream in the first half of the previous century. I remember the scene from the wonderful movie *Chariots of Fire* where Sam Mussabini spends time with Harold Abrahams explaining, with coins on a table, how he must increase his stride rate. He also shows Abrahams a picture of Charley Paddock breasting the tape in the Olympic Games in Antwerp in 1920. No videotape available then, no opportunity to view his own performance...just a still shot of his opponent and Mussabini's eyeball analysis of his major opponent...such was coaching at that time.

As a coach I like to have a quick and easy way to assess momentum and the quality of our play. In the early years we kept a record of goal shots and circle penetrations to help assist in this process. I would view these at half time and game end and receive updates as requested.

We all have a sense of a game's momentum and flow and coaches must be good at reading this aspect of the game. In hockey the SCORE can deceive. The score can go against a dominant team and so the reality of what lies behind the score must always be kept in mind.

While circle penetration for and against and shots, for and against, were useful I was keen to get more detail...some qualitative as well as quantitative information. It was okay to know the number of goal shots or penetrations but what about the quality of those shots or penetrations. For it is true that 'every goal shot is not the same'. My quest for more detail about the quality of the chances created by our team and our opponent meant that we must look at more than just the number of shots.

Goal Opportunity Total...GOT

Accordingly, we developed the GOT or 'Goal Opportunity Total'. As I have already indicated, my simple belief has always been that the way to success is to make as many quality scoring chances as is possible and limit our opponents to as few as possible. By measuring our opportunity against that of the opponent you developed a picture of exactly how effectively you are penetrating and how you are being penetrated.

I started doing this myself and eventually our statisticians would be able to provide the tally with the statistics package for each game. The beauty of this measure was that I was able to watch the game at the same time as I was writing down the scores for every opportunity for both teams. I was able to have a continuous update of the game's progress. It should be clear that in hockey it is only possible to score a goal from inside the scoring semicircle at each end of the ground. The scoring system for our GOT was like this:

0… any ball fired through the circle touched by nobody…these events are recorded as zero and if there are a number of them that indicates the method of circle entry is ineffective.

½… any ball passed into or through the circle that was intercepted by an opponent.

1… anytime a team gets possession of the ball in the attacking scoring circle or indeed we should have possessed the ball but failed to do so because of a skill error. Note, we are measuring opportunity not outcomes! Any shot taken may be difficult but it still may require saving.

2… goal shot taken from an angle or pressured but with some chance to score and usually requiring a save if on target.

3… goal shot taken better angle less pressure.

4… goal shot taken…very good scoring chance.

5… goal shot taken with time, close to the goal right in front or open opportunity.

5… penalty corner (can be won from outside the circle if a deliberate foul occurs). By convention all shots taken in a penalty corner are included in this score, i.e. rebounds and subsequent chances while the ball remains in the circle area.

2… repeat penalty corner.

7… penalty stroke awarded.

Effectively, the range from 1-5 describes the quality of the goal scoring chance. One would merely have possession of the ball in the scoring zone. It might also be applied to a mis-trapped ball in the scoring zone. As a scoring opportunity that is easily a '1' but a skill error failed to make it eventuate.

Shots with time, not under tackling pressure and close to goal are rare and attract a 5 usually, but if the goalkeeper is close and advancing such an opportunity might be a 4 or 3 depending on the angle available to shoot.

Every penalty corner is a great scoring chance and so opens up the possibility of a clear and powerful goal shot and so it attracts a 5. Sometimes it might lead to multiple shots but it is still designated a 5! If the shot is blocked and another penalty corner is awarded then that attracts a 2. Consecutive penalty corners are very good opportunities.

A penalty stroke...is almost a certain goal but still has to be converted and is designated a 7.

The GOT gave us a lot of ways to measure our performance, which could be used to track our progress and the relative worth of our team's efforts. Of course, things like goal difference are important but in a two-week competition in which seven games are played, such rudimentary data is not sufficient to give a real measure of what is happening or what has happened. It allowed us to measure many more data points and certainly more depth than goals scored in such a low scoring game as field hockey.

In the hockey tournaments we play, goal difference offers nowhere near enough data to be able to make sense of it. There are just too few data points and indeed some of the measures can be very unfair.

I believe in cricket it would make sense to develop a better way to measure how well someone is bowling rather than wickets and runs! Over a career wickets and runs are valid but in any small sample these things can deceive. The long hop or full toss that brings a wicket is a bad ball whereas the snicked ball that deceived the batsman and goes for 4 is actually a good ball!

Whatever the tactics or method used by any opponent, the GOT still allows for one to measure the effectiveness of the method utilised. It also allows the effectiveness of your team in making opportunities, defending efficiently and denying opportunities to opponents to be measured. Teams operate in many different ways; each committed to their own way of playing and each with their own rationale for playing the way they do.

Some will argue that to defend and just aim to make a few good chances is a legitimate way to operate. Is that not what some European teams and definitely Argentina are up to? Maybe that's risky as you will need to be very efficient in attack and you will perhaps draw more and lose less. It probably reflects a lack of confidence in your defence being able to do their job without extra help.

Whatever the way of playing it will be reflected in the GOT scores and allow us this insight. I am of the view that this measure gives quite a lot of data to assess what our opponents are up to. I like to be able to measure teams over a tournament. During the last few years I was with the Kookaburras our aim was to always decisively win the GOT score. We wanted to keep our opponents scores low (single figures for a half) and have ours as high as possible (over thirty for a half was a good start).

Some of the cumulative data from recent competitions is below and some of the observations about the team are also outlined.

Table...World Cup June, 2014

Teams (order)		Goals	Goal diff	GOT	Net GOT	GOT/Goal
No. of games		F/A	F-A	F/A	F-A	F/A
Australia	7	30/3	+27	486/177	+309	16.2 / 59.0
Netherlands	7	16/10	+6	352/250	+102	22.0 / 25.0
Argentina	7	18/10	+8	256/272	-16	14.2 / 27.2
England	7	8/12	-4	259/312	-53	32.5 / 26.0
Belgium	6	21/14	+7	378/222	+156	18.0 / 15.8
Germany	6	17/10	+7	338/235	+103	19.9 / 23.5

These figures allow you to make a number of observations, which are confirmed by the 'in-tournament' results. The interesting thing is that a team can do well in any particular tournament with great success in one part of their game or with even a few good results. Such is the nature of a game with relatively low scoring. This is even more evident in tournaments where quarterfinals are now the norm as there is less reliance on finishing top two in your pool.

Easily our most difficult game of the pool round was against Belgium. We won 3-1 but the GOT score was close (51.5 to 45) and after a good start we were pressured but led 2-0 at half time. An early goal by the brilliant Ockenden should have made us comfortable but Belgium was still pushing at the end. We were never assured.

Characteristically, Belgium had 12 halves...they always fired lots of hard balls into the scoring circle which required lots of good trapping in the scoring zone...any error can easily become a penalty corner. Whenever we played against Belgium we knew we had to be ready for these speculative balls fired with speed into the circle. A team like Germany would not try so many of these balls but would attempt deflections and sometimes make five more passes before trying to enter. They were perhaps more patient or just trying to get into a better position to increase their odds of success.

After that game I fully expected Belgium to make the semi-finals. Had they done so I believed we might well have played them in the final! Surprisingly, they lost to England in the final match of the round. It was a game they should have won with the better chances and superior GOT (55-38). England finished second in the pool but by almost every other measure should have been third in the pool. The one area where they exceeded Belgium was GOT per goal against...England defended better in spite of conceding more opportunities. It was the area where Belgium were the worst of the top six teams and probably the reason they missed the semi-finals.

Argentina's form was predicated on their exceptional efficiency in scoring; they required only 14.2 GOT for every goal. This was the best in the tournament. Australia was very good at 16.2 whereas England were nearly double that! This efficiency reflects their brilliant penalty corner taker Peillat and Argentina's emphasis on that part of their game when in scoring positions. They will win a corner rather than take a low percentage shot! That is really just smart play when you have a weapon like Peillat. Argentina also defended well with each conceded goal coming from a GOT of 27.2.

Of course attacking and defending cannot be just assessed by a GOT score per goal because good defending entails limiting the GOT available to one's opponent as well as not allowing a score once they get there! Similarly, our aim is to maximise our GOT score by making numerous quality chances as well as being efficient once they are made. Hence total GOT as well as GOT per goal are important.

Equally, within any GOT score the elements that make it up are important as those elements go to the quality of the opportunities. The total picture for Germany (6th) and the Netherlands (2nd) shows that these teams were very close and in almost every measure there was hardly any variation. Germany's loss to the Netherlands 0-1 (GOT 38.5 to 52) in the round game after a surprise loss to

Argentina was enough to derail them. That Belgium defeated them for 5th place merely underlined Belgium's quality, which they had signalled before the World Cup and confirmed in 2015 by making the World League final. Their progress is reflected in the 'behind the result' stats as outlined above.

Of course the winning performance by Australia was exceptional and confirmed what the GOT told us six months earlier. The biggest strength was again to get high GOT totals, which in every game exceeded 50, while our opponents averaged about 25. With those figures you have given yourself the required platform. Exceptional, however, was the GOT score per goal in defence of 59. From our experience with these numbers we now believe a figure above 25 is pretty good so this number reflects exceptionally good work in the defensive circle and by the goalkeeper. In particular, it reflects real quality in defending set plays, such as penalty corners. This was very pleasing because we had made this one of our specific aims after it slipped up in London after the round games.

Interesting also is the information GOT tells you about the various teams against which you play. Going into the World Cup final against the Netherlands I looked at the recent matches we had played. My view was that the average GOT over a few games is usually quite a good predictor of the likely GOT score in the next match. This of course says nothing about the result on the day but it does describe the likely opportunities that will be created if you play to your recent standard.

In the previous year we had played Holland five times for three wins and two losses. The losses in January occurred in Delhi where we had been without about ten players who were in the final World Cup team so I knew we could improve. The Netherlands on the other hand had played in Delhi with effectively their best team and although we lost in neither game were we outplayed while being out-scored!

The results were as follows…

Rotterdam…friendly	won 3-1…GOT F/A	51/27.5
Rotterdam…friendly	won 5-2…GOT F/A	54.5/33
Rotterdam…WL3 S final	won 4-3…GOT F/A	69.5/26
Delhi…WL4 round match	lost 0-1…GOT F/A	67/30
Delhi…WL4 S final	lost 3-4…GOT F/A	53/37

Thus the average GOT was 59 to 30; therefore given equal efficiency by both teams this should translate into a doubling of the opponents score. The important point is of course that even when we lost to the Netherlands we had been making the game and providing ourselves with twice the opportunities of our opponents. This is better than our recent games against Belgium for example.

So what was the GOT score on the big day? It was 64 to 27.5. The actual sheet I kept that day is reproduced in the Appendix 5 for the record. It offers an insight into the way I used to measure the progress of the match and some matters such as our prepared corner plans. It is interesting how the score was so very close to the predicted average! Having kept these numbers for a few years now it is reassuring to see the analytical as well as predictive value they represent.

As a coaching tool the GOT score enabled us to identify when we were being inefficient in the scoring circle and it was always our aim to convert ½s, 1s and 2s into 3s, 4s or 5s. We wanted to improve the quality of our chances. It would also allow some accessible and objective measure of the quality of our work in the scoring circle.

In January 2014 we were disappointed to finish 4th in the World League final in Delhi yet with ten players who would play in The Hague not being there the performance took on a new perspective. Once again the GOT provided me with some reassurance about our trajectory and preparation. With polishing the small details we were still on track to perform well in The Hague. The chart below outlines some figures from that competition. While the gross figures have not been able to be found the net figure is equally revealing.

Table...World league 4. Jan 2014				
Teams (finish order)		Goals	Goal Diff	Net GOT
	No of games	F/A	F-A	F-A
1. Netherlands	6	18/13	+5	+ 5
2. New Zealand	6	11/23	-12	-58
3. England	6	15/6	+9	-66
4. Australia	6	20/12	+8	+211
5. Belgium	6	9/11	-2	+31
6. India	6	12/21	-9	-129
7. Argentina	6	12/14	-2	-32
8. Germany	6	17/14	+3	+48

Interestingly, the quarterfinal system delivered two teams into the semi-finals that had a negative GOT which was quite unusual. Also in the 5-8 positions, Belgium, Argentina and Germany are clearly better than their finishing positions according to this analysis. There are always 'outliers' and in this set of figures England is one of those as their goal difference reflects a brilliant defensive effort rather than a great scoring performance.

It seems clear that FIH is keen to have more upsets and surprises in the major tournaments. Their move to play quarters, introduce quarterfinals, the elimination of extra time and introduction of shoot-outs will, I predict, cause this to occur! For coaches, who endeavour to win by making their teams above such vagaries, it is a cause for nervousness.

The search for better and more instructive and objective figures to measure efficiency and performance is a critical tool utilised by coaches and without these aids coaches will not be able to assess quality with the accuracy they desire. The boffins who work behind the scenes in this area of data analysis are indispensable to the elite coach.

However, in the GOT I believe I have outlined a tool that is very useful and low tech that can be easily collected in real-time while observing the performance. As you can see in my sheet from the World Cup final (Appendix 5) it is possible to watch and manage the game while keeping this measure of progress and momentum as the game is being played.

Any coach at any level can design and utilise such a tool to allow them to assess the momentum and quality of their team's game as they watch it. I hope that it might prove as useful to some of you as it has to myself.

Whatever else, the numbers of sport are tools to be embraced by all. While in some disciplines there is blindness to the value of such analysis I find very few elite coaches who do not want accurate and objective data collected. These are the numbers that tell us a lot about what is going on out there on the field!

Preparing for the 1976 Olympics forty years ago. Hockey silver medalists were Australia's best performed athletes. Ric Charlesworth, Mal Poole, Merv Adams (coach), David Bell and Terry Walsh. Merv was instrumental in awakening our horizons. All four players would go on to be lifelong contributors to the game.

1996 Atlanta Gold medalists at a reunion in 2010. Kate Allen, Bob Haigh, Alyson Annan, Lisa Powell, Juliet Haslam, Rechelle Hawkes Ric Charlesworth, Claire Mitchell-Taverner and Louise Dobson. Allen and Mitchell-Taverner were travelling reserves and along with Bob Haigh (an assistant coach) would be in Sydney in 2000.

Holi Day (Hindu Spring Festival of colours) in Lucknow. I have just arrived at the Sports Authority of India (SAI) facility to be greeted by coaches MK Kaushik and Harendra Singh. In a minute I was covered in colours!

KPS Gill and Jothikumaran at Mr Gill's bungalow in Delhi with my 'new' contract in March 2008. At the end of April the IHF would suspend them after the two were implicated in a 'sting operation' caught on video taking a bribe for player selections!

Early morning training in Lucknow with the Indian women's team.

Fergus Kavanagh pops the ball over the head of German Goalkeeper Max Weinhold to seal the result 5-3 in the last seconds of the final of the Champions Trophy. We came back from 1-3 at half time.

A delighted group. Winners of the Champions Trophy in Melbourne in December 2009. My first major success with the Kookaburras.

Morning of the World Cup final March 2010. We stopped after training to have our photo taken in front of India Gate a short distance from the National Stadium.

March 13th 2010 triumphant in the World Cup in Delhi after defeating Germany 2-1 in the final. 24 years earlier I had played in our first win at that tournament in London when we beat England by the same score.

Oscar and Hugo accompany me across the field after defeating England 4-0 in another Champions Trophy final in Monchengladbach in 2010.

The coaching staff in our expansive apartment at the Commonwealth Games in Delhi 2010. Our emphatic performance in stifling heat was the perfect end to the year. Paul Gaudoin, Neil Mclean, Graham Reid, David Hatt, Ric Charlesworth and Jason Duff.

Jonathon playing against Spain outside Barcelona in 2011. David Alegre in pursuit. We won 3-2.

Graham Reid was my valued assistant for six years. Graham and I only played together briefly at the end of my career. We didn't always agree but were always able to work through issues and complemented one another.

Champions Trophy 2011… four in a row! After a tough year in which our form dipped we fought hard to beat an emerging Spanish team 1-0 in the final…going into London I expected Spain to be a real force but devastating injuries in the first two games derailed their plans.

Carmen, Oscar and Hugo went to London and enjoyed the Olympics at various venues…mostly we met up after hockey games and were happy except for the devastation of the semi final. This was after the bronze medal match.

We aimed for the top of the podium in London but a bronze medal was still important.

After London I spent six weeks with the Mumbai Magicians in the growing Hockey India League (HIL). Unfortunately Shiv Sena, a far right party aligned with the Hindu nationalists, did not want our four Pakistani players to play. Their protests stopped us training till the Pakistanis left. We started the league five players short (a Spaniard also did not make it) and lost a lot!

After the HIL debacle 2013 developed promisingly as the 'rebuild' gained momentum. At the Azlan Shah tournament we were again champions in a tournament we had first won in 1983 in Kuala Lumpur. There are many new Kookaburras in this team.

Our 'Hockey 9s' series in 2013 was fun. Here Jamie Dwyer joins in the fun…if only he read the book how his game would improve! Jamie is, in my view, the best male hockey player Australia has produced.

At Rotterdam Hockey Club, in the middle of 2013, we secured a place at the 2014 World Cup when we qualified through the World league semi final process. We were assured a place in The Hague a year later. We were aiming to repeat what we had achieved in Delhi.

Our last game in Rotterdam saw us upset by Belgium. We lost in a shootout and after the match we knew we had much to do in order to play well a year later.

Tristan White receiving a message as we watch play at the World League finals in Delhi in early 2014. Tristan went very close to selection for The Hague and two years later made the Rio team only to be replaced when injured a couple of weeks before the team departed.

On the way to the World Cup. Libby came to visit me at Bishem Abbey and we spent a relaxed afternoon in Marlow ('Wind in the Willows' country) meeting some Kookaburras in the town.

Next to the water at Scheveningen for a stroll and stretch. This was a daily ritual. The pier and beach are in the background. It was an ideal location.

"Readiness is all"…from the Bard. Players break from the huddle ready to play in The Hague.

Corinne Reid whose wisdom is found within this book. She was a brilliant contributor to our effort after London. At Klein Switzerland during training heading off for coffee!

After the final with Carlos Retegui of Argentina. Full of energy and purpose he is a super coach who guided both men and women from that county to medals in The Hague.

'Winners are grinners'. Four very satisfied coaches after the 6-1 win in the final. Graham Reid, Ric Charlesworth, Paul Gaudoin and Ben Bishop holding the magnificent trophy.

Our whole group together just after the players left the dais... pure relief and satisfaction washes over you.

What some of the Hockeyroos have been doing since playing! Claire Mitchell-Taverner and Chris Dobson with Molly and Max.

The best reason to step off the coaching roundabout. Daughter Kate with husband Emanuel and beautiful grandchildren Harriet and Georgina.

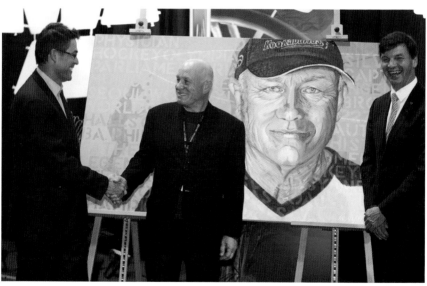

My portrait painted by Leslie Meaney (artist, teacher, swimmer and former Hockeyroo) presented to the Australian Sports Commission Chairman John Wiley after my retirement. It hangs in the lecture theatre that bears my name. I received the inaugural 'AIS World's Best' award.

8

T E A M W O R K

Hockey is a complex integrated team activity. To succeed in it, as in any invasion game like basketball, soccer, AFL or rugby, you need to penetrate the opposition territory and get at their goal – you aim to score goals while defending your citadel whenever the other team has the ball.

You are part of a team who all share the same ambition – to outscore your opponent. Mostly, at the elite level teams aim to defend and counterattack. Few teams play 'devil may care' and so getting close to the opposition goal is not easy. The big matches often involve attrition, and the ability to withstand an onslaught and endure is critical. The whole group has to be part of this experience, buy into it, understand it and be able to enact it.

Organisation and discipline are required and the whole group needs to be aware and switched on to achieve your aim of scoring, and only very rarely is it achieved by an individual piece of brilliance. Normally, it is the result of consecutive co-ordinated plans and actions. The initiating factor in creating a scoring opportunity might sometimes be a brilliant piece of individual skill. However, often it is an error of skill made by an opponent that you are able to take advantage of.

Likewise, to defend properly, organisation and discipline are also prerequisites. I rarely saw a goal against where there were not at least four or more consecutive errors or failings that led to a score against us. Avoiding such errors – especially when tired, stressed or under siege – was essential to being a resilient unit.

It's a Moral Issue...

But here is the thing! It is chaotic and often confusing on the pitch. The athletes are required to co-operate, work and act together, solve problems and be persistent. This is not easy. You do not succeed if you do not have character – you need individuals who care and who do the **right thing** at the **right time** for the **right reason**. This is analogous with many moral choices we are asked to make in our lives.

Moral choices are practical choices about what to do in any particular circumstance. We usually have a sense of what the right thing to do is but often it is not our preferred option. We may not want to do it!

The best teams are replete with athletes who make the right choice at the right time for the right reason. Teams with a critical mass of such characters are stubborn and resilient in defence and organised and determined in attack. They can, of course, also be brilliantly skilled and creative but best of all they choose the right time to utilise their gifts.

Why is the reason important? It is important because it goes to motivation and motivation goes to our investment in the task and understanding of why that choice is right. If, for instance, we do it because we want to avoid criticism or we are afraid to err or afraid of punishment, then the internal drivers are not likely to be able to operate when something different comes along or we are in a really chaotic moment.

It may not be complicated as for many, sport and the execution of the skills is an end in itself. Athletes can lose themselves in the moment and be absorbed by the task and as such they are often at their best and perfectly focussed on task. It is the ability to be totally task focussed that brings with it mastery of any task. It allows us to invest the time required to perfect the task.

'Mastery' easily slips off the tongue but it is much more than a glib descriptor and it seldom is evidenced in sport in isolation. One of the most eye opening shifts that occurred in my life was the shift I embarked on when I left politics and embarked on my coaching experience with the Hockeyroos. I had learnt little about teamwork from my time in politics! That is unsurprising but I started to understand teamwork better when coaching.

I found myself then in an environment where I was going to work in shorts and a T-shirt rather than a suit and tie but I was working with a group of individuals who were skilled, highly ambitious, hard-working and wanted to become the best they could be. They wanted to be the best in the world. Not much difference from politics there, except that they all understood or came to understand that they could only be really, really good if they worked together.

It is a great pity that this message does not seem to have penetrated the political consciousness of those leading our nation!

To develop and extend the players in your team must be the aim of the coach, and it doesn't happen with rules or external disciplines. It requires the coach to trust and guide not always direct and instruct. One doesn't get to that place without a profound engagement with the task and the individuals, and an understanding of the absolute necessity for co-operation.

Real team play requires an understanding of why we ought to do something and putting aside ego so the individual's personal ambitions and desires are secondary to the team's goals and ambitions. This does not disenfranchise the individual at all. It just puts them is a place where it is clear that for one of us to succeed we all need to work together. We all need to succeed.

These things are neither easy nor instinctive. Given the drive of our primitive mechanisms we are likely to be swamped with adrenalin and testosterone in an intense competitive environment. The poise and composure to see through these drivers allow the champion team player to pass across the face of goal for the 'tip in' rather than shoot ferociously into a well-positioned goalkeeper or powerfully into the side of the goal.

This team ethos, when embedded, becomes infectious and redoubles itself when evident in the match. It becomes contagious. The midfielder pressures and chases to force a poor pass that a teammate may then intercept. A poorly positioned defender stays in the contest to harass and delay so teammates can recover their positions. The brilliant dribbler plays the simple pass to a better-positioned teammate rather than win plaudits from an unknowing audience for an elaborate but perhaps risky and less effective display of dribbling. Defenders force an attacker wide so the attacker's scoring chance is diminished. This defender knows that the goalkeeper, correctly positioned, can save any shot from such an angle.

These actions all require a trust and belief that teammates will play their part. Trust that they can be relied on and that together their actions will deny opportunities for the opposition or make opportunities for the team to score.

Once these habits become embedded in the group, once they are part of the DNA, then your team is on the way to realising its potential. Your aim is to reach a place where the team's performance is much greater than the sum of all the individual parts.

Of course, there is more – such understanding doesn't develop overnight and you cannot put together a team that displays these characteristics in a few months. There was a time when this was not possible with our national team. We usually had a few weeks in a year when we were together and that was likely in a competitive environment. This was the case before the mid-1980s in my experience and as a consequence our teams of that era were at times brilliant but usually erratic and unable to sustain consistent performances.

With national teams this is very difficult and so it can be plausibly argued in soccer, for instance, that the big club teams are in fact stronger and better than national teams. Certainly, during my time of viewing the World Cup and football since the 1960s, it has been the case that national teams spend only a few weeks preparing for this tournament whereas club teams are honed over years in competitive leagues.

In more recent times it appears the regular matches played by international teams through the World Cup qualifiers in regional competitions have helped coaches prepare them more thoroughly. Our Australian team now qualifies and prepares for the World Cup through Asia. They now spend more time preparing for the World Cup than was previously the case when World Cup qualification was distilled into a couple of matches against the fifth ranked team in South America.

In hockey it was not until the mid-80s that we were able to have a centralised training environment where players were able to build real understanding and get to know one another as intimately as club players might do. Before that time, building understanding and team cohesiveness were not really possible. One thing that explains the ascendency of the subcontinental hockey teams during the first part of the last century was their capacity to hold centralised training camps in their preparation for major tournaments.

I have a copy of *Sports Illustrated* from the 1960s showing the Pakistan team preparing for the Olympic Games at their camp in the Himalayas. Because of the military and government sponsorship of teams, the subcontinental teams had a tradition of training camps and preparation far more sophisticated than anything we experienced as true amateurs in that time.

Thus, as a result of the establishment of the centralised training programs with access to the latest sport science analysis and rehabilitation facilities, the previous amateurs became more professional.

There are other factors too. In Australia, geography plays an important role. Only since we developed centralised training bases, have we have been able to do this. In the Netherlands, however, the players are able to live at home and train together regularly as the distances are so short and travel easy.

Similarly, access to international competition is assisted by geography in many of those places. In 2013, we (Australia) had to spend nearly half a million dollars to compete in World Cup qualifying events to make the World Cup. For Belgium and Holland, with the competition held in the Netherlands, the expenditure was in the order of tens of thousands of dollars. This fact underlines an issue, which the international body needs to address.

If competing in these environments forges real teamwork and understanding then an aspirational country or team must travel and challenge itself against high-quality teams. This 'tyranny of distance' is part of the disadvantage Australians face when they want to take on the rest of the world no matter what the sport. The exception perhaps is netball where the only real competition (New Zealand) is on our doorstep.

So how do you really build a team that contains players who will cover for one another, who will 'run in case' something happens, who will do their own job and help someone else to do their job when required? How do you develop the sort of empathy and understanding of one another and for one another's roles so that your team becomes bulletproof?

You do it iteratively – bit by bit and you encourage them to think about the game that way. You reward and praise good examples of such behaviours and you redirect when instances occur where such things are ignored. Bit by bit your players understand that they cannot realise their potential without these actions. They might be good individually but will they be really good together and will the team in which they play win competitions consistently? Those with ambition and drive eventually reach the place where they understand that teams cannot perform optimally without co-operation.

Conscious Interlocking Individuality...

Of course, there is still more to be really WORLD'S BEST – to go further. Corinne Reid used the term **conscious interlocking individuality** when referring to team cohesiveness. This is not a state where everyone is on the same page and does exactly what is expected of them! Indeed, if everyone did exactly as expected your team could be too predictable, and being too predictable can be a problem.

In this ideal place individuals are encouraged to express their individuality and be difficult to anticipate and therefore hard to read by opponents. Yet, their teammates are 'aware' and they are 'aware' of what might be coming and what they can do. Conscious interlocking individuality allows for flexibility and unpredictability, while at the same time the individual and teammates understand the nuance and context of what they are trying to do.

The best teams allow brilliant individuals to be just that, yet they also do it in the umbrella of a shared understanding and awareness. Equally, individuals feel responsibility to the team and so their actions are coloured by the motivation of the team. Their egos must come second to the team and the measure of every action is 'was this good for the team, does this benefit the team'?

Phil Jackson in his successful time as coach of the LA Lakers talked about 'mindfulness' and indeed I recently saw Seattle Seahawks coach Pete Carroll talking about the same stuff. It is the need for relationships to be at the centre of what happens in a team. It isn't new but it is hard to measure and takes time and energy to develop and extend. It isn't the stuff of technique or tactics or strength and conditioning, which of course requires constant nurturing too. It is about understanding interdependence and the need for players to be aware of themselves and aware of each other and to tie that understanding together in a way in which the team and their teammates support and assist each other to succeed.

Mumbo jumbo you might say, but for Ray McLean, founder of consultancy Leading teams, it has been the cornerstone of a very successful business. His organisation provides team building, culture creation, collective and coherent standard setting for several AFL teams along with many businesses and organisations. The programs require sharing an experience of knowledge and make the leaders of the team responsible for maintaining standards on and off the field. Everyone commits to upholding an elite level of performance to be answerable to one another. It is not always comfortable and fun and it requires rigour and discipline to be accountable openly to one another. The cornerstone of such a system must be mutual respect and trust in one another. The success of Ray's business is testimony to Ray McLean's model.

Absolute Clarity of Purpose
In the best teams, there is absolute clarity about where you are going together, what you want to achieve and how you might get there. In order to get to this point there needs to be trust in one another and openness to feedback, criticism and praise. Honest praise not sycophantic following.

My experience in coaching tells me that getting to this position can be more difficult in men's teams as there tends to be more testosterone and ego and less willingness to sublimate one's personal ambitions for the team. Perhaps women are socialised to put the family and children first and thus are better at this.

Real Openness

Tensions and stresses between individuals are inevitable and require mature, grown-up conversations to adequately deal with them. Children, when they don't get their own way, have outbursts and tantrums whereas you would hope adults are able to understand that we all make mistakes and don't always get what we want. We understand how the world is while trying to take it to an idealised 'perfect' place. With a sporting team or individuals in sport we endeavour to achieve a perfect performance but we are equally aware that things will go wrong and we will have to deal with difficulties that come along.

So when we don't achieve what we want or we come up short we can admit our errors and work to find solutions to do better and keep going until we get it right or make improvements.

Candour

To be really open we need to admit our errors and ask for help while working co-operatively to help others. What sort of conversations does this entail? Tough ones!

"When you do that it hurts our team, you must try to change that."

"What are you going to do to rectify your weakness at…?"

"I don't think it is like that…I think…"

To create that environment the coach has to be able to listen and admit his or her own foibles and relinquish some control. This for me was possible because I firmly believed the team had to own the tactics and methods we employed. Some of these conversations were really tough and were of a nature that you wanted to avoid. There were disagreements; they were important and they involved emotion.

No Hierarchy

I firmly believe teamwork thrives where there is no rigid hierarchy or a rigid 'order-laden' culture, like the military or even the public service. There is no doubt that such organisations can get things done, but they do not allow for the exceptional to be achieved, or real creativity to be expressed and released. If you want exceptional then it is necessary to throw away the rulebook.

This is not saying there is no discipline or accountability. It is, of course, self-discipline and accountability to one another that is encouraged and thrives in such an environment. This environment values all contributions and its diversity is its strength.

Mostly, it should be understood that teams are evolving, changing dynamic bodies that are never the same from one day to the next. Constant vigilance is required to measure the temperature and tone of the team. It is never harmonious for more than a few days without tensions and stresses emerging. Players and staff ought to become skilled at dealing with these blow-ups. Sometimes they are minor and sometimes they look minor but underneath lie chronic tensions and deep-seated resentments. You ignore and avoid these things at your peril.

So when we talk about teamwork we ought to be clear that you need to 'work' at being a team every day. The staff, the players and the administration have to be on the same page. This is easier said than done as individuals have egos and outside interests, and many an administrator has had too much to say or allowed personal opinions to be misconstrued as club policy.

We need to express a *shared identity and purpose, agreement about how we will behave and how we want to be seen, real honesty and candour in our interactions and communication, and willingness to all contribute and co-operate to achieve our goals.* If you put all that together you have the formula for teamwork which is critical for an exceptional culture and performances.

9

THE MORE THINGS CHANGE ...

Fifty years ago Cyril Walter, a legendary figure in New Zealand hockey published *The Theory and Practice of Hockey*. During my time in New Zealand I picked the book up at a second-hand bookstore in Christchurch. Many of Cyril's charges from Christchurch made up the bulk of the New Zealand team at the Montreal Olympics where they famously beat us in 1976. Like all books of that era it is dated and tired looking. It was printed in Great Britain and the language of Walter is proper and precise.

Taking the time to browse through it recently I was struck by how much of it was still salient and relevant to modern hockey. Yes, the game has developed dramatically since those times so as to be largely unrecognisable from today's game. Synthetic pitches and compound carbon fibre sticks, plastic dimple balls, no offside, unlimited interchanges, high density foam protecting goalkeepers, quarters of 15 minutes rather than 35 minute halves – the list is seemingly endless. A whole range of new skills is now part of the framework that accompanies the basics of yesteryear. Hitting with the edge, catching and throwing overheads and the penalty corner flinging foremost amongst them.

In spite of all this the field and goal dimensions are unchanged and many of the principles of coaching remain as relevant today as they were in 1966, when Walter wrote the book.

I was struck by the central emphasis on skill and quality skill development, and by the tactical awareness exhibited – Walter's continual emphasis on the need for the player not in possession to 'make the play' – create danger, position to defend or be available. Young players of all persuasions need emphasis on the two minutes of the game when they have the ball but they also must work at what they do when their team or they themselves are without the ball. Such lessons are timeless and such knowledge and actions remain central no matter what has changed in the game.

Similarly, Walter emphasizes the importance of trapping – being able to safely stop and control the ball to keep it safe and in one's orbit. One who hasn't mastered this skill can never be effective whether the game is football, soccer, hockey (ice or field), basketball or water polo.

In many games this may simply mean being able to catch it but in soccer where control is with the feet or hockey (with the stick) the skill required is much more difficult and needs constant refining and development so as to allow one to execute beyond simple play to complex play.

When one ponders the pace of change in the past twenty years it is staggering, and for those with greying hair or indeed without much hair, it can be very difficult to keep track of the changes...of the possibilities, the nuances, the technology and the tactics.

Video...

"The camera is an instrument that teaches people how to see without a camera."

Dorothea Lange (1895-1965)

The famous photojournalist of days gone by makes a wonderful observation about how live images have changed our lives in the past century. The introduction of television in the home and video in the second half of the last century and now digital media has changed so many aspects of our lives. News reporting, documentary and live current affairs programs added to the cinematographic world of movies are all examples. But of course sport too has been profoundly changed and especially the art of coaching. This is because it allows us 'reality testing' when we play back the action of the game.

In 1996, when we competed in the Centenary Olympics in Atlanta the possibilities of digital analysis in sport were beginning to dawn. Video was still in analogue mode and VHS was still the mode of choice as we coaches sought to find the moments we needed to illustrate our coaching. Video was, of course, the big change of the 70s that allowed coaches to see and show exactly what happened. Before that we only had reels of celluloid with ponderous editing and fragile technology.

Twenty years earlier in 1976, there was no videotape possibility and the most potent coaching tool in my time was not accessible in the way we are able to use it these days.

Coaching in my earliest days occurred via anecdote, recollection, memory and recall. Over time games that were mainly discovered and invented in the 19th century by the British grew and developed. Coaches, of course, were not part of the scene at the very beginning when groups of gentlemen organised themselves and 'played'. In Jonathan Wilson's excellent book *Inverting the Pyramid* (a history of football tactics), he describes how in the early 20th century Herbert Chapman, (1878-1934) hit upon the idea of instituting 'team talks' to help players prepare for the games and to organise for victory. Chapman was famed as the one who introduced the WM formation, championed floodlighting, European club competitions and numbered shirts! At that time he was one of the FA's most influential and innovative managers having success with Huddersfield Town and Arsenal before his untimely and sudden death in 1934. All these things that seem everyday now were great innovations then.

Innovation

It is not so long ago (late 70s) that cricket under lights, coloured clothing and helmets were seen as ground breaking. Indeed, the march for progress and change pervades every sport and competition. The great challenge for coaches is to be on the right side of these changes and to anticipate them, embrace them when they arrive and be willing to push the envelope to give your team/ players the opportunity to be the agents of change and to be at the vanguard of change.

In the cauldron of elite sport it is the players or practitioners who are the engines of greatest change. They are the innovators who try new things, experiment with technique or equipment, and advance the game. Any coach/manager not attuned to these developments misses opportunities and can harm the team's prospects to distinguish and differentiate itself.

I believe this may be one area of sport where the changes have been more dramatic and yet I wonder if it is different? Did coaches in bygone eras have to deal with players so keen to ask "why", rather than ones who were just willing to do as they were told?

When I first played, a one-to-one meeting with the coach was a rarity. Now it is expected to occur on a regular basis.

Similarly, when I coached the Hockeyroos in the 1990s, our approach to having an expanded leadership group was outside normal practice and considered unusual. Now it appears most sporting franchises embrace leadership programs and groups that are a shift from the hierarchical view of the early 20th century.

Technology

In 1996, before the Olympic Games in Atlanta we travelled to Europe in May and June for matches against Great Britain, Germany and the Netherlands. While watching a practice match in Reading I saw that the British goalkeeper had new equipment in the form of high-density foam gloves, bigger and with better protection than anything I had seen before. The gloves (or mitts) were part of the 'rebound revolution' that was changing goalkeeping forever. I purchased three sets of these revolutionary gloves to bring back to Australia. Initially, our goalkeepers were reluctant the use the unfamiliar equipment. After only a week they were convinced of its utility and embraced its use. In the Olympic tournament only two months later most teams used this equipment.

Rule Changes

Throughout my coaching stints with national teams, changes have been constant. In 1993 the interchange rule was introduced. At the end of 1996 the removal of offside was introduced. Hitting on the reverse with the edge of the stick seeped into the rules in the late 1990s. Auto play from free hits began in 2009 and the use of overheads from free hits was later introduced. And now quarters and time stopping for penalty corners are the norm. The penalty corner rules and its adjudication have likewise been regularly changed, and along with this the play of goalkeepers, their equipment and myriad other regulations. All of this change introduces opportunity to experiment and postulate, which organisations, teams and coaches ought to utilise. Continually, these adjustments require flexibility and an open mind in order to stay at the cutting edge in your sport.

Indeed, in hockey in the first half of the 20th century it was the Indians who dominated the 'British owned' game largely on the back of their fresh approach as well as technological change in the development of smaller stick hooks and dribbling skills.

Given this obsession with change and innovation, and the need to counteract the disruption and the shifts of the modern game, what is the place of the traditional skills and fundamentals in sport? To me they remain just that, FUNDAMENTALS, on which one's game is built. Hockey is a complicated game, as is cricket, and there are many, many skills to be mastered. Football (soccer) or basketball on the other hand, are much simpler games. The ball is big, hands, feet or head are used to control the ball and the parameters are relatively simple compared with bat and ball games. Tennis without any interference is in another category. All these sports are different and none I am identifying are necessarily 'better' than another, but some do not require the scope and difficulty of skills. Swimming requires the same perfect action again and again, also with no interference. This requires closed skills for execution. Golf has no interference but the ball is small and distances large. The skill required is precise. In cycling, swimming or rowing physiology is a much greater component of success than most team ball games.

However, whatever the detail and parameters, exquisite and reproducible skill is a prerequisite for brilliant, exceptional performance. To reach such proficiency the athlete must work very hard and have an approach towards uncompromising quality all the time.

In the beginning of 2012, I read Chad Harbach's novel *The Art of Fielding,* an engaging read which I enjoyed very much. This work touched on the sporting metaphors that had always been a part of my life. The tale is of Henry Skrimshander's journey to realise his potential in baseball. Potential that could be realised by being drafted into the pro ranks from college baseball.

One piece that I really liked was: *"Baseball was an art, but to excel at it you had to become a machine. It didn't matter how beautifully you performed sometimes, what you did on your best day, how many spectacular plays you made. You weren't a painter or a writer – you didn't work in private and discard your mistakes, and it wasn't just your masterpieces that counted. What mattered, as for any machine was repeatability. Moments of inspiration were nothing compared to elimination of error... Can you perform on demand, like a car, a furnace, a gun? Can you make that throw one hundred times out of a hundred? If it can't be a hundred, it had better be ninety-nine."*

This piece from the pen of a fictional storyteller is a piece of pure gold sporting philosophy. 'Repeatability' – one of my favourite phrases – is players need "reproducible skill under pressure". Skill execution must become automatic, instinctive, reliable and ingrained.

As I have outlined elsewhere, in "Comfort the Troubled and Trouble the Comfortable", part of the pathway to excellent and reproducible skill is of course the highest quality practice.

Repetition is essential to solidify any skill but this ought to be accompanied by quality feedback to ensure technique is correct. To advance the level of skill the tasks should be continuously more difficult. Once we embark on this pathway we ensure progressive learning. The end point is achieved when we develop the competence to reproduce these new skills under the pressure of competition. That entails being able to execute skills in an environment of the disruption and chaos of a match situation. Skill honed by this process in a competitive environment ensures mastery is complete.

This is as true today as it always has been and indeed perhaps the only thing to have changed is the sophistication of the methods available, particularly the methods for feedback and the time available to apply to the skills. These are the things that have changed.

I was recently fascinated to read the coach's report from the 1956 Olympic Games. F.W. Browne was stationed at RAAF station Richmond, New South Wales, when the report was sent in early 1957.

Squadron Leader Fred Browne made a number of recommendations while indicating that the standard of the game had improved markedly since his arrival in Australia in 1947. He was in the vanguard of migrants from the subcontinent after partition in India. He believed the Olympic tournament had given Australia a real perspective about the game elsewhere and what was needed to progress. No longer was the country operating in a void away from outside influence, ideas and developments.

His recommendations and ideas were constructive. While the selected Olympians had taken time to adjust to a full-time training program of 2-3 sessions per day they had advanced considerably. The need for more than three weeks preparation was clear!! He suggested at least six weeks were required. These days we might laugh at such a short period of preparation.

Browne suggested overseas competition would be vital for Australia to advance its game and to learn what other teams and countries had to offer. This would allow us to refine our approach and techniques as we challenged the world.

His final two recommendations, I believe, were part of an approach that would see Australia on the podium eight years later in Tokyo. Australia's first Olympic hockey medal, bronze, would be won there. He suggested that we ought to start to play more hockey in summer on harder surfaces in order to improve skills and play a faster game and he clearly railed at the selection process by suggesting the team have its coach as a selector!

In 1960, Victorian coach Charlie Morley, would take over as Olympic coach and so Browne never again had stewardship of the team.

The ideas of Fred Browne are of course consistent with the approach that Australia has taken. During the 1960s and 1970s our national men's team began to travel overseas and experience increasing amounts of success. The international exposure afforded by the Melbourne Olympics was clearly a catalyst. The knowledge returned to Australia from these teams was transferred and shared and our game grew and developed. In 1964 in Tokyo we won our first Olympic medal when third and in 1968, Australia would lose the Olympic final against Pakistan coming so close to gold.

It is interesting to reflect that arguably our best player of the sixties, Julian Pearce who made his debut in 1960 and last played in 1970, only played forty three times for Australia. Today such a career would realise nearly three hundred games!

By 1976, after beating India twice and Pakistan in the semi-final, Australia contested the final with New Zealand. As a contender at the elite level we had arrived. In 1983 we won the Champions Trophy for the first time and won again in 1984 and 1985. The World Cup, inaugurated in 1971, eluded us for 15 years before winning it in 1986 for the first time. This was merely 30 years after Browne's report.

Full-time training, international exposure, a focus on skills yet our own style, selection by the coaches and the best training surfaces are now all taken for granted. The modern players stand on the shoulders of pioneers like Browne and Morley

It is unquestionably the rhythm of all sport that requires a search for better, stronger, faster, and in hockey it was the international interaction that very much accelerated that. In Australian football, for instance, it took 100 years to realise that sometimes you should kick the ball backwards and sideways to keep possession and achieve better and more effective penetrations.

In the 1960s, when I played as a schoolboy footballer, it was completely anathema to do so (kick backwards and sideways) and not until the 1990s did this start to come into the game. It was the influence of other sports, such as basketball and water polo, observed by coaches that brought about this shift.

There are many things that have shaped modern sport and many options likely to be in the future. During the last 50 years the big shifts for coaches have been advances in physiology and training, the utilisation of video, measurements of motion and speed, digital analysis and many more innovations have meant we are better able to analyse performance, prepare and train.

Central to the successes of our hockey teams in Australia has been the establishment of centralised training opportunities and a willingness to learn from others while still being true to our way of playing. Fred Browne would be pleased that those who followed have implemented much that he recommended in 1956.

The continued search for brilliant skill and technical innovation, tactical sophistication and co-operation and relentless determination remain. They always have been the things that make the difference. They are as old as time. They were recognised by writers like Shakespeare, Sun Tzu and Tolstoy as crucial to prevail in earlier times and they still work today.

FUTURE concerns...

Elsewhere in this book I have expressed my concern about the direction our sport might be taking. I have been particularly worried about the reports of an attraction to small-sided games as used in the Youth Olympics. While this does allow some smaller countries access it completely changes the game so as to make it practically unrecognisable. As such it dumbs down some of the skills, which give the game its charm and grace.

Our sport as it is now played can always be improved, and from time to time changes that have been made have been disappointing. However, the majority have increased the speed and flow and maintained the level of skill required so as to make it an extraordinary spectacle. It is a very fast and skilful game. So much so that not everyone can appreciate the spectacle but we should resist attempts to go for the five-a-side formula espoused by some.

I have been a champion of nine-a-side as the game's dimensions and essence is maintained and defending is made more difficult so requiring an emphasis on attack. As the athleticism of the participants has improved this move would release more space for creativity and risk-taking and, with other adjustments, increase scoring. This improves the likelihood of quality play winning in the end. As such it encourages coaches to focus on scoring rather than defending.

I suspect administrators in soccer do not want such reliability. They are unwilling to change rules in their game as upsets and shootouts bring drama, conflict and publicity. Fanaticism and uncertainty fuel the passions of the game in which defence has precedence over attack. In the 2016 European Championships the winner, Portugal, only won once in normal time in seven matches! In that game it is too easy to defend and so defence is rewarded. I believe the best sport values defence but tips the balance slightly the other way. Basketball is perhaps a game where it is too easy to score!

Soccer's leaders seem opposed to video referral even on the goal line in spite of the controversies, and when Brazil was knocked out of the recent Copa America on a blatant act of cheating it was as if this was normal practice! The practise of 'diving' and faking injury is endemic in the game and attempts to change it seem impotent.

In hockey such ideas as widening the goal could assist scoring as the goalkeeper has become a different beast given the size and quality of their equipment but such a move would also require corner rules to change. Again, I would support this as the present rule is dangerous and places too much value on one closed skill. Of course those in Europe seem attached to this aspect of the game so the practicality of change is unlikely despite the obvious utility and safety of such change.

Any adjustments should I believe encapsulate three things... *simplicity, safety and reward skill*. If we do this our game will have an exciting pathway. The move to shorter quarters, which has less playing time, ought to have been resisted unless the quarters were 20 minutes. The removal of extra time and so direct shootouts ought to have been resisted. Here we see the insidious influence of media, which I cover elsewhere for that seems to be the reason the sport has changed these things.

The recent penchant for players to 'stage theatrically' is an unwanted introduction which then gets rewarded with opponents suspended. Vigilance is required here as suspensions that go for five or ten minutes are in fact much longer as time stopped for corners makes the penalty effectively extended.

Finally, we have the issue of umpiring. The problem is that umpiring matters a lot, especially in a low scoring game like hockey. At the elite level we need to get that right. And at every level we need it to be understandable.

I firmly believe it is time for two extra umpires to be stationed above the goal in a cage (safe from balls flying at speed) to adjudicate goal circle action. Video referral usage would be reduced and the field umpires could track along both sides of the field not concerned so much about being 'in position' for the sudden breakaway. Any such break would be able to be handled by the 'in situ' umpire above the goal at the other end.

This situation could extend the umpiring life of some of the best umpires who retire too early and would enable a 'birds-eye view' of an ever more crowded and messy scoring circle. It need only apply for the major competitions and I believe the number of the appeals for video adjudication would fall as a result.

Our game has been progressive enough to adjust and modernise and will need to continue to do so to remain contemporary. I only hope that those in charge make their judgements without undue influence from some of the corporate factors that I outline in my chapter on corporate sport.

1 0

"OUR DOUBTS ARE TRAITORS..."

"Thou art a monument without tomb
And art alive still, while thy booke doth live,
And we have wits to read, and praise to give."

In 1623, seven years after Shakespeare's death, when the First Folio of his plays was published, Ben Jonson said this of his friend and fellow writer. Now four hundred years after his death we still marvel at the extraordinary body of the Bard's work.

When one looks at the record book it appears the world record holder or the world champion only wins at the Olympics one event in two or three. Regardless of technical pedigree or past form, physical qualities or tactical nous, there is another factor that is crucial if you are to be successful. That essential ingredient is the mental strength or resilience to persist and endure through the rigours of competition. Whether you call it single-mindedness or calmness or poise or determination it amounts to a competitive quality that is essential in all champion athletes at the highest level.

Shakespeare may well have been the first psychologist in English literature. He put meat on the bones of his characters in a way that gave us an understanding of their foibles and failures, their strengths and weaknesses. He understood their very beating hearts and their motivations. He was an observer of human nature and he taught us about the motivations of his characters.

Harold Bloom is one of the world's most passionate lovers of the Bard. In his wonderful book *Shakespeare, the Invention of the Human*, he proposes the idea that Shakespeare taught us to understand human nature – he inaugurated personality as we know it, and this is one of the reasons for Shakespeare's pervasiveness and enduring quality.

Coaches are about change. We want to change the habits and behaviours of our athletes and should never be satisfied by short-term changes. We want deep personal change. Some suggest change is just a reorientation of our priorities, resources, skills and abilities that we already possess. I would suggest it is much more than that.

It is a reinvention of ourselves in which we recognise a grander or different purpose for ourselves. We realise we are able to perform at a much higher standard than at present. In Shakespeare's work there are the themes of life. Many of these themes are also the themes of sport. The competition for power, the challenge of achievement and the search for success. Shakespeare, through his characters, espoused the need for continual learning and co-operation, the quality of humility, the dealing with doubt and uncertainty and the art of planning and leadership.

Coaches are always looking for examples of these things and for a different voice to pass on the message. I often used quotes from statesmen like Nelson Mandela and Winston Churchill, from great athletes like Wayne Gretzky, Martina Navratilova and Herb Elliott, and from coaches like Wayne Bennett and Alex Ferguson. But easily the most fertile source of knowledge was the Bard.

Accordingly, I have included some of my favourite and most relevant quotes from my little book *Shakespeare the Coach*. I believe these few pieces of wisdom exemplify why we ought to be sure that we give appropriate attention to our mental clarity and capacity to be calm and composed when in the contest. In the Bard's time the scientific actions of neurotransmitters and hormones were not understood yet man's passions and the way in which emotion could interfere with decision-making was understood. Through observation and experience men knew what worked and what distracted in decision making.

Whether a king leading an army or a lowly commoner seeking justice or a way to find their path in the world, or a father offering advice to his son, Shakespeare had advice to give and a story to tell.

Here are some of my favourite 'Bardisms' which go to such issues as dealing with doubt, building resilience and the need for coaching and direction. We see how action is more important than talk, the virtue of humility, the value of strategy, the importance of good preparation, leadership's crucial input and the need for objectivity and self-awareness. Before modern-day gurus started talking about social intelligence, the keenest observer of human nature was aware of the importance and relevance of it.

These are only some of the topics explored in this chapter and the flavour of my book *Shakespeare the Coach* is sprinkled across the pages. I hope it serves to emphasize that the mental challenges in sport and life are not new and remain the same challenges that Elizabethans experienced over four hundred year ago.

No. 1. **"Our doubts are traitors,**
      And makes us lose the good we oft might win
      By fearing to attempt…" *Measure for Measure,* 1.iv, lines 77-79

Every athlete and competitor is beset with doubts about their ability to perform or succeed on occasions. In this quote Lucio is convincing Isabella that she should plead for the life of her brother Claudio who has been unfairly sentenced in a fanciful Viennese setting. One imagined Shakespeare is holding up to ridicule the corruption of his own time in civic London! It is a theme used elsewhere by the Bard, which has as much relevance today as it did four hundred years ago.

In sport our performances are often on display for all to see and we are measured in a way that is extremely challenging. If our actions in everyday life were thus measured it would make life stressful. Professional athletes are publically measured on a weekly basis (every kick, catch, fumble and error or miss is counted) in a way in which most of us would not like ourselves to be measured in our own work environment!

Yet Shakespeare is saying we need to overcome our doubts and fears to act and perform if we are to operate in the world…if we are to achieve our aims.

In most sports the 'away from home' performance is a real phenomenon and indeed in soccer the 'away goal' is valued more than a 'home goal'. What does this come down to? Once travel fatigue and environmental conditions, like the home pitch and umpire bias are taken into account, it is clear there are reasons that influence the outcome.

I would contend that the story is also one of mental strength in winning the struggle between doubt and belief that takes place every time we compete. Something goes wrong – your best player gets injured or the umpire makes an error, or the opponent plays well for a time or the crowd is loud and not supporting you – and the resolve and conviction of the individual wanes. The doubts surface and belief diminishes. Herb Elliott talked about that little voice that suggests you might slow down or give in. The best competitors do not submit to such doubts!

No. 2. **"Sweet are the uses of adversity…"** *As you Like it,* 2.i, line12

The Bard understood that it is only through trials and challenges that we build real resilience and the capacity to overcome difficulties. There are numerous such references in his works. Another that comes to mind is the danger of comfort and value of hardship.

"Plenty and Peace breeds cowards:
Hardness ever
Of hardiness is mother..." *Cymbeline,* 3.vi, lines 21-22.

As a coach you are always trying to find ways in which you can provide experiences wherein your players are challenged and tested at the edge of their capacity. By doing so you hope they will be able to develop the resilience that will stand them in good stead when challenged and tested in real games. It was always my view that you should try to create, at training, situations which are harder than that which might be faced in the contest.

Sometimes you overload one team, you give the athletes less time and space in which to perform, you get them tired, you make them deal with unfair decision-making. There are many ways to lift the degree of difficulty to test and build resilience and skill execution under pressure.

Requiring your players to deal with the loss of a teammate through temporary suspension in practice scenarios is essential if your team is to be able to work their way through such situations in international matches.

No. 3. **"Men's faults do seldom to themselves appear."** *The Rape of Lucrece,* line 633.

As analytical and self-aware as we may be, there is always a place for an outside opinion on what we do. The coach can be a technical advisor or director, analyst, strategist, teacher and motivator. Some of the best are all of these things. As the Bard points out, we all need someone holding up the mirror to allow us to view our own performances because we are not inclined to do it very objectively ourselves!!

While in everyday life we often are able to play hide and seek with reality, the sporting life at elite level does not allow this. There is public scrutiny of performance!

The best coaches challenge and hold athletes to account and work with them to rectify deficiencies. Only then can we expect to change and improve. We all learn best from our mistakes and the best coaches deliver really candid feedback. This is not an easy thing to do, but done well it plays an important role in reinforcing change and development.

The best performers do have self-awareness, and over time it is learnt and developed in those seeking self-improvement. Later in this chapter we go further into this topic yet often at the early stages of development it is necessary for the coach or mentor to call out our over-estimation of ourselves!

No. 4. **"Talkers are no good doers…"** *Richard III*, 1.iii, line 351
   "Action is eloquence." *Coriolanus*, 3.ii, line 76

These two quotes outline the need for decisiveness rather than hesitancy or pontificating. In a famous Australian football game, famed coach of Hawthorn in days gone by, John Kennedy, is reputed to have implored his players to not think but act. "Don't think act," was his advice as his team was wallowing in a place where they were unable to execute their skills that day.

Usually, being decisive rather than procrastinating and being unsure is the thing that creates opportunity and enables things to happen. Real definition in your action is required to deal with acute moments in a match. Of course there are always different actions available in any moment but it is not helpful to dither and be indecisive.

Take action and prepare for what may happen next is the best thing to do. The very best performers make firm decisions and judgements and yet are flexible enough to adjust strategy and change course when appropriate. Likewise, in a sporting sense teammates are able to adjust and cover or create opportunity when they see decisive action further up the field.

All of this is predicated on the time frame for action for any set of circumstances, and as Shakespeare was well aware it is easy to be the critic on the sideline when one is not being measured or assessed. However, the ability to act and be decisive is the currency of sporting excellence.

No. 5. **"It is a witness still of excellency**
   To put a strange face on his own perfection." *Much Ado About Nothing*, 2.iii, lines 43-44

In his insightful book *Good to Great* Jim Collins examines what makes companies great. Collins' analysis indicates that companies that do best are led by humble and determined CEOs. The highly paid, high profile, noisy bosses are not the ones who take good businesses to great performances. There is a common misconception that brash, confident, even arrogant demeanour is the stuff of champion sporting performers. In my view nothing could be further from the truth. The best performers and performances are born in an environment of genuine humility, and that accompanies a desire to continually improve and add to what has already been achieved. Champions are seldom satisfied with one triumph or victory; they search for perfection and longevity in the activity closest to their hearts. To wit: Federer seeks another grand slam and Djokovich aims to surpass him; Hawthorn FC wants to keep winning as do Manchester United, Bayern Munich and Real Madrid; Bolt aims at a third Olympic triumph (and succeeds) and the All Blacks keep on working for improvement.

In the teams I coached I was proud of the attitude of humility that resided in the leaders and staff as we went about our work. There was resolve to improve and be better yet seldom did I feel we got ahead of ourselves. It is indeed a defining quality of the best teams as it underpins a desire to improve and the discipline required to make that improvement through hard work and co-operation.

In his work *The Checklist Manifesto* Atul Gawande expounds the checklist as an important tool in getting better outcomes in a whole range of endeavours…surgery, flying planes, building skyscrapers – even playing games. Specifically, he suggests its power resides in the humility inherent in the belief that we might fail or make mistakes and so we embrace its discipline and the need to communicate and co-operate before embarking on such endeavours.

No. 6. **"…the readiness is all…"** *Hamlet*, 5, ii, line 215

"…defences, musters, preparations
should be maintain'd, assembled, and collected,
As were a war in expectation." *Henry V*, 2, iv. Lines 18-20

Coaches understand that there are three things required for consistent performance and those three requirements are; preparation, preparation and preparation! In Shakespeare's day the great contests of the time did not take place on Wembley stadium or Twickenham or at the Olympic Games. They occurred on the battlefields of Europe. At Agincourt the French were underprepared and suffered accordingly.

Good preparation and vigilance about knowing what to expect gives us confidence and belief that we will be able to handle whatever comes along whatever the challenge we may face. The best athletes understand the need for periods of training away from competition wherein technique is honed, fitness and agility built and tactics and strategy imagined and formulated. Only by taking the time for such periods can constant progress be assured. With the Kookaburras and the Hockeyroos such blocks of training solidified and underpinned great competition play.

No. 7a. **"Till then 'tis wisdom to conceal our meaning."** *Henry V*,
1, Part III, 4.vii, line 60.

"Have more than thou showest,
Speak less than thou knowest,
Lend less than thou owest,
Ride more than thou goest…" *King Lear*, 1.iv, lines 117-120

Edward IV wants time to organise and build his forces and so recognises the need to disguise his intentions, and in Lear even the Fool knows the need to disguise ones intentions! In the contest (mainly military in Shakespeare's time) the value of surprise is clear, as is the advantage that can come from being underestimated.

It is best to appear, as you are not: If you are slow, try to appear fast; if flexible, appear rigid; if light, appear heavy; if hard, appear soft. This is the essence of deception and the cornerstone of strategy.

Of course having a strategy is not enough once the contest begins. There is the need for decisive action and flexibility so that poor strategies can be discarded and adjusted in the heat of battle. In a sporting contest an action on one side of the pitch often creates an overreaction to the threat and thereby vulnerability on the other side of the pitch allowing for a quick transfer to allow penetration and perhaps a scoring chance.

Teams transfer the play for exactly this reason and transferring the ball from side to side can disorientate and distract defenders when done well. There are sometimes advantages in creating an impression or image of being unbeatable but it is equally true that being underestimated can be a great motivator. It was always my view that it is quite handy to lose enough for the opposition to think that you are not as good as you actually are! Hence, I was always happy to experiment and take risks and try things in the lesser competitions.

I must say I find it incredible that modern day sporting contests on television are replete with the sideline interview. These days these interviews are carried out 'in the game' or 'on the bench' as players exit at half time or enter the field. Do we really think for a moment that anything central to team strategy or tactics would be shared with a worldwide audience!! We really are kidding ourselves!! I find these interviews some of the most banal and uninteresting one ever hears.

No. 7b. "We few, we happy few, we band of brothers..."
Henry V, 4.iii, line 60

Co-operation is the glue that holds organisations, families and teams together and is indispensable if you are to succeed in any endeavour where you cannot achieve it alone. This famous line is delivered before the battle of Agincourt when Henry V, now the mature leader, calls on his men to join together in the life and death challenge that lies ahead.

As an actor, playwright, owner and investor Shakespeare knew his business well. He understood the need for a group of players to combine together and co-operate in the production of a play. The theatre at that time largely operated as a repertory system, with a considerable variety of plays available and a different one played every afternoon. Shakespeare understood that teamwork was required to succeed in business, and his success as a businessman reflected that approach. Around 1612 he retired to Stratford-upon-Avon a wealthy man.

Team sports as we know them today were not on the agenda in Elizabethan England and so the activity most identified with co-operative adversarial enterprises was the military. At Agincourt the English win an improbable victory against a much larger French force which underestimated English resolve and ingenuity. The English longbow played a significant role. Henry's rousing St Crispin's Day speech before the battle played a role in the victory.

Interestingly, Shakespeare gives considerable coverage to the night before the battle and the quiet time the King spends with his troops. The Bard clearly understands that while rhetoric is important there is also a need to understand these men better.

> "We few, we happy few, we band of brothers;
> For he today that sheds his blood with me
> Shall be my brother; be he ne'er so vile,
> This day shall gentle his condition;

And gentlemen in England now a-bed
Shall think themselves accurs'd they were not here,
And hold their manhoods cheap whiles any speaks
That fought with us upon St Crispin's Day." *Henry V,* 4.iii
lines 60-67

The appeal to 'brotherhood' and togetherness in the words and the use of 'we' and 'us' is very much the emotion of modern team sport and business and conveys the pride inherent in doing something important and challenging well.

No. 8. **"The speciality of rule hath been neglected."**
Troilus and Cressida, 1.iii, line 78

Ulysses laments the fragmentation that has occurred in the Greek camp at the seven-year point of the siege of Troy. Where leadership falters, discipline, order and harmony have been eroded and morale is low. Even the great Achilles idles away his time without direction or purpose.

Shakespeare understood how crucial leadership was to the success of an endeavour…it gives direction and purpose and meaning. The best leaders are able to persuade others to join them and can inspire loyalty and motivation.

The Bard made plentiful reference to the quality of leadership and the need for purpose and direction in the lives of men and women.

Sometimes, the goals and direction seem impossible, yet without aiming to achieve the seemingly impossible great advances are seldom made. **"…we are such stuff as dreams are made on…"** (*Tempest*)

As for persuasion, Shakespeare was a master, and the speech by Mark Anthony over the body of Caesar is a fine example of the power of rhetoric to persuade and convince which many of the best leaders have in abundance.

This is, of course, a sentiment that is ever present in modern literature and politics. The Kennedys utilised the poignant words

of George Bernard Shaw's serpent in *Back to Methuselah* to outline aspirational ambitions to great effect. *"You see things and ask 'Why'?*
   "But I dream things that never were and ask 'why not'?"

Leadership is as crucial today as in Shakespeare's time when the very hierarchical nature of power limited the individual's ability to be heard. Maybe today we can all be heard but the problem is who is listening?

No. 9. **"Greatness knows itself…"** *Henry IV*, Part 1, 4.iii, line 76
   "A fool doth think he is wise, but the wise man knows himself to be a fool." *As You Like It*, 5.i, line 31

While these two quotes may seem paradoxical what they do is touch the need for true insight and self-reflection. Outstanding performers understand their strengths and weaknesses and are able to operate within the boundaries of these to produce the results they seek.

Self-awareness is an indispensable accompaniment to any successful performer whatever the activity. Socrates decried the fact that men looked ridiculous when trying to know obscure things before they knew themselves. The words 'know thyself' were chiselled into the wall of the Arts Department at the University of Western Australia. It has stayed with me since my undergraduate days.

From Shakespeare's most famous work, *Hamlet*, comes the advice from the oily Polonius to his son Laertes.

   "This above all – to thine own self be true,
   And it must follow, as the night the day,
   Thou canst not then be false to any man." *Hamlet*, 1.iii, lines 78-80.

It has been suggested that this quote promotes greed and selfishness, yet a more sympathetic interpretation is that it is an appeal to honesty and empathy. Being analytical and introspective about motives and purpose is the stuff of mature and reasoned decision making.

Few athletes can fulfil their potential without knowing themselves well and understanding their inner drives. It involves an active awareness of how our actions will affect others. In improving and rebuilding the Kookaburras after our disappointment in London one of our important tasks was to get our team to be explicit about their signatures and to understand how their individual signature impacted others.

The process was confronting and required candour and self-reflection. The capacity to give honest feedback to each other and hold one another to account requires such emotional intelligence. While a fool will overestimate himself and underestimate opponents, and therefore cut corners, a wise competitor knows better.

No. 10. **"But men may construe things after their fashion,**
　　　　Clean from the purpose of the things themselves."
　　　　Julius Caesar, 1.iii, lines 34-35.

Cicero is less than impressed by Casca's assertion that there are ominous portents afoot. While unlikely to be swayed by soothsayers and predictors today we are subject to our own and others prejudices and biases.

There is always a need for objectivity and dispassionate analysis when it comes to making decisions in business or sport. We can easily fall into the mistake of seeing what we want to see. The growth in statistical analysis in sport and for objective assessments of what is going on has been rapid and significant. The *Moneyball* story and the more recent tale about three-point shooting by the Golden State Warriors shows there is real benefit for those overseeing sporting teams to make their judgements on the best information available.

The anecdotal tale, or preconception, is reinforced by some action on the field and thus becomes a mindset. "He's always been a poor kick," can be reinforced and then becomes the 'reality' in the minds of some.

Accordingly, we need to look at what is actually happening and over time the true picture can emerge. Someone who has improved a weakness in their game or been unfairly assessed from a small sample needs to be reconsidered. Thus the numbers reveal the present reality and progress in eradicating a weakness and can be plotted. We would be foolish to allow our biases and preconceptions to influence our judgement and decision-making.

Along with these samples of the Bard's wide repertoire of messages goes advice on the pitfalls of youth and the declines of old age; the need to balance reprimand with praise; the power of the mind to overcome challenges of the flesh and fears; the importance of learning and the need for change. Critically, he understood the value of patience: *"What wound did ever heal but by degrees?"* (*Othello*), and courage, physical sometimes, but also the ability to turn the other cheek: *"He's truly valiant that can wisely suffer, The worst that man can breathe..."* (*Timon of Athens*)

I have always believed that there is no such thing as an 'elite sporting personality'. The best and greatest performers in sport over the decades have been people from the full spectrum of the human psychological range. Some are more anxious than others; some are more neurotic, some more conscientious, and some more extroverted, while others prefer their own council.

They are often gifted in terms of their physical prowess, have developed in unique and different ways, and manage and develop strategies that enable them to perform under pressure in a highly competitive environment. As with Shakespeare's characters, elite performers have the foibles and faults which are common to us all and yet they are still able to operate and perform.

I hope this chapter provides an interesting insight into the human condition from the perspective of arguably literature's greatest writer and first psychologist – four hundred years dead.

" C O M E T O T H E E D G E "

Corinne Reid

"Come to the edge," he said.
"We can't, we're afraid!" they responded.
"Come to the edge," he said.
"We can't, we will fall!" they responded.
"Come to the edge," he said.
And so they came.
And he pushed them.
And they flew.
— Guillaume Apollinaire

Come to the edge

In early 2013, in a café in Western Australia I listened as Richard (Ric) Charlesworth reflected on the Kookaburras' London Olympic campaign. It was reminiscent of a similar conversation 20 years earlier, about the Hockeyroos' performance in Barcelona. Both teams had been gold-medal favourites, both had returned disappointed. Richard had been head coach in one campaign and was a coaching beneficiary of the other. In both conversations I was struck by the same qualities – by 2013, I recognised these as the essence of the man – a sometimes brutal, often searing, always analytical and remorseless gaze, no stone unturned, no corner to hide, a rollercoaster of interpretation, re-interpretation, looking for 'the truth' amongst grains of evidence and ideas. In the latter case, he did not escape his own scrutiny – indeed he was at the epicentre – he has never been one to shirk responsibility. *Never expect more of others that you expect of yourself.* His purpose went beyond remorse or regret. In both cases, he was searching for points of difference, new possibilities, a vantage point on the edge of a new landscape. In both cases standing on the cliff top with him in these conversations persuaded me to accept his offer to come work with him. Over the years, it has also persuaded many athletes to step out of the comfort zone of being the best junior in their state of origin, to walk on that cliff top.

We can't, we're afraid!

Being the best in the world at anything is hard. Being a Hockeyroo or a Kookaburra with Richard is immeasurably harder – it is as much about becoming the best person you can be, as it is about becoming the best hockey player you can be. Fear is an ever-present and important part of that life as it is in all human endeavour on new frontiers. Richard's view, and mine, is that great feats of human endeavour are about character, not just abilities. And character is forged in fire. Stuck to my hotel room door on many tours were the following words of wisdom from Nelson Mandela:

"I learned that courage was not the absence of fear, but the triumph over it. The brave man is not he who does not feel afraid, but he who conquers that fear."

Athletes experience Richard's gaze intensely. Sometimes they find it hard to bear. Always they crave it. In both the Hockeyroos and the Kookaburras, athletes male and female, have often only been able to see the rubble at the foot of the cliff – they cannot see the top of the mountain let alone the cliff top. Surviving involves learning to tolerate fear. Thriving involves valuing what fear brings. In both cases, trust is a necessary, and challenging, requirement. Daily life requires athletes to wrangle with their own desire to keep doing what has worked for them in the past (a position often supported by family, friends and local coaches) or to sign up to the altogether more terrifying option of giving up that control and trusting an unclear direction that feels unfamiliar, uncomfortable and uncertain.

It is not only athletes who feel this fear when working with Richard. Often staff will feel the weight of expectation of working with a very successful team and a very successful coach. Doing what is 'known', even 'gold standard practice', will not be enough – creating the *new* gold standard is a minimum requirement. Sometimes this can be seen in chaotic and reactive group dynamics that parallel the fear-based dynamics in the player group when they are under pressure. Sometimes it is best captured in what is not seen. In 2013 when I joined Richard at the Kookaburras, there were conversations in which it was suggested to me that perhaps the reason for the Kookaburras underperformance in London was that Richard was 'past his prime'. Examples of disorganised thinking were provided. I entertained this as a serious possibility – my job would then have been to gently persuade him to step aside. Over the next week, I watched and listened, and tuned in again to 'life on Mars' (which is how players have referred to Richard's unique thinking style). What I saw, once again, was that while his thinking could seem chaotic it was in fact orbiting on another plane altogether and held within it new possibilities for the team to progress. One of the challenges for an exceptional coach is to truly understand that what is obvious to him may not be at all obvious to his athletes or to his staff. Sometimes, what he needs is a translator. At other times what he needs is a critical friend to give him this feedback. My role in this context is to be both translator to athletes and staff and critical friend to Richard – to help create a safe space in which to be terrified.

Richard also feels fear. Richard's inward gaze is just as intense as his outward gaze – he does not escape his own scrutiny or recriminations. Richard's intellect and character is such that he sees an infinity of constellations of cause, and yet fears that which he cannot see, that he may have missed something important. It drives him on. Perhaps the most rare and wonderful quality of this process is that invariably the search for clues has an emergent property that illuminates solutions, and more than that, new possibilities. I have lost count of the number of conversations that start in one place and 'escape'. My initial urge to fight this meandering and keep him 'on task' has long since been replaced with a deep appreciation of both the exceptionality and the value of this apparently chaotic, driven, iterative, elliptical, problem solving style. While evolution is often linear and incremental, revolution is not – progress sometimes requires step-shifts in thinking that bystanders cannot see. But it does not leave the thinker in a calm space – Richard is rarely calm.

Come to the edge

Richard draws to him people that are prepared to walk the clifftop. Those who work with him, athlete and staff alike, will know they are alive! He does not want acolytes – he wants activists. Being an activist comes with opportunities to create impressive change, and it comes with responsibilities to be conscious in creating the disruptions, discomfort and distress that are required to make those changes. It is rare to work with an elite coach who is truly open to new possibilities – rarer still to work with one who demands them. By the time coaches reach the elite level they are often strongly persuaded by their own experience and success to the point where they imagine that further progress is about doing more of the same, just a little better. Athletes and assistants are brought in to bring this vision to life rather than to challenge and contribute to an emergent and organic vision. To allow a greater contribution requires a rare and complex elixir; (i) a willingness to give up control (perhaps the most difficult ingredient for elite coaches); (ii) a belief that the people around you have something valuable to offer; (iii) faith that each individual will work to their best potential when they know you have faith in them, and (iv) a trust that, despite the intense pressure and struggles, there is an 'us' – that we are all in it together, we are on the same side and that we have 'signed up' to something larger than ourselves. So, who made the grade?

Perhaps the two most impressive assistant coaches that have worked with Richard have been Chris Spice in charge of the GB Olympic swimming team for Rio and Herbie (Robert) Haigh (no doubt creating trouble in retirement somewhere in Adelaide). Both were skilled players in their own right, but more importantly, they are exceptional people. What was noteworthy about them as coaches is that they were never followers in their relationship with Richard – they did not hide behind him or bask in reflected glory. They stood firmly with him side by side, in good times and in bad. They laughed, they conspired, they argued with him. They are very different men – each marched to the beat of their own drum, but both brought an exceptional energy and passion for the job, myriad organic ideas and a work ethic second to none. They pushed him, and he flew!

Wendy Pritchard, a former national player and captain herself, became the best team manager I have worked with. In her youth – one of the youngest players to have been selected for her state and known for her performance under pressure – she brought the same tenacity to the job as manager. She led the young women in her care by example – setting the standard in independence of thought, ethical conduct, toughness and just getting the job done. She provided a safe space for athletes to 'land' when stressed on tour, not by being a mother figure, but by being the epitome of a strong woman that could cope with whatever came her way. I remember being in awe of her ability to land in a foreign country with a jet-lagged team of young women, a fractious coach, mountains of luggage and no local language, and to 'magic' us to our destination. Tricia Heberle was another formidable role model – a tour de force in the drive for excellence. Her role morphed from videographer, to coaching assistant and ultimately to high performance director of the Kookaburras. A successful national player and coach herself, as an administrator she both demanded and supported excellence in national teams, and in return provided excellence in leadership. I had ringside seats on many behind-the-scenes crises that were averted or managed with grace and efficiency by Trish and Wendy, leaving not a ripple on the lives of our team. The steadfastness of both women created an anchor, a grounding point for our players and our staff team – an invaluable commodity in the crazy, frenetic backrooms of elite sport. Richard provided them the opportunity to carve out these roles, to break new ground, and they delivered.

In 1993 I was intrigued to see that rather than the scorched earth policy that usually accompanies a change in coaching team, Richard kept the former national coach, Brian Glencross, in his team as high performance manager. He could see that Brian had been a 'frontiers man' and had what it took to carve out a new landscape for women's hockey over more than a decade. Brian used that experience to 'clear the decks' for Richard and the new coaching team. He knew the practicalities of the business and the many bureaucratic obstacles facing coaches – he acted as a 'look-out', minesweeper and fixer.

Perhaps finally, Steve Lawrence, then sports physiologist, now director of the WA Institute of Sport, was a powerhouse of future thinking. Steve's relaxed walk belies the ferocity of his thinking. He pushed new boundaries for us on all things fitness and physical. He metaphorically held a mirror up to the players to encourage honesty with themselves. It was not shaming, but empowering. He had faith in their ability to be fitter, faster and stronger. And they came to believe in themselves as much as he did.

These exceptional individuals shared in common a loyalty to Richard and a desire to put their own egos and individual achievements second to the achievements of the team. It is no surprise to me that each has gone on to new and challenging horizons. Still, 20 years later, in times of personal joy and in times of trouble, we seek each other out.

We can't, we will fall!

Working with Richard has never simply been about winning. As a goal, winning has never been enough. Working with Richard has been about being the best you can be – as an individual and, additionally and more challenging, as a team. Being the best you can be may not be enough to win, or it may be just enough to win, but if it is *more* than enough to win, then winning is not enough. Being the best you can be, remains the goal – it may be enough to change the landscape of the sport and of the person. It always redefines what is possible.

In pushing themselves to these new boundaries, it is also important for athletes to understand their 'signature' for coping under stress. Richard's commitment to the psychological development of his players is unmatched in my experience. Each week he sat in on our evening team psychology sessions after long days at training and in meetings. He listened attentively as athletes revealed their hopes, vulnerabilities and frustrations. He worked on his own discipline – he learned to say nothing and let the athletes find their own solutions – he trusted me that this would make the solutions stronger than if he offered them up. When invited, he was an active participant as the players searched for new ways to build connections and create the fabric of the team. Sometimes he shared with them his own frustrations. There were many honest and challenging conversations – but always, he was fully present... and he gave them the valuable gift of *time*, to work out their own solutions to the innumerable challenges of living on the edge.

He saw this as an investment in their wellbeing and also saw that it was this fabric, woven many miles away and many months ahead of time, that would hold them together under fire in an Olympic final.

Come to the edge
Richard's strength and his vulnerability as a coach lies in the fact that he truly *invites* athletes to come to the edge – he invites them into the inner sanctum, to make their own choices, create their own destiny and to own their journey. Whilst his own achievements as an athlete would have made it possible for Richard to demand respect and dictate terms, he has not chosen this path. Rather he *commands* respect through his work ethic, determination, razor sharp intellect and his willingness to engage with his athletes in all aspects of training and competition.

Although altruism is not his driving motive, in many ways he sees himself as in the service of his athletes – creating environments in which they can be their best selves and go further than they believe they can. Yes, he has an ego – a desire to be the best coach he can be and to be appreciated for these achievements, but he has continued to choose a field of battle in which his own achievements are closely interdependent upon the efforts and achievements of many others – coaching a team is not a low-risk option if you are all about ego! It has been a curious and impressive thing to me that Richard carries his expertise so lightly that athletes are often at the same time drawn to his mentorship and also willing to be openly and naively critical of it. Encouraging debates about coaching methods is a sign of incredible grounding and self-belief in a coach. Not everyone gets to the Olympics, not everyone wins a gold medal but everyone has been given an opportunity to make the best of the abilities and talents they have been gifted.

And so they came

For many years, I have watched athletes move into and out of Richard's national squads and competition teams. This is a process necessarily filled with hope, frustration, enthusiasm, exasperation, exhilaration, anger, passion, reluctance, doubt and sometimes incredible self-confidence. Each athlete brings with them their own strengths and vulnerabilities – some known to them, most not. Most also do not know how lucky they are to be arriving in a place that values those differences, with a coach who sees the individual as the master of their own destiny. In this place strength is seen as the by-product of creating an environment in which your unique constellation of abilities can be best expressed. Achieving this is a difficult feat in individual sports, in team sports it is usually not considered relevant, or at least not a priority. Richard has always been an outlier himself – he understands that others will also have their eccentricities. Indeed, he has selected players into his squads who have not been obvious choices, some who have a history of personal challenges, others in whom he sees untapped potential that others don't see. His job, our job, is to weave those eccentricities into the warp and weft of an indestructible team.

And he pushed them

What Richard asks of his players really is a leap of faith, but not blind faith in him, rather faith in themselves and in each other – in all of the work, all of the preparation, all of the commitment that has brought them to the edge of the cliff. His final gift to his athletes is to offer *his* faith in *them* to launch them on their journey.

Richard's coaching philosophy is one of engineering his own redundancy. Months are spent with athletes encouraging independence of thought, rigour of action, tolerance of stress, strength of relationship and steadfastness of aim. Leadership and self-direction are prioritised and rehearsed – sometimes coaches unexpectedly don't show up at training or at a game, athletes must fend for themselves. In the end, he trains them to be their own guide and to reflexively look to one another for support.

He pushes them beyond where they imagine their limits are. He invites them to push themselves further still. We have developed a philosophy of 'not-quite-readiness' in which athletes are given responsibilities and opportunities that lie just beyond their current level of competency. This is done so that they will take the final step in uncertainty, finding their way as they go and creating new neural pathways second by second so that they do not fall and burning them into a new map that is uniquely of their making. We are training them to be pioneers and leaders – ready for anything.

And they flew

The prevailing winds at the cliff edge are fuelled by Richard's values. These values are imbued in the culture of his teams. They provide a reliable current on which athletes may launch themselves as elite hockey players and as strong men and women. These values include:

- The team is greater than the individual.

- Every incident, every moment is a choice.

- Excellence is even more important than success.

- The greatest gift we can give to others is our belief in them.

- In elite sport the only thing that is certain is uncertainty. Learn to appreciate uncertainty.

- The privilege of being an elite athlete brings a responsibility to make the most of this opportunity – to search for continual improvement and be our best selves.

So how far did they fly? In the two Olympic cycles that we worked with the Hockeyroos, they evolved from being a very disciplined team that needed a coach to lead from the front, to a group of passionate, confident, self-directed athletes who found their voices and became the authors of their own story. This was not an instant transformation but one that emerged with time (see table below) – each step enabling the next, there was no short cut to be taken. By Atlanta we had managed to move from a hierarchical coaching model to a more collegial one in which players and staff worked side by side in planning and decision making. The culture of the group became more participative; the athletes more active 'learners' than passive 'doers'; the coach more expert teacher than dictator. A fledgling but growing trust had emerged that withstood the pressure of Olympic selection and competition. The team triumphed...but we had become a target for others to pursue and more was required. Already Richard was back at the cliff edge surveying the territory.

Cultural Evolution of the Hockeyroos

Post Barcalona	Pre Altanta	Post Atlanta	Pre-Sydney
Discipline	Professionalism	Participation	Self-determination
Coach Driven	Athlete Contribution	Athlete Participation	Athlete Driven
'Doing' Culture	'Learning' Culture	'Exploring' Culture	'Seeking' Culture
Hierarchical	Participative Student Model	Collegial	Mentor Model

We recognised that the ultimate strength comes from connections born within the team. To be invincible, the group that takes the field in an Olympic final must be forged from one piece of steel that has no fault lines and is not dependent on direction from the bench – it must be able to respond fluently and fluidly to the unfolding game. Between Atlanta and Sydney, Richard worked harder to make himself redundant. Athletes were encouraged to bring more to the table, to be 'seekers' of knowledge, to drive the team to the next level, to create their own connections, to take to the field of play as a 'leader-full' team. Richard became more adept at making space for them to do so. He became an expert at leading from behind – becoming more a mentor than a coach. At first they wrestled him back into the space. Eventually they stepped into it themselves. In Sydney, the girls flew.

At the beginning of my time with the Kookaburras there was a similar disciplined passivity from the playing group and also from the assistant coaching team. They expressed a familiar expectation of 'firm' leadership from a coach who seemed reluctant to provide the greater detail or the 'clearer vision' that was being called for. This was seen as a weakness. Again he stood firm – 'holding the space' for the athletes rather than filling it himself. Again, an invitation was issued for athletes to 'come to the edge'. The necessity for self-direction was once again presented to the playing group in our weekly psychology sessions – there was ambivalence, anger, fear and dissent, hope, excitement and determination. A core group stood up and accepted the challenge. Others followed in time. The first steps on the gold medal winning journey to the World Cup had begun. In June of 2014 they sat the exam and showed over two weeks in The Hague that they were flying. Many of that group continue on to Rio…where again they will be tested to find their best selves…

The men and women of the Hockeyroos and the Kookaburras have stood on the shoulders of a giant. But they have been given the freedom to stretch their own wings. He did not seek to make them in his own image but rather to help them define their own horizons and re-define hockey. And they have done so.

PART 3

SPORTS

1 2

CHAMPIONS

Decathlete Ashton Eaton is arguably the greatest athlete on the planet at the time of writing yet he is largely unknown to the public in Australia. Perhaps it is because the mainstream media has its own interests and biases, which it reinforces, promotes and proselytises.

In the Australian media he does not seem to warrant any time or space. It is a pity that someone who I would describe as a truly exceptional athlete, yet whose sport is outside the traditional framework garners so little attention here. Perhaps if we had an Australian contender in this event it would be of interest.

Eaton was the gold medallist in the decathlon at the 2012 and 2016 Olympics and set a new world record at the 2015 World Athletics Championships in Beijing. He can run, jump, throw, hurdle, putt and vault better than anyone in the world yet he has nowhere near the fame of Federer, Woods, Ronaldo or Messi. He is not considered in the same breath with Jordan Speith, Djokovic, Serena Williams or many others.

Few in Australia would remember Glynis Nunn who won a gold medal at the 1984 Olympics in the heptathlon although her all-round ability was exceptional. As a hurdler she was 5th and in long jump came 7th at the same Olympics.

One could argue that Usain Bolt is an exceptional or special case as he is someone from athletics who truly is amongst the best known in the world. I would argue that while the 100 metres sprint has a 'special place' in the athletic pantheon, it is only Bolt's repeated and exceptional performances that have put him there. Not many people can name the athletes he regularly competes against yet they also are very, very good.

In truth it is difficult to compare athletes and athletic performance across different sports and so we are better off not trying to go there. Each sport has its own competitive environment which can define part of its worth. Who plays it, i.e. which countries? Is it a primary or secondary sport in the places it is played? What numbers are involved? How complicated is the sport? What are the barriers to entry and what conflicts and biases are involved in its promotion and dissemination?

For instance, equestrian activities or car or yacht racing are hardly sports available to ordinary citizens. Athletics ought to be the biggest sport for participants as nearly every child somewhere at sometime runs a race or jumps or tests out their strength against others. Yet once puberty is negotiated very few persist in competing in running races. The problem for athletics worldwide is that such testing of personal abilities and traits doesn't necessarily convert into lifelong participation. Distance running seems the exception.

Participation is more likely to occur in games where players compete against one another in teams. Trying to help one's team overcome another team. Competitive leagues that exist in countries or regions are often the models for such sports. Also, countries compete against one another in what is usually the highest level of competition.

Clearly some of the simplest games have the highest number of active participants. Perhaps one of the simplest games in the world is the biggest – football, or soccer as it is known in Australia – and is now a dual gender sport, which truly makes it the world game. One only requires a round ball to play, and as no other equipment is needed, it can be played whenever a few friends get together to enjoy the experience of play.

Rugby has never been my favourite sport but at the highest level almost any sport is exciting and the skills and teamwork on display in the contests are uplifting. As a devotee of sport, such qualities can be appreciated and admired. For the fans, performances are lauded and for young aspirants these skills are mimicked and pursued.

I recall staying up to watch the Wallabies play the All Blacks at Twickenham on October 31, 2015 and was not disappointed. The results went against Australia but the New Zealand team played at a skill level and tempo that was outstanding and in the end overwhelmed their opponents.

Having lived in Christchurch, New Zealand for two years when working with New Zealand Cricket in 2005-07, I watched the Crusaders regularly and even played my last cricket game against the Crusaders for New Zealand Cricket staff at Hagley Park in 2005. Robbie Deans, the then coach of the Crusaders, was a keen cricketer himself and organised and played in the game!

Rugby is practically a religious commitment to all New Zealanders and I learned about the game and its place in New Zealand while there. The team that won unprecedented back-to-back World Cups is being widely branded the "best ever" with good reason. Richie McGraw and Dan Carter are unquestionably special having been at the forefront for well over a decade.

The question every sports watcher usually gets to at some stage is who is the best? Which team was the greatest? How do the present champions match up with the current crop? Here is the source of many pub debates and expert assessments. It will continue through the ages. We have some faltering footage of Bradman batting and Babe Ruth at the plate but where would they stand in today's contest.

While clearly Bradman was special in his time one wonders about where he would fit in the modern game. Such speculation could fill chapters. I will not go there except to say I firmly sit in the camp that believes today's champions are better than those from the past. In the last 15 years many of the games we play and watch have made dramatic improvements and some are barely recognisable from 50 years ago, let alone 100 years ago!

Early this century cricket was in need of a three-hour product, as the anachronism that is test cricket, could not attract a new impatient audience who wanted instant results and had lost touch with the iconic history and tales of years gone by. During my time as high performance manager with NZ Cricket, T20 arrived on the scene and was seized upon as the potential saviour of the game. Some resisted and, extraordinarily, India objected to these games being on the itinerary when visiting New Zealand!

For the women's game T20 has been fantastic and as a quick cricket fix it has drawn many back to watch cricket. However, I believe cricket erred when T20 emerged as this short version of the game does not bear close enough resemblance to the 50-over game or indeed test cricket. I believe T20 with "five out all out" would have preserved the traditional balance between risk and reward that underpins the guile and finesse of the longer game.

This schism between traditional cricket and T20 will no doubt play itself out but in teaching the game to youngsters, coaches face a very difficult task. The power game that is developing in T20 may in 50 years be the only cricket that exists. Those running the game vow this will not occur but I am not so sure. Maybe that development is inevitable anyway. Many would argue that Viv Richards in this new game would be special with his brilliant power game and athleticism in the field. Perhaps he was merely a harbinger of this change!

The AFL in its aim to keep the sport exciting and dramatic, searches for ways to avoid a crowded game played with increasing stoppages. It is tinkering with interchange rules and considering ways to decrease stoppages. Yet isn't it at stoppages that a Nat Fyfe excels?

In the largest of all international games individual champions like Messi or Ronaldo draw crowds and excite but on the biggest stage at the World Cup it is also the exploits of champion teams such as Germany or Spain that can galvanise a nation to follow their exploits.

Hockey's evolution

In my book *The Coach* I endeavoured to identify the best hockey players in my period playing and coaching the game. That has now been extended another decade and a half. I feel there is a place to update and expand on that exercise. At the same time I feel inclined to consider the recent players in the new millennium. Accordingly, I have tried to settle on my considerations after the 2000 Olympics in Sydney.

It has been the Kookaburras most successful era in the game. In 16 years to the end of 2016, we have won seven Champions Trophies, played in four World Cup finals (2 gold and 2 silver) and won two bronze medals and one gold at four Olympics. Over the same period only Germany has a better record of winning gold at major competitions yet they have not been anywhere near as reliable and consistent over the period in all major competitions. The Netherlands have always been in the finals but without the big wins that characterised their brilliant teams of the 90s. Including Champions Trophies and two World Leagues, the figures since 2000 look like this.

	Olympic Games	World Cup	Champion Trophy	World Leagues
Germany **(14-7 Gold)**	2 Gold 2 Bronze	2 Gold 1 Silver	3 Gold 3 Silver 1 Bronze	
Australia **(19-11 Gold)**	1 Gold 2 Bronze	2 Gold 2 Silver	7 Gold 3 Silver 1 Bronze	Gold
Netherlands **(16-4 Gold)**	2 Silver	1 Silver 2 Bronze	3 Gold 3 Silver 4 Bronze	Gold

For the Hockeyroos the story has been quite different, as they have failed to reach the heights of the 90s when they were easily the best team in the world. The table below shows the dominance of the Netherlands and Argentina since the Sydney Olympics with Australia and Germany well behind in the last decade and a half. Australia has risen up the rankings in recent times but the emphatic performances of the 90s could not be sustained. One hopes they will come again…

	Olympic Games	World Cup	Champion Trophy	World Leagues
Netherlands **(23-9 Gold)**	2 Gold 2 Silver	2 Gold 2 Silver	4 Gold 3 Silver 7 Bronze	1 Gold
Argentina **(19-10 Gold)**	2 Bronze 1 Silver	2 Gold 2 Bronze	7 Gold 3 Silver 1 Bronze	1 Gold
Australia **(8-1 Gold)**		2 Silver	1 Gold 3 Silver 1 Bronze	1 Silver
Germany **(7-2 Gold)**	1 Gold 1 Bronze		1 Gold 2 Silver 1 Bronze	1 Bronze

With England as the next team in the men's and women's games, the Netherlands, Germany, Argentina and Australia are clearly the pre-eminent teams in the world game at the moment.

Extraordinarily, as this book was being finalised, at Rio Argentina's men and GB's women would win gold medals…both were ranked seventh in the pre tournament rankings!

When Richard Aggiss (who coached the Kookaburras in the 80s) conducted his informal poll at the end of the millennium to identify our sport's best, our Olympic history was only 44 years old for the men and less than two decades for the women. The question was only asked of the men's game, and as I outlined in my book *The Coach*, the figures were indeed flattering for me at that time in the 90s.

My twentieth century group was first selected in *The Coach*. At the time it was a considered calculation yet in retrospect it did not include the likes of Warren Birmingham and Paul Lewis who would have been mighty close. Paul Gaudoin, Michael Brennan, Daniel Sproule and Stephen Davies were considered but were still playing in the national team at the time. 2000 was pretty much a watershed for the men and the women, with many retirements and a new group coming through.

So here is my latest attempt with the licence that teams now have 18 players and I am allowed two reserves.

I would not change the goalkeepers but given Lachie Dreher's longevity and quality he comes into consideration. Paul Dearing is no longer with us sadly but was outstanding for a decade and Damon Diletti was often preferred to Dreher when they played together in the team.

Bob Haigh was outstanding and so reliable at left defence. The speedy and courageous Ken Wark and the poised Craig Davies all complement one another. Versatile Michael York gives balance and flexibility. I would not change the deep defenders and Brain Glencross is just outside the group.

In the defensive midfield I would add Birmingham to the combination of Jay Stacy, the great long passer and corner exponent, Julian Pearce the dominant central general and David Bell the exquisite tackler and feeder. At a time when Australia was transitioning to a newer group Birmingham dominated the midfield. No one has been as good as Pearce there but Warren was a very fine player. David Wansborough misses out because he was perhaps in between being a defender and attacker and didn't settle in either spot. Des Piper's toughness and nous wasn't enough to change my mind but old-timers all include him in their teams.

In attacking midfield I would likewise stick with Trevor Smith, a fabulous all-rounder, Colin Batch and Peter Haselhurst, great schemers, and I still get a game by virtue of Richard Aggiss' survey! However, here Michael Brennan comes in for consideration. He was a brilliant and creative ball carrier who stopped in 2000 but then came back in 2004. Good as Brennan was, one who played 73 more games and scored 25 more goals was Paul Lewis and so he sneaks in as one reserve. Lewis had a terrific engine and was a smart and creative midfielder.

At the front I would insist on Ron Riley and Mark Hager, the two with the best scoring percentage…77.2 per cent and 78.3 per cent respectively. Don Smart, so skilled, and Walsh, so forceful, would join them. My final selection as a reserve yet unlucky not to make the first 18 is Steven Davies. He was prolific, enigmatic and always lively. Never to be underestimated. I have demoted Grant Mitton, who was brilliant on the right wing but perhaps not as versatile as the others, and Eric Pearce – perhaps because I never saw him at his best.

	Selection	*Reserves*	*Others*
Goal Keeping	Damon Dilletti Paul Dearing		Lachie Dreher
Defenders	Bob Haigh Michael York Ken Wark Craig Davies		Brian Glencross
Defensive Midfield	Jay Stacy Julian Pearce David Bell Warren Birmingham		Des Piper David Wansborough
Attacking Midfield	Trevor Smith Ric Charlesworth Colin Batch Peter Haselhurst	Paul Lewis	Michael Brennan
Strikers	Don Smart Ron Riley Terry Walsh Mark Hager	Steven Davies	Grant Mitton Eric Pearce

Post 2000

Such exercises, of course, are only a snapshot in time and as the world moves on and our experiences in the sport expand, the perspective is enhanced, broadened and fresher. All that is being considered here is my best shot at the post-2000 era. As I have already mentioned this has been Australia's greatest period during which we have exceeded our greatest rivals, Germany and Holland, in nearly every category. Interestingly, nine of this group were eligible for Rio this year.

In 2003 I watched the Champions Trophy in Amsterdam and saw Australia lose in the final 3-1 against the Netherlands. It was a gripping encounter and in the end decided – as such a game often is – by goalkeeping errors. Australia had a terrific all-round team but did not have outstanding goalkeeping. I left for Italy thinking that if I was Barry Dancer this needed a solution if the team was to win in Athens. Equally, Jamie Dwyer, quickly establishing himself as an outstanding player, injured his knee and he would need to recover from his reconstruction before Athens.

As 2004 began Stephen Mowlam emerged and played first for Australia in the Azlan Shah tournament in January. Mowlam had been 'hidden' in Victoria where he had been understudy to Lachlan Dreher. Dreher played 14 consecutive seasons in the Kookaburras from 1989 to 2002 and it was not until his retirement that Mowlam was on display at the nationals in 2003. Mowlam had attitude to back up his saving skills and throughout 2003 started to show his worth. By the Olympics he was the first choice for Australia and would remain so at all the majors for the next four years until he lost his way in 2008 when Lambert played the main games in Beijing.

It was a pity when Mowlam and Lambert did not continue after Beijing and we had to start all over again in such an important position. I would select Mowlam joined by Charter, a present day player, who has now played with calm and authority in many tournaments. His 2014 World Cup was quite brilliant.

Gaudoin could have been selected in the twentieth century group as he played more before 2000. He was chosen captain of the team for Athens only to be withdrawn through injury. I have included him here. I have told him that I thought he should have played midfield much more where his quickness and skill would have had even greater effect. He played alongside Bevan George and Mathew Wells, the two best deep defenders of the era. Wells was a wonderful passer with one of the sweetest hits in the game and he complimented George whose defensive tackling and interceptions were outstanding.

Fergus Kavanagh was first selected for the Junior WC in 2005 but an injury ruled him out. By 2008 he was playing midfield in Beijing and subsequently we have used him mainly as a defender. Easily one of the best tacklers in the game, he is assured, calm and able to make good decisions, which are the hallmark of the best defenders. He has completed his engineering degree while playing international hockey and also playing in the Netherlands and

India. This is a mark of his capable and organised mind and ability to apply himself.

On the bench behind these four we have our latest addition, Mathew Swann, who first emerged in 2009 after a brilliant Junior World Cup performance in Singapore. With an outstanding aerobic engine Swann is fast becoming a crucial cog in the Australian defence where his tackling and intercepting are often the beginning of Australia's counterattack. Versatile, courageous and able to stop and turn on a pinhead, Swann is rarely beaten and always able to recover and harass.

Brent Livermore was captain of the team that won in Athens and also played in Sydney where he is remembered for having his penalty saved in a shootout. He was at the centre of the national team for a decade and indeed missed out on Beijing through injury concerns. He was aerobically elite and one of the first players to introduce a trademark spin manoeuvre to evade tackles in the midfield. After 2008 I maintained him in the squad, as I believed he could make it to the New Delhi World Cup. He proved a dedicated trainer who worked extremely hard and was one of our most difficult selections in 2010 when he lost his place to an emerging Matthew Butturini. I felt for him as he gave everything and was a victim of the deep squad we were developing.

Rob Hammond and Liam De Young had arrived around the same time and both played for well over a decade. Hammond, the creative midfielder and wing defender, had the ability to do the unexpected and create goals with his dynamic and aggressive style. He was nearly left out of the WC team in 2014. I'm glad we did not make that mistake! As a team member he was a leader and thoughtful contributor adding value to those around him. Liam De Young was both speedy and skilful. Mainly on the sideline in 2004 when new to the team, over the next decade his calmness and quiet brilliance made him an often unnoticed but critical contributor.

Both Hammond and De Young scored and created crucial goals throughout my time with the Kookaburras.

Mark Knowles was selected in 2014 as FIH Player of the Year after leading Australia to their triumph in The Hague. I first saw him as a junior member of the 2004 team in Athens, where as a newly selected tyro, he first made his mark. In 2005 he led the junior team (U/21) to their World Cup final in Rotterdam. Quick, skilful and creative, he was the force behind that team often making dynamic interventions to create a goal or save one! Throughout my time with the Kookaburras he was a central part of the defence where he has become the consummate play reader. His interceptions and tackles are critical and his passing over distance is often of the most penetrating kind.

As a defensive midfield these players provide panache and stability and the capacity to make a difference at both ends of the field.

In the attacking midfield Dwyer and Ockenden are in my view the best we have ever had with Eddie not as adventurous as his brilliant teammate but equally valuable. Troy Elder was named player of the tournament at the 2002 World Cup in Kuala Lumpur where Australia just slipped up at the final hurdle. Strong ball control and elimination skills were complemented by an astute game sense and the added skill of being a very competent corner taker. He was a midfielder of the highest order.

Orchard, who came into his own after Beijing, had a different set of skills which in combination gave the midfield depth and diversity. He had tremendous speed and very thorough basics to go with a penchant for the unusual, and therefore a capacity to be unpredictable. Sometimes moody and easily distracted, when Orchard put his mind to it he presented as a match winner of the highest order. These attacking midfielders together would be a best-ever combination. Unfortunately, left on the substitute bench is Nathan Eglington. He was a different type of player who had the pace and dynamic athleticism to always reach the ball before an unsuspecting defender, leaving them stranded. Again, injuries cut short his brilliant progress in the game after missing Beijing. I was very keen for Nathan to continue after I became coach but his body did not allow it to happen.

Michael Brennan was an unusual player who Barry Dancer wisely brought back to play in Athens. He then moved on to his passion – training horses! Brennan made his debut in 1995 and played through to Sydney before his remarkable return to play in Athens. Skilled in eliminating opponents speedy and enigmatic, his contribution in Athens at critical moments was telling. He played mainly before Sydney and was probably at his best then but made a cameo entrance for the Athens Olympics.

The goal scorers are critical in every game and in Grant Schubert and Michael McCann, Turner and Abbott we have had some special ones. The bustling and aggressive Schubert scored 98 times in 180 games; he made things happen and like his contemporary McCann (72 goals in 165 games) was a great goal poacher from close range. Abbott, a finisher of enormous skill, was unfortunately curtailed by injuries more than by his opponents. With uncanny judgement and superb eliminations he utilised his size and strength to demand extra attention whenever near the ball. His 62 goals in 111 matches (57 per 100 games) is a very good return but does not do justice to his ability. Des was a truly special player.

Perhaps the best story at the front in my time was the emergence of Glenn Turner who has endured and thrived after many thought he would never make it. Skilful in eliminating, strong in holding position against the toughest defender and able to finish so consistently, Turner's record of scoring is exceptional. Still playing when I last looked, he was scoring at a rate of about 77 goals per 100 matches. This gives him a scoring percentage the equal of Ron Riley and Mark Hager. It is right up there with the best ever scoring rate for an Australian player.

I believe the team is pretty well balanced but perhaps it lacks an outstanding penalty corner exponent with only Elder and Gaudoin being used in that role during that time. Luke Doerner and Chris Ciriello would have been the main contenders and both of them were match winners during my time. However, I concentrated on the whole game for these players, and supplemented by Matthew Wells on corners, this team probably would have had the firepower to win.

	Selection	Reserves	Others
Goal Keeping	Stephen Mowlam Andrew Charter		Stephen Lambert
Defenders	Bevan George Fergus Kavanagh Matt Wells Paul Gaudoin	Matt Swann	
Defensive Midfield	Rob Hammond Brent Livermore Liam De Young Mark Knowles		
Attacking Midfield	Jamie Dwyer Troy Elder Eddie Ockenden Simon Orchard	Nathan Eglington	
Strikers	Glenn Turner Des Abbott Grant Schubert Mike McCann		Kieran Govers

Recently, I had occasion to be involved in a discussion as to our greatest ever player. My good friend, John Morgan, with whom I work in a little business developing SUPAGOLF, opined that he had heard two sporting commentators debating the merits of Jamie Dwyer and myself. He suggested the 'expert' who espoused my case won the argument. It should not be that I ought go there but having 'lived' my own career over 17 years in the national team and observed Jamie over his 16 years (six of which I was his coach). I do have a view.

Since his May, 2001 debut against New Zealand, Jamie has broken all the records for matches, goals and awards. He has been in the middle of teams throughout the sport's most successful era. He is in my view in the half dozen best male hockey players I have seen in my lifetime.

As Jamie's coach I marvelled at what he could do – his level of technical skill, his ability to improvise, his training ethic, his physical agility and endurance. Jamie ticked all the boxes. He saw passes others didn't see; he understood the tactical necessities of a situation and game. If that is not enough he has had the versatility to play effectively as striker and midfielder and his goal-scoring penchant puts him at the top of Australia's all-time goal scoring list.

I might have competed with him or even exceeded him on competitiveness, tackling and defending, tactical nous, endurance, passing depth and range but for technical brilliance, goal scoring, agility and his ability to play across the lines he is way in front.

The expert on my side may have won the debate but he was wrong! Jamie Dwyer is the best Australian male player I have seen – he is much, much better than I ever was, and indeed I believe another player, Eddie Ockenden, when he finally hangs up his boots, may prove to be not so far behind Jamie. He too, is much, much better than I ever was.

It is indicative of what a lucky coach I was that these two outstanding players were part of the Kookaburras in my time as coach.

Given this exercise is completed for the men's game perhaps it would be of similar interest for the women's game. My pre-2000 team selected after Sydney I would revise slightly. In Nikki Hudson, Katrina Powell, Alyson Annan and Rachel Imison there are four players who were in the pre-2000 team. They would all fit into the post-2000 group as they continued to play after the Sydney Olympics. Accordingly, I have put them in both teams.

Annan did not play long into the new century because she moved to the Netherlands and Australia surprisingly chose not to select her. All the others in the group played a considerable amount after 2000 and would have easily been in the best post-2000 team. As we have space for 20 now I would promote Shirley Tonkin, the best woman player and goal scorer I saw in 70s, and keep Michelle Andrews in her place as a reserve.

Elspeth Clement the first woman to play 100 matches when she reached that target at the Seoul Olympics comes in as a defender, and Juliet Haslam, so versatile and such a great competitor, wins a place in the defensive midfield. The goalkeepers and attacking midfield are unchanged. This is a terrific team in a group that won three Olympic gold medals in four Olympic appearances from 1988 to 2000.

	Selection	Reserves	Others
Goal Keeping	Kathleen Partridge Rachel Imison		Clover Maitland
Defenders	Jenny Morris Elspeth Clement Michelle Hager Liane Tooth	Juliet Haslam	
Defensive Midfield	Kate Starre Lisa Carruthers Renita Garard Wendy Pritchard		
Attacking Midfield	Alyson Annan Sharon Buchanan Rechelle Hawkes Marian Aylmore		
Strikers	Katrina Powell Nikki Hudson Shirley Tonkin Jackie Periera	Michelle Mitchell (Andrews)	

I have not had close contact with the women's program since my departure in 2000 and accordingly I asked Adam Commens and Frank Murray to provide their perspectives regarding a twenty-first century team and those who have been the best in this century. Unlike the men there are a considerable number of players who crossed the eras and four have been selected in both teams. They are Annan, K Powell, Hudson and Imison. Three others also played in Sydney; Katie Allen, Angie Skirving and Julie Towers.

Extraordinarily, Annan hardly played in the post 2000 era as she was living in the Netherlands and considered too distant and therefore overlooked. I think David Bell erred in not including her. Toni Cronk played in three Olympics in goal, and in London gave what is probably the best performance in a tournament by an Australian goalkeeper to concede only two goals. Imison's 12 seasons is testimony to her quality and Rachael Lynch, still playing, is close but behind those two.

Allen was exceedingly brave and resilient and Nicole Arrold and Kobie McGurk were, at different times and sometimes together, rocks in a defensive wall. Jodie Schultz-Kenny is the most outstanding defender in the team at present and also our most prolific penalty corner scorer ever.

The defensive midfield has Skirving-Lambert, Emilie Halliday and Melanie Twitt-Wells who were all there at the start of the decade. Tall and angular with a very good corner and great tackling, Skirving was hard to pass. Twitt, the midfield worker, was agile and always busy while Halliday's speed and ability to break the play open made her dangerous as a counterattacker. Teneal Attard endured many injuries to play over 200 matches in an tough and uncompromising career.

In the midfield Madonna Blyth is our most capped player ever. She is world class, and Casey Eastham-Sablowski, who first played as a teenager, complements with her strength and dynamism. Karen

Smith, so unlucky not to make the big teams in the 90s came into her own and represented nearly 300 times over eleven years. Annan was of course simply the best player of her era from any nation but didn't play much after 2000. Accordingly, I would select Hope Munro as an attacking midfielder...she was skilled and could score.

At the front Powell and Hudson were great before 2000 and continued on. Hudson scored 99 goals in 303 games and was the first to reach 300. Julie Towers similarly continued to score one goal for every three games, and Hope Munro, whether at the front or midfield, made things happen. I expected Emily Smith and Ashleigh Nelson (my reserve) to eventually exceed Towers as a goal scorer... perhaps later in 2016 although an injury has now ruled Nelson out. In prospect Smith will play longer and score more.

	Selection	Reserves	Others
Goal Keeping	Rachel Imison Toni Kronk	Rachael Lynch	
Defenders	Katie Allen Jodi Schultz-Kenny Nicole Arrold Kobi McGurk		
Defensive Midfield	Emily Halliday Angie Skirving-Lambert Melanie Twitt-Wells Teneal Attard		
Attacking Midfield	Madonna Blyth Karen Smith Casey Eastham (Sablowski) Alyson Annan		
Strikers	Katrina Powell Nikki Hudson Julie Towers Hope Munro	Ashleigh Nelson	Megan Rivers Emily Smith

Finally as I did previously I will look at players from other nations and try to do justice to post-2000 teams of champions. For the men I am comfortable with what I saw up until I coached and then during my tenure as national coach until 2015. Here is the list I considered with my two reserves and others who I considered but could not include.

	Selection	**Reserves**	**Others**
Goal Keeping	Max Weinhold Guus Vogels		Jaap Stockmann
Defenders	Max Muller Waseem Ahmed Timo Wess Rodrigo Garca		Phillip Crone Pedro Ibarra Rashid Mehmood
Defensive Midfield	Moritz Furste Tobias Hauke Jeroen Delmee Robert Van der Horst		Christian Mayerhofer Christoph Eimer Emmanuel Stockbroekx
Attacking Midfield	Teun De Nooijer Ashley Jackson Tibor Weissenborn Felix Denayer	Sardar Singh	Namyong Lee Barry Middleton Simon Gougnard Robbert Kemperman
Strikers	Pol Amat Christopher Zeller Eddie Tubau Florian Fuchs	Lucas Vila	Matthias Witthaus Ronald Brouwer Seo Jongho Simon Child Tom Boon Agustin Mazzilli Santi Friexa Rob Reckers

The final 20 is difficult because so many impressed and indeed there are teams that have recently emerged, like Belgium, that have some tremendous players in their midst but who could not be fitted in when one looks over the last 15 years. As time passes Belgium will have more worthy players for consideration in such an exercise.

Max Weinhold was the exceptional goalkeeper at the centre of Germany's two Olympic gold medals in 2008 and 2012. His performance in the critical games of those tournaments was pivotal. Guus Vogels, at first an understudy to Ronald Jansen, became his country's custodian for a decade. He finished at the World Cup in 2010 where he was selected as player of the tournament. Jaap Stockmann is still playing and probably has more to do.

My four defenders are difficult to select. Max Muller was not the most skilful but for toughness, bravery and thorough commitment he is hard to overlook. Timo Wess also has a spot because his leadership and commitment were also special. Perhaps Robert Van der Horst could not be called a defender given his attacking edge and, similarly, Ibarra might miss out. I struggle with the rest although Waseem Ahmed when at left-half for Pakistan was complete in that position...he would later distinguish himself in the midfield. I also included the wonderful Spaniard Rodrigo Garca who was at the centre of the Spanish teams that did so well.

In defensive midfield I go for Tobias Hauke, Moritz Furste and Jeroen Delmee. Robert Van der Horst, could move from the back in view of his penchant to go forward. All could change the course of a game with a single action and provided play-reading and playmaking that was central to the success of their teams. Hauke in the pivot and Furste beside him were intensely competitive and always made things happen. Delmee, who as a novice missed a penalty in a shootout way back in the 1994 World Cup final, seemingly played forever and was so reliable and so important to the tone and direction of the teams from the Netherlands.

In attacking midfield Teun De Nooijer and Ashley Jackson stand out with De Nooijer one of the best I have ever seen and Jackson still competing as a vibrant and brilliant playmaker who makes great passes and always surprises with his inventiveness. Felix Denayer gets the nod from an emerging group of Belgium players...still very young, he defends and makes goals with fantastic ground coverage and vision. Tibor Weissenborn gets the nod ahead of Sardar Singh perhaps because his German team had more success but both proved crucial match winners for their teams. Sardar would be one of my reserves and he is indeed versatile being able to play right across the lines. De Nooijer is in the 'best-ever' group for me and Ashley, if he lasts a few more years, may join him. The others are as yet less credentialed at the moment but match winners all.

There were of course many other deserving midfielders, and Christian Mayerhofer and Christoph Eimer were notable at the beginning of the period. Current players Robbert Kemperman, Simon Gougnard and Namyong Lee come to mind as well as Barry Middleton who can also play at the front.

Of my list of strikers I can only pick four and so have gone for Pol Amat who lit up the game for well over a decade with blistering pace and superb skill and cunning. Christopher Zeller at his best was powerful, potent and creative and his penalty corner work added another dimension. From Eddie Tubau, Florian Fuchs, Barry Middleton, Santi Friexa, Simon Child, Seo Jongho, Tom Boon, Lucas Vila, Ronald Brouwer, Rob Reckers, Agustin Mazzilli and Matthias Witthaus I really do struggle to choose two more as all have a good case. I think I lean towards one who is no longer playing in Eddie Tubau and one still at his peak in Florian Fuchs who, true to his name, is cunning, wily and quick. Lucas Vila, the brilliant Argentinian, gets the spot as my other reserve. I first saw him at the Junior World Cup in 2005 in Rotterdam where he won player of the tournament. That promise has been realised most recently with his team securing a podium finish in The Hague in 2014. Boon, Mazzilli, Witthaus, Seo, Child, Freixa, Reckers and Brouwer are all worthy of mention but in choosing this twenty I could not find a place for them.

With the women the task is even more taxing and again I have called on colleagues in the women's game including Adam Commens, Alyson Annan and Mark Hager to help me fill in the picture. I have settled on the following group but no doubt there are others who have fallen under the radar.

	Selection	Reserves	Others
Goal Keeping	Beth Storry Joyce Sombroek		Louisa Walter Maddie Hinch Belen Succi
Defenders	Tina Bachmann Minke Booij Noel Barrionuevo Kate Richardson-Walsh	Ma Yibo	Magdelena Aicega Janneke Schopman Crista Cullen
Defensive Midfield	Fanny Rinne Kayla Sharland-Whitlock Maartje Paumen Eva De Goede		
Attacking Midfield	Luciana Aymar Naomi Van As Lidewij Welten Ellen Hoog	Stacey Michelsen	Song Quinling Minke Smabers Alex Danson
Strikers	Fu Baorong Natascha Keller Carla Rebecchi Mintje Donners		Park Mi Hyun Soledad Garcia Anita McLaren (Punt)

During the decade and a half since Sydney, the Netherlands and Argentina have been the dominant teams with the Netherlands again 'unbackable' favourites for Rio, as another Olympic cycle draws to a close. Extraordinarily, six are selected in this team who are still playing! Accordingly, my group of twenty players from outside Australia includes eight from the Netherlands with three from Argentina and three from Germany all who played in the surprising gold medal team from Athens.

Goalkeepers Beth Storry and Joyce Sombroek get the nod ahead of Louisa Walter who was Germany's hero in 2004 and current custodians Maddie Hinch and Belen Succi.

Minke Booij led the Netherlands defence so successfully and Barrionuevo, Tina Bachmann and England's most capped player, Kate Richardson-Walsh, join her. All are team leaders and uncompromising defenders. Ma Yibo was central to the Chinese team that won silver in Beijing and she gets the nod as a reserve. Crista Cullen (Eng), Magdelena Aicega (Arg) and Janneke Schopman (Neth) miss out but only by a whisker and are characteristically tough and skilled defenders.

There is more variety in the defensive midfield where New Zealand's best player in the era, Kayla Sharland-Whitlock, is represented. She could play further up the field as could Rinne from Germany. Eva De Goede has been a great foil for Maartje Paumen who I could also have placed as a defender. Paumen's brilliant corners make her an essential selection.

Luciana Aymar leads the attacking midfield and is with Alyson Annan one of the best two players I have seen in the women's game. I first saw her play in the junior World Cup in Seoul in 1998 and her stamp on the game lasted another decade and a half. The others in the attacking midfield are all from the Netherlands in Ellen Hoog, Naomi Van As and Lidewij Welten who, at the moment, is the most dangerous player in the women's game.

At the front I have chosen Mintje Donners who led the Dutch at the turn of the century. She was a fast, powerful and uncompromising striker who made goals. Natascha Keller played forever it seemed and was one of the smartest and most skilful players in the women's game. She scored and set up goals and was part of Germany's most famous hockey family. Father Carsten Keller and her brothers were all Olympic gold medallists! Carla Rebecchi is the best striker of the period for Argentina and Fu Baorong was the focal point of China's teams for a decade.

I went for Stacey Michelsen as my other reserve. She has been a key player in a fine New Zealand team over the past few years. Others worthy of consideration include Song Quinling, Minke Smabers, Park Mi Hyun, Alex Danson, Soledad Garcia and Anita McLaren – all attacking players and all capable of providing balance and versatility to the group.

I found this a challenging piece to write and I am sure there will be a range of views as to its value. However, for our game it is important to recognise those who have lit up the international hockey stage. These are the athletes who continue to develop and embellish their skills and make their teams and our game the fantastic spectacle it has become.

With just a two inch (5.1cm) wide stick they can catch and control a 160 gram hockey ball and hit, slap, flick, dribble and scoop it with remarkable precision and at great speed. I have seen so much in our game over decades yet I am in awe of what the modern players can do and long may it continue. This game, principally about speed, skill, strategy, ingenuity and fortitude, is a spectacle worth seeing.

Coaching...

I thought I should take the opportunity to write a little about the coaches who influenced me most and against whom my teams played. Many have been colleagues in competition during my time as coach of Australia.

Growing up in Perth I was fortunate to be at the heart of a period in which I played against many of the country's best players on a regular basis as the local competition was strong and many West Australians were in the National Team. In the 1950s, 1960s, 1970s and into the 1980s National teams were replete with West Australian players. Accordingly, many aspired to be National coaches and Merv Adams, Richard Aggiss, and Frank Murray were all coaches who influenced me.

Of course it all started with my primary school teacher Wilfred Thorpe who was followed by Doug McKenzie and then at Christ Church by Ray House. All three were influential in my development during my school days when their enthusiasm and guidance helped me fall in love with the game's rhythms and beauty.

My first coach for Australia was Arthur Sturgess who coached the team to the Olympic final in 1968 in Mexico. Arthur's team in Munich four years later was the last Australian men's team to not make the semi finals. Arthur experimented with tactics and ignited my interest in analysis. He was very much a progressive thinker and planner following the legendary Charlie Morley who led the team to its first ever Olympic medal in Tokyo.

Recently when I wrote to Arthur about my project to discover our best ever group, he reminded me of his involvement in earlier times and his deep attachment to the game. Like every one of those who did the job he had invested much of his energy and passion into this endeavour.

Adams coming from India after partition was exotic and different. He was a great motivator who pushed us very hard and helped us believe that we could beat the subcontinental giants who dominated the game for half a century. Our victories over them in 1976 at Montreal were very much his creation and a result of his efforts and deep-seated belief. Don McWatters, an innovative Queenslander who, unluckily did not get to take our team to Moscow, followed Adams. Don had captained Australia in 1968 when injury limited his involvement. Don built on Merv Adams' legacy and worked hard on helping us overcome the emerging Europeans.

Next came Richard Aggiss who was very successful with our state team and led Australia to our first Champions Trophy win in 1983 and our first World Cup win in 1986. Aggiss a teacher and motivator was a beneficiary of the Australian Institute of Sport which established its first decentralised program in Perth in 1984. For the first time Australian Teams were able to prepare for competition in a centralised environment and our consistency on the international stage improved dramatically. Richard Aggiss was the coach when I started to believe that we from the antipodes could beat the world at this game.

As a player the coach who taught me the most was Frank Murray who was in my view the one of the most analytical and thoughtful coaches I have ever played for and worked with. Frank coached National teams of men and women for 14 years and his teams were always in contention.

Of Australia's successful elite coaches two led teams to Olympic gold medals and although I never saw them coaching 'up close' Brian Glencross and Barry Dancer both have the runs on the board with those special results. Dancer's record is exceptional as his team also twice made the World Cup final in 2002 and 2006.

During the nineties Korean coach Song-Ryul Choi was perhaps my most difficult opponent as his Korean team in 1996 was exceptional. When I began with the Hockeyroos Jose Brasa had just coached Spain to an Olympic gold medal in Barcelona. We had many difficult tussles and later when with the Kookaburras we were again opponents when he coached India in 2010.

Jose did a really good job in India and I was very surprised when he was sacked after leading India to a silver medal in the Commonwealth Games in Delhi. Tom van't Hek coached a very competitive Netherlands women's team for nearly six years and we seldom had an easy match against them. He had played against me in the 1980s when a brilliant and creative left winger. Another coach who I would meet later on was Mark Lammers a Dutchman who coached the Spanish women in Sydney. He did a fine job with a limited team to make the semi-finals. Fourteen years later when coaching Belgium at the World Cup in The Hague his team was again so difficult to beat. His teams were always so thoroughly organised and well prepared.

Berti Rauth was at the helm of the German women in Atlanta and Sydney and they were one of those teams that were so close to a medal yet had little luck. I always enjoyed our discussions on hockey. Unfortunately, I could not converse with Sergio Vigil against whom I had played in the eighties. My Spanish was not good enough but when his Argentinian team broke through to win silver in Sydney he had done a terrific job.

Another who I admired during the 90s was Rolant Oltmans who led the Netherlands men's team so well during that time. When I watched the men during that era his team played the best hockey. Presently leading India, he has done a marvellous job building their team up as evidenced by a recent Champions trophy medal. Paul Lissek the meticulous tactician and organiser oversaw successful German teams and passed the baton to Bernard Peters who in 2002 made the breakthrough for Germany in Kuala Lumpur when they won their first ever World Cup. Four years later they repeated that performance and hockey lost Bernard to soccer when he moved to Hoffenheim.

By 2009 when I began another stint at the helm of a national team there were new faces on the scene. Markus Weise had just coached the German men's team to Olympic gold in Beijing. It was a remarkable double as he led their women's team to an unlikely gold in Athens four years earlier. Markus, who I have mentioned elsewhere in the book, is the most successful coach in our sport at the Olympics. He became so at my expense when Germany defeated us in London. His teams were always so tough to defeat and in the best German tradition exhaustively competitive for every minute.

I believe that Bernard Peters and then Markus were responsible for a more assertive and aggressive German approach, which combined the typical resilience of prior German teams with more penetration and some of the game's most brilliant attackers

Michel van den Heuvel led the Netherlands after the Beijing Olympics and, it seemed to me, was unfortunate to lose the job after finishing third in the Delhi World Cup. His replacement Paul van

Ass produced two silver medals but that was not enough for the ambitious Dutch. He lost the job to Max Caldas who had success with the women in 2012 and 2014.

Of those who are in the frame now I believe the most impressive of all is Carlos Retegui. He took the Argentinian women to a World Cup success and in The Hague, in a feat of extraordinary stamina and skill, saw both men and women from Argentina win medals. Carlos has great enthusiasm and passion and engenders belief and purpose in his teams. As a player he was full of drive and energy and this comes through in his squads yet he also guides smart players and tactical teams. In my view at the moment he is the best in the business with Markus Weise retreating to soccer like his predecessor.

Finally, I should mention one of the giants of the game who has been one of the most important coaches and educators in our game. Horst Wein was a presence strutting the fields of the Olympic tournament in Munich in 1972. As a young Olympic hopeful I was informed that Horst, a recently past player, was responsible for the tournament organisation. Later I would read his first book *The Science of Hockey* and meet him at tournaments when he was coach of Spain.

I remember spending time in Karachi assisting him with his English translation of a newer version of that book and on many occasions we had the most interesting discussions about the game and its many aspects. I even had occasion to suggest his heart murmur, which was palpable, might need further investigation... this episode led to him having surgery at a later date! Horst, a great thinker and brilliant teacher developed many programs in hockey and soccer and his books on game intelligence are totally relevant to developing smart players.

During my time in New Zealand I again had cause to meet up with Horst who travelled the world teaching. He was not only a very generous and gracious man but he is irreplaceable as a thinker on the game. His death early in 2016 saddened so many in hockey. I was pleased to be able to communicate with his son Christian and express gratitude for all he had done for our game.

1 3

THE EXCELLENCE DELUSION

Corinne Reid

"...the harder the conflict, the more glorious the triumph. What we obtain too cheap, we esteem too lightly; 'tis dearness only that gives everything its value."

(Thomas Paine 1776, The Day of Freedom)

A team's culture is its psychological DNA – its influence can be felt in every task, on and off the field. Perhaps most importantly, it delimits potential. Achieving a culture of excellence, is arguably then, the apex KPI (Key Performance Indicator) for psychologists working in elite sport. Yet the notion of excellence has become so common, such a cliché, that it is elusive. This is not a sporting crisis, but a societal one. The challenge for the team psychologist is to invite athletes to set a higher bar.

Faking it 'til we make it

Our culture craves excellence and is committed to creating the illusion of it. From the earliest age, we inculcate our children into thinking they are excellent at everything. Giving 'positive feedback' is seen as key to good parenting and 'critical feedback' as potentially damaging to self-esteem. At birthday parties, everyone wins a prize

– we teach our children about excellence at the same time we teach them about cheating. Children are given medals, certificates and awards for everything they do. This is meant to provide them with evidence that they can achieve anything they put their minds to but in reality it tells us that we can achieve excellence without trying – excellence will 'happen' if you turn up.

As adults, we become more obsessed with, and more removed from, excellence. We have plastic surgery to make us physically excellent. We construct social media personas, airbrush photos and massage our CVs to create an image of excellence. Paradoxically, our potential for authentic excellence recedes with every hour spent creating the artifice of excellence. Even when we do have the real potential for excellence (and not everyone does), this artifice blurs the distinction between talent and achievement. Premature attribution of excellence creates a vulnerability – a sense that they have already 'arrived' before they have begun. We don't need to look far to see examples in sport.

Media, as the nanotechnology of modern civilisation, feeds this deception in visible and invisible ways. Sound bites both accommodate and generate the oversimplification of excellence. We love narratives of exceptional success and gut-wrenching failure – a 'little bit' of success does not make the news. The worship of celebrity is about the ordinary being elevated to excellence. In this domain, drama wins, hyperbole rules. Every episode needs its highs and lows. Celebrities – including celebrity sport stars – oblige! Politicians too have a delusion dialect – 'spin' – media advisors 'create' the politician and craft the story. They live down to our cultural expectations. These are just some of the many ways in which we lower the bar on excellence in our community.

Emperors with no clothes

Nowhere can our growing cultural confusion about excellence be seen more clearly than in elite sport. We elevate young athletes with talent to the status of excellence. Before they have a chance to know themselves and their potential they are lauded as icons, their 'character' is created. It is easy to believe the hype and to be drowned by it. I have seen many talented juniors not make the transition to senior elite ranks or underachieve when they get there because they have skipped a critical part of their trajectory toward excellence. Five minutes of fame seduces talented juniors out of the transformative process of punishingly hard work, self-reflection, self-doubt, and self-exploration. A critical rite of passage from talent to excellence is lost. They are left exposed.

The artifice is also illuminated when our icons are revealed to be less than we expect. In recent times we have seen Lance Armstrong catapult from hero to pariah; the Russian track and field team banned from international competition for widespread doping; and closer to home, the Essendon football team, also paying the price for doping transgressions, or at least, for 'looking the other way'. It is not just doping – there are public conversations about fairness and sportsmanship that also highlight that at this point in our history, excellence has an Achilles heel – excellence comes cheap. Win at all costs. Claim 'no-goals'. Put in the illegal tackle if you can get away with it. Sledging is 'part of the game'. If you win, there are no questions asked, no one is called to account. The culture of excellence has a dark side. It has become a quest without values.

Rocking the boat: Creating space for excellence

So what do we do about the excellence delusion? We call it. We do this knowing that we are in for a rough ride, that it can be professional suicide. Ask Brian Clough on Leeds United, Mickey Arthur on Australian cricket or Ewan McKenzie on rugby. All systemic change can feel tectonic – indeed our excellence delusion breeds passivity and dependence. But far worse than this, when challenged, our excellence delusion can ignite latent (and not so latent!), defensiveness, aggression and denial. This was the lion's den that I walked into with both the Hockeyroos and the Kookaburras – both returning from unexpected defeat at the Olympics.

> *"The hardest thing was (and continues to be) maintaining true honesty. Individually in our own reflections, athlete to athlete and coach to athlete. Previously we were too worried about ruffling feathers or rocking the boat when this challenging of ways was exactly what we needed."*
> Tristan Clemons, Kookaburras

My first meeting with each of these teams was like walking into a freezer. Crossed arms, averted gaze, glares, conspiratorial silence, withering eye rolling, open hostility. But if I listened carefully, there was also grief, fear, hurt, determination and grudging awareness. Perhaps most importantly, there were individuals with no time to lose who were desperate for change – they were ready to accept the invitation to honesty. In addition to their own momentum toward change, these individuals were enormously important as Trojan horses that were ready to pierce the defences of their own team in the interests of not repeating history – the pain of losing an attainable gold medal.

Noticing, naming and acknowledging these complex and conflicted emotions was the first step in creating the bedrock for a culture of excellence. Instability was necessary to create the potential for stability. Not wavering in this difficult conversation was a pivotal moment. Equally, acknowledging the risks of change was a Rubicon to be crossed. These risks cannot be denied, bypassed or avoided – learning to live with risk is a vital step toward building a culture of excellence. Paradoxically, each of these confronting conversations was necessary for getting past defences, for having the drawbridge lowered so that a conversation about excellence could begin.

Redefining excellence

Embracing a new culture of excellence often requires the re-writing of childhood memories – excellence is not an award or a certificate, nor the applause of a proud parent, nor of a crowd, nor the media. The essence of excellence is a set of values, an attitude that encompasses commitment, curiosity, consciousness, persistence, honesty and integrity. Excellence is also about exceptionality. By definition then it is rare, difficult, uncomfortable and often invisible. Excellence is a personal quest, not just following a program or doing what is asked, not emulating another – these things are enough to be very good, but none of these things are enough for excellence.

Excellence requires openness and vulnerability, a willingness to live with perpetual uncertainty as we push up against the edges of what is known and what has been done and then push further still into uncharted territory. Excellence is about continual improvement and absolute determination not to stop in the search for better. This determination comes with the acceptance of pain and disappointment along the way and an understanding that these experiences forge stronger character and afford greater potential.

> *"I came to understand that it was about striving for excellence, not success as such (we were on the longest winning streak in history but it wasn't enough); it was wanting the person beside you to be as good as they could be so the whole team and your own performance lifted."*
> Clover Maitland, Hockeyroos

In a team environment, excellence also requires understanding that team-first means that sometimes our individual interests come second. It requires pushing each other to do better, even those who are competing with us for a position. It is knowing that we may do everything we possibly can, and still be found wanting, still not get selected because a team-mate is a better 'fit' in this team at this time. It is about sportsmanship and honouring the excellence of others. These are difficult commitments to make and the mark of champions.

A culture of excellence is an emergent property of these foundational values. To bring these values to life we need more than a *desire* for excellence – this is a relatively common commodity. We need a willingness to have critical conversations that are reflective of those values; prioritise actions that are consistent with those values; develop strong relationships to support the expression of those values; and place ourselves in the line of fire with critical experiences to test our commitment to these values.

Trojan horses

> *"The hardest step for me...was to first understand that our culture was not resilient, not team-first, closed minded (and therefore lacked the honesty that would become the backbone of our identity). Yeah we were 'good' as a team, but by no means were we truly great when we set out on this challenge."*
> Rob Hammond, Leadership Group, Kookaburras

Athletes and coaches ready to accept an invitation to responsibility are a powerful force for their teams in achieving a culture of excellence. Leadership is required here but so are 'first followers' – individuals prepared to look back unflinchingly at where things went wrong and to support a new course of action. Perhaps critically, these individuals are prepared to 'give ground' and understand that more of the same will get more of the same – they are prepared to 'undo' in the service of 'creating'. It is a hard ask to recognise that, despite very close outcomes, a wrong turn has been taken, that an artifice has been created that would, again, be sufficient to get the team to the foot of success but prevent that final step being taken. When an outcome is desired so strongly, it is hard to let go of any step taken in its service. The bravery required to 'let go' flourishes with illumination and support.

> *"The most important part of change by far for me was building a critical mass/buy in. It wasn't easy but the more people who bought in the easier it was to see change."*
> Mark Knowles, Captain, Kookaburras

Trojan athletes carrying the message of change has far more transformative potential than a psychologist (or indeed a coach) carrying this message. It feels more possible when peers feel it is possible. The potential for change, indeed the evidence of change, is carried right into the heart of the group by trusted team-mates. Our job is to provide the scaffolding for this task and the reflective space to reinforce the process as it unfolds and as it butts up against fortress walls. Being a Trojan athlete comes with risks – team-mates committed to the old path may feel betrayed and their excellence delusion exposed. New ground is, as yet, untrodden and the path unclear.

Fifty shades of 'no'
Resistance is an integral part of exceptionality. Resistance is a strength and a weakness in different measure, at different moments. Single-mindedness is what allows exceptional athletes to get up each morning to train and to push through fatigue without being distracted by the easier path. It is also the thing that prevents flexibility and sometimes obscures more successful paths.

Athletes and coaches like control. Giving up control, changing direction, evaluating weaknesses, can make them feel vulnerable.

> *"The hardest thing is giving up what has worked before when it has outlived its usefulness. Knowing when to move on and how to take that leap of faith is hard. Sometimes it feels like a fight to the death."*
> Kate Starre, Hockeyroos

Becoming a translator in the many dialects of 'no' is critical if cultural change is to be possible. These languages seem different, but are often counter-melodies in a symphony of fear. Remember, most cultural intervention occurs after a cultural inflection point becomes a tipping point. This usually follows a dramatically poor performance or a public indiscretion – sometimes both (think the Australian swim team following the London Olympics). Fear is everywhere. This is not an ideal time to address a cultural malaise (prevention is better) but it is the usual reality.

'No' comes in many guises. There is the angry 'no', which functions as an aversive roar to push away attempts at change. There is the pathologising 'no' in which the role of the change agent is diminished, ridiculed or demonised to minimise the requirement to engage. There is the fearful 'no' in which athletes are more able to acknowledge their concern but are not able to transition to a new way of doing things, very much 'the devil you know' approach. Then there is the ambivalent 'no' – the athletes who can see the need for change when in session but lose the vision and the volition when other influences and anxieties creep in. Finally there is the 'yes-no'. This is the most invisible at first glance – the athlete that seems keen to join with change – there is no push back but they just never seem to get around to doing what it takes to change; something always comes up, there is always a reason. Becoming fluent in 'no' is critical. Understanding this as a fear response allows movement toward cracking the code of 'no'.

Beyond the individual 'no', there are other forms of resistance that occur within teams. Sometimes the group allows uncertainties to be represented on their behalf by an individual team member or staff member. These are the gladiators and boundary riders within the team. Gladiators are the individuals who take a vocal combative stance and prevent others from having to confront their fears – they become the lightning rod for discontent. Boundary riders are individuals who maintain a silent vigil on the periphery of the group and function as an anchor for old ways and a safe place of retreat for those who are ambivalent. In understanding the possibilities for change, it is important not to engage with these relationships as a battleground but rather to value the qualities inherent in these roles that can potentially be harnessed to change: There is courage in speaking up, there is courage in defending hard fought ground. If these qualities are acknowledged and respected there is the potential for your greatest adversary to become your greatest ally in the process of change.

Naming 'no' is, again, a fundamental part of the call to excellence. The second step is to withstand the onslaught of 'no', to remain present and continue to invite athletes and coaches to responsibility for their past choices, for their present choices and for their future. This requires creating a safe space for grief – for the lost opportunities and missed moments. Strong emotions should not be thwarted but welcomed as a process of 'letting go' and becoming 'unstuck'. Understanding that strong emotions are not personal (though often personally directed) can help the practitioner in these moments.

An invitation to excellence: Critical conversations

Once the drawbridge has been lowered, do not enter. Instead invite the athletes and coaches to leave the fort and join the search for excellence. While it is tempting to pave the way, and make it feel safe, it would defeat the purpose. Inviting athletes to be uncomfortable, to be afraid, is to invite them to do the hard thing for the right reason and to demonstrate your confidence in their capacity to do so. This approach is a foundational element of not creating yet another artifice of excellence. The invitation begins with critical conversations.

For the Hockeyroos and the Kookaburras, critical conversations have been the foundation for cultural change and the touchstone for excellence. Facing our fears and confronting the unknown provides an authentic platform for excellence. Creating space for excellence requires honest self-appraisal and honest conversations with others about vulnerabilities and strengths that need attention from coaches and athletes alike. The purpose is to illuminate fractures, fissures and fault-lines so they can be repaired prior to competition. This is a process that was accorded a weekly timeslot but which was also expected to set the tone for all conversations within the playing team and the staff group.

"It is your personal responsibility to be honest with yourself and directly to each other. You can lead from anywhere. No title required."
Jenny Morris, Leadership Group, Hockeyroos

There are a few important rules for critical conversations.

- Don't waste time on 'fake issues' – focus on issues that are real points of vulnerability for the team.

- Decide who the key parties are that need to be involved in this conversation if all perspectives are to be represented.

- Adopt a stance of openness, curiosity, willingness to change.

- Do not rush to a solution, spend the time fully hearing the message.

- Invite emotion into the conversation – emotions will be there in vulnerable moments so best that they be there when planning solutions.

- Keep each other honest by 'calling it' when you hear avoidance, distraction, minimisation or fabrication.

Perhaps the most confronting conversations for athletes are those which highlight that excellence is not talent (or flair), nor is excellence simply achievement – it is possible to reach the top in ways that are morally bankrupt. Excellence is about how you get there. Excellence is not Maradona's 'hand of God'. Excellence is Kieran Govers conceding a goal in the World League semi-final decider by admitting to a foul before the goal was scored – it is also about his teammates who supported this admission. Excellence is about character that has in its DNA a drive for being the best you can be and to recognise and value that in others, even (or perhaps, especially) in our closest competitors. Defining, and then holding each other to these standards is what critical conversations are about.

"I think the critical conversations were the hardest to practice/ put into place. Although I think we got the most reward out of persisting with this. …on a multitude of levels the team was able to continually improve and perform at a very high standard without continual fractures throughout the group holding us back."
Tim Deavin, Leadership Group, Kookaburras

The challenges in critical conversations are many: Truly listening and hearing; remaining open to hard messages; managing emotion;

being empathic. Critical conversations may continue for days, weeks or months – sometimes we need to try again and again until we can find a path forward. To paraphrase John F. Kennedy, 'we choose to do this thing not because it is easy but *because* it is hard'. Each attempt, each effort creates a greater depth in our team culture. Critical conversations require a real commitment to 'being in it together', even when we disagree. These critical conversations provide the platform from which we can create a path to excellence. The sum total of months of critical conversations is more than individual growth, more than strong connections between teammates, and even more than a deeper respect for one another. It is an emergent sense of a clear commitment to a team vision and an unwavering strength in holding its course.

Uncharted territory: setting the compass and finding our way

Achieving exceptional feats invariably requires venturing into uncharted waters. This is often where our excellence delusion is exposed. On the brink of success, a step from gold, under extreme pressure, the artifice crumbles, fear escapes and raw talent is found wanting. In these moments, so far removed in time and place from our weekly psychology sessions, our hard-fought culture of excellence must provide the compass and the ballast. A culture of excellence is about creating an environment in which we can be our best selves. Once this culture is created, excellence is what happens when times are tough, when the easy thing would be possible but instead, individuals, and the team, step up and create something exceptional. Both the Hockeyroos and the Kookaburras accepted this invitation to excellence and found their 'true north'. It guided them to victory and beyond…to excellence.

14

CAPTAIN'S PICK...
THAT'S NOT LEADERSHIP

I spent a decade in Federal Parliament between 1983 and 1993 during which time I saw up close the way in which decisions are made and policy enacted in our national parliament...the clearinghouse of ideas in our country. I learnt little about teamwork during my time there but I did see men and women of talent and good purpose work at changing and improving our country. It was not a perfect system as there was great frustration for those ambitious to advance. I did not leave thinking it was an environment where merit determined progress.

Unfortunately, I think in recent times we have in many senses lost our way. The recent phenomenon of the 'captain's pick' and the loss of a moral compass to direct the values that ought to underpin government policy have gone hand in hand. The nation's leadership has lost its way amidst an unruly array of short-term pragmatism and populist simplicity. I firmly believe in collective decision-making as a way of ensuring the widest ranges of views are aired. With a background honed in scientific enquiry, I also believe we ought to listen to the considerable expertise available when making public policy.

Tony Abbott's predilection for making decisions on his own when in The Lodge turned out to be the reason for some of his worst decisions in government. These decisions underline the folly of such a way of operating when the wisdom of collective judgement is available. In *The Coach* I spent time outlining my observation, still valid, that without real teamwork governments fail to utilise their resources of talent and diversity.

Abbott's list of captain's picks tells the story of his demise. Unfunded, expensive paid parental leave started the rot and was never agreed nor was it enacted. Never increasing taxes on wealthy superannuants was simply silly public policy in times of budgetary pressure. Peter Costello's decisions which were very generous to the wealthy, made in earlier times, were simply bad policy. Co-payments for medical services never saw the light of day and made many enemies for no gain. Abbott's appointment of Bronwyn Bishop as Speaker raised the temperature of the parliament as she ejected record numbers. Banning MPs from ABC appearances was a sign of a boxer with a glass jaw! Reinstating knights and dames was a return to the past out of step with contemporary Australia and of course a knighthood for Prince Philip was the barbecue stopper! For Tony Abbott it was a knockout blow.

The whole idea of the captain's pick is anathema to our modern concept of how families, businesses and teams ought to be organised and run. When in the 1990s we moved the Hockeyroos towards the model of a broader leadership group and a critical mass of leaders we were putting aside the anachronistic model of leadership that came from 19th century thinking when hierarchical structures were in vogue and when the games we play were invented.

It was resisted at the time yet when one looks around professional sports in this country now the landscape is replete with 'leadership groups'. These groups are centrally involved in the management of the playing group, team dynamics, the setting of standards of behaviour and development of tactics and strategy – indeed everything directed at team performance. The players are, of course, grown-ups who are heavily invested in the team's performance. It is well understood that all knowledge does not reside in the captain, boss or even prime minister!

When recently John Howard was happily projecting the mantra that *"my operating principle is to keep the Labor Party from government"*, I was dismayed. Our recent and widely respected senior statesman seemed comfortable with this. Surely, as prime minister public good and right policy and justice rate a place in the guiding principle of our leader! When Malcolm Turnbull lost the Liberal leadership over his position on climate change I felt at least there was still some backbone to that leader. Yet then Rudd repudiated his stance on the great moral challenge of climate change. No wonder he lost many of us!

Later, the argument espoused by government regarding our nation's position on climate change was that we should not take a position contrary to our interests. Short term interests at that. If other countries won't take action, even if it might be the right thing to do, then we should not act unilaterally! This is apparently a respectable argument in the modern world. It is, in essence, a view that we cannot have any guiding principles or values that inform our actions…what counts is that we see what everyone else is doing and act according to their behaviour.

That is a sad position as it limits our capacity to make our own judgements based on the evidence. It limits our capacity to be creative and innovative and to take a position of leadership on an issue that may be the most important for the future of our planet, the environment and our children. Bonhoeffer had something to say about that in an earlier chapter: *"The ultimate test of a moral society is the kind of world it leaves to its children"*

The investigation of ideas and analysis of policy options should be the task of government and lawmakers. Innovation and the search for policy clarity while ensuring fairness and justice are essential activities if we are to improve our society and govern well. It remains a truism that the best way to be re-elected is to govern well, and good government requires the capacity to listen, learn, evolve, adjust, reflect, recalibrate and advance. The same qualities required in evaluating performance and planning for excellence in sport or business.

It is never a good idea to avoid reality, to hope it will be all right on the day or at some time hence problems will go away. A method for confronting, addressing, analysing and dealing with the problems that confront us is central, and the moral compass to guide such a process is fundamental to effective policy formulation.

Without a process that values diversity and the wide spectrum of ideas within a society, we fall short of achieving outcomes that genuinely advance our society. Equally, by involving team members in the process of decision-making and respecting their positions, any team functions better.

The problems are not simple – they are complex – yet they are not insurmountable and we have demonstrably failed in dealing with some of them as a nation over successive administrations. On the backbench, one often felt powerless to effect change and have an influence. One also saw close up the frustrations of ministers whose daily battles consumed so much energy that fundamental changes, so necessary, seemed so far away. Change is difficult to achieve and powerful sectional interests often diverted good ideas.

More recently, the need to oppose everything suggested by one's opponent has created many false dichotomies that polarised debates, often appealing to lowest common denominator determinations. This polarisation lowers our tolerance for compassion and consideration of others whose needs may be greater than our own.

The moral compass has been lost in the frenzy to be liked or popular or tough.

The position at which we have come on asylum seekers and the treatment of those detained is, I believe, a cause for national shame. We have arrived here because it is politically expedient to be seen as hard on these people who have committed no crimes and who only seek to find a better and safer life for their families. We use simple utilitarian arguments to assuage our guilt when we deny fundamental rights to needy, distressed and desperate people. Worse still, what we are doing is hidden from the public. It appears at one stage we even paid the so-called smugglers to return their passengers to the place of origin! The irony is shocking.

We are not even being even-handed in how we deal with asylum seekers who might arrive via alternative routes. Arrive by plane and you are treated differently...where is the fairness in this situation?

I was 11 years old when I first saw the grainy images of the final moments of Thich Quang Duc's life when in protest against the treatment of the Buddhist minority he self-immolated on a street corner in Saigon. Some months later the repressive Diem Government fell. Yet, now we as a country have such extreme protests made against our treatment of asylum seekers. Our Immigration Minister, Peter Dutton, has the temerity to deny agency to those so traumatised by Australia's action that they would take such drastic action to protest their plight.

Our position is our country's great shame and so at odds with the position taken by Malcolm Fraser and the Opposition when leading the nation some four decades ago. When I ask myself how we got to this place I think the answer can only be that those in power saw advantage for themselves and didn't really want to increase our intake of refugees. It is clear that with regional co-operation and an orderly assessment in neighbouring countries the post-Vietnam War solution would have worked. The real paucity of fairness in the policy is underlined by the fact that a 'queue jumper' arriving by plane can slip through!

I am not trying to simplify what is very complex but along the way choices were made that led us to this outcome and some of the results are quite absurd. Resettlement in Cambodia as an option is so bizarre that in itself it underlines the folly and stupidity of where we have come to. That Australia as a wealthy and proud nation has come to this is indeed shameful. Here in this piece I hope I am making a case for jettisoning this really shoddy and deplorable mess that is our nation's shame...this is an example of leadership lost and both sides of politics are to blame.

Of course it is never simply about making the right decision or knowing what is best to do. The finesse required to garner support or accumulate credits to be applied to convince naysayers is part of the art of persuasion. When I first coached the Kookaburras I was keen to play a pressing game rather than the 'half-court' favoured by the Europeans. As many of the players played in Europe and were comfortable with these tactics the task of persuasion took some time but together we eventually settled on such an approach. It was not without some disagreements and trial and error but it was a collective process that came out of robust discussion and analysis of what we were doing and aiming to achieve.

I have always believed that leadership has at its core two elements. Firstly, it requires real definition and purpose about where you want to go. Secondly, one needs the ability to get people to come with you through persuasion, through one's example and via rational argument. The force of the case and the way one engages and explains the challenges to the community also adds weight to the cause. Always in such deliberation we ought to be guided by our values and by an appeal to the better angels of our nature...our moral compass.

Also required is a sense of timing and good judgement. One needs to seize the opportunities that present themselves. The nation still celebrates John Howard's stance and timing in the reform of gun control law in 1996 after the terrible Port Arthur slaughter of that year. When opportunity presents itself a good leader is ready and able to utilise the circumstances. The other side of Howard's opportunism unfortunately surfaced in October 2001 when, in an election campaign he used the lie of the 'children overboard' saga to save his sliding electoral chances. That sorry episode would be the beginning of our slide into asylum seeker politics that has been characterised by a race to the bottom.

My experience...

I was proud to be part of what I believed was a period of very good government. Bob Hawke and Paul Keating, in different ways yet together, led Australia through 1983 to 1996. As time passes the quality of their stewardship of Australia is increasingly evident.

Hailing from Western Australia, Peter Walsh was a farmer who studied economics and who established a reputation as a parsimonious and rigorous finance minister in Bob Hawke's ministry. Peter was keen to eliminate government excess and played a part in shaping budgets that balanced in difficult times. Peter was constantly searching to eliminate excesses and control expenditure. He was not about being popular – perhaps senators need be less attuned to the electorate's temperature.

Perhaps his greatest legacy was the establishment, as a piece of public policy, of the petroleum products resource rental tax enacted in 1987. In contrast to the bungled attempts to establish a profit based mining tax in the Rudd era, the preparation and selling of this reform was done effectively even in the face of opposition from many vested interests. Walsh's tax still operates effectively and has not caused the end of petroleum product exploration as predicted.

Walsh of course was not the salesman of this policy but he was the rock-solid finance minister behind the detail.

Keating was the salesman of government budgetary policy in that time but he needed allies and Walsh was the perfect foil. In Kerry O'Brien's book *Keating* he said of Walsh: *"Peter made a great contribution but the political job of shaping change and then selling it was not one of his strengths."* The point here is that such shifts cannot be delivered or indeed advanced without teamwork or co-operation and the captain's pick is not a sign of strength but one of weakness and insecurity.

What Keating had was an acute sense of where he wanted to go (as did Walsh) but along with that went the political skills to finesse the pathway, gather the support and take the community with him. These skills are necessary to enable one to fight another day and fight the next battle too. Keating had an eye for the electorate and for the team. "You have to pull caucus colleagues onto the task and sign them up, not confront and alienate them."

It may seem out of place to raise questions of public policy in the context of an exploration of World's Best sporting practice yet I would argue that our expectation from our leaders in public policy and government ought to entail rigour, analysis, a search for options and possibilities and a transparent collaborative decision-making process. The same approach is appropriate for every family, company, business, non-profit organisation and, of course, sporting teams, clubs and national bodies.

When it comes to public policy making I think we have reason to feel let down by our leaders. Two areas absolutely central to the wellbeing and efficiency of a modern progressive nation are education and health care. We have our heads above water perhaps but are we world's best? The resounding response is no and indeed we are in danger of sliding further down the rankings in each area.

In education we have evolved, for several reasons, a system that is based on choice and competition. The competition between private and public education is wasteful and unseemly and the choice is unfortunately about money – who can afford it? I have always believed the only criteria for an education system ought to be quality, and in our wealthy country we ought to aim for the highest quality of education for all. Certainly, the best education ought not to be only for the wealthy.

The very best education system would garner all the resources available and focus them on having the highest quality for all, as is the case in the Scandinavian countries where such an ethos exists. This is not only good public policy from a fairness and equity position but it is economically sensible. By building a clever country with a well-trained and capable workforce you improve productivity and efficiency and innovate.

Given the historical mess that has created a system for the rich and poor the use of government resources to redress the imbalance is critical. All of history ought to tell us of the centrality of education to economic advancement and wellbeing. So surely this should be policy priority number one!

The other major area of public policy divergence is that of health care which gobbles up vast sums of taxpayers' dollars. It has for a long time been my view that the whole designation of the portfolio as being responsible for 'health' is wrong. It is, as it stands and operates, a *'sickness care'* ministry. Mainly it administers to the treatment of people who are already sick. The incentives inherent in fee-for-service medicine underpin that.

A 'health policy' would contain incentives for doctors to see patients less by virtue of making them healthier and have preventative medicine up front and central. Lifestyle change and health education from an early age would be critical. Exercise, dietary oversight, environmental hazard reduction, living conditions and many other preventative strategies would assume more prominence.

This would entail more salaried doctors and challenge entrepreneurial practice to get the economic incentives right. There would need to be difficult debates about the best way to treat the old and fragile. Excessive expenditure in the twilight years would obviously need oversight.

Of course our 'sickness care' system does, thanks to tenacious Labor governments, remain universal and so we have been able to contain expenditures better than countries like the US, yet the public-private tension is ever present.

Unfortunately, the blemishes of everyday political life do not allow for such sense and rationality, and as a nation our policy makers have sorely let us down. As my time in the public policy making space subsided in 1993 I was horrified by the tendency towards focus group sampling as a way of reinforcing policy direction. This was especially so in the election environment. Diligent, considered, serious policy creation took a back seat to the necessity of political imperative. In the election campaign it was about the leader and slogans hitting the mark with undecided voters. This is akin to picking the team with the best captain and the most resonant club song to win. Unfortunately, the best team is always determined by the performances of all the players on the field!!

In my lifetime the worst public policy decision was made by the Howard Government when in 2003 it determined to join the 'Coalition of the Willing' and enter the second Gulf War with George W. Bush and Tony Blair, leading the way into a folly of the highest order. The weapons of mass destruction did not exist (they were the pretext for our intervention), and the subsequent turmoil and heartache that is the Middle East today are the consequence of an ill thought through, illegal, violent and society-smashing action.

It is parallel to the US arming the Taliban in the early 1980s to counteract the Russian invasion of Afghanistan. This led to long-standing consequences in the region. The consequences of the Iraq foolishness will likely be with us for many generations. The present turmoil and instability in the Middle East, and the resultant worldwide refugee migrations, are largely a consequence.

It is interesting to look at how such blunders as the Iraq involvement were arrived at, and again it seemed John Howard's personal involvement and motivations swayed the cause of good policy making. Howard was in Washington at the time of the 9/11 attacks and this seemingly cemented his attachment to the aggressive reaction to Iraq that was borne out of those events. Iraq, a secular entity led by a tyrant, was a great distance from those responsible and the justifications for the war and our involvement were tenuous at best.

I cannot help but think that a process that included truly divergent and diverse views would have come to a different conclusion. Any forensic appraisal of the shaky justifications would have revealed the truth and the false dichotomy presented by Bush, (you're either with us or you're unpatriotic), was misleading and perverse. Single powerful decision makers very often get it wrong and in 2003 three powerful leaders in three different countries got it wrong when the checks and balances of good decision making were ignored.

With a federal election in full swing (2016) we have had competing sides contesting the space for ideas yet the big changes required by our nation are mostly ignored and denied. Broadening the tax base in order to improve fairness and efficiency makes sense. Nobody will take it on. Things like land tax and stamp duty reform, broadening and increasing GST (with compensations for low and fixed income earners) inter-generational transfer taxes and revisions on negative gearing and capital gains tax are necessary. At least both parties are acting to reduce overly generous superannuation concessions!

Fairness is something we should all be able to expect and the greater equality, which should fall from this, can be a bonus for our economy. It is pretty clear that low and middle-income people spend a greater percentage of their income and so the economic benefit of a fair distribution of wealth works.

Leaders have a responsibility to create an environment in which decisions that effect the direction and detail of public policy are fair for all, do not discriminate against minorities, share the costs and benefits and provide resources to enable all citizens access to equal opportunities. These may seem laudable aims and some may say unrealistic, yet such outcomes are achievable with good will and with respect for the diversity that is inherent in our global living space.

In great teams player involvement in decision-making is critical for performance. It is measured on the field of play and the players are front and centre there. Great teams share the load, co-operate fully, critique one another, set high standards and are encouraged to participate. They are able to disagree and still share a common goal and they work together to solve problems and repair damage caused by mistakes. This is a collective endeavour and there is no place for the captain's pick!

CORPORATE SPORT

In my book *The Coach* I wrote a chapter titled "Let Sport Own Sport". It was a plea, forlorn I suspect, for sport to be in control of its own destiny. It was a commentary on what I saw happening and a hope, in the fashion of King Canute, to somehow stop it.

The story of Canute I first heard was of his own vainglorious attempt to hold back the tide. It was apparently recorded first in Henry of Huntington's 12th century chronicle of the history of England. Now a more accepted version is that Canute was informed by sycophantic courtiers that the King of England was entitled to sit on the sea without getting wet.

On discovering the folly of this advice (Canute got wet), he decided to take his own counsel in the future and became a wise and successful leader, hence the memorable proverb "paddle your own Canute".

Anyway, since *The Coach* the commercialisation of sport has continued apace and any attempt to slow or change its progress would certainly seem to be forlorn.

I played my sports at the highest levels yet when I examine my motivation it is clear it was never financial. There was a rhythm to the movement of sport, the desire to score and do well, the physical and mental challenges and testing that the contest brought forth. It was a mental exercise as much as a physical one. The environment of competition could be hostile and fierce, even chaotic, but it was also played within the guidance of rules and conventions designed to promote fairness and an even playing field.

Team sport brought more complexity and the additional element of co-operation and co-ordination of actions and thoughts. Without these elements nobody could succeed. The lessons from team sport, of course, were relevant to almost every element of human endeavour. Families, businesses, schools, indeed any group activity, required these things to function properly.

So, is the place of sport in the future as relevant as it once was? Or is the world changing inexorably so that sport no longer has a place in developing our youth, promoting fitness, teaching values, learning to love movement and engaging in 'play'?

I quoted David Malouf in *The Coach,* and that quote taken from *The Australian* newspaper in January 2001 said something of Australia's progress as a nation. Malouf, unlike others, did not undervalue the role of sport in Australia's development as a nation.

"Sport has continued to be the place where we are most aware of ourselves as a people; and when we consider the alternatives there can be few healthier or more benign, more civilised ways in which a nation might discover a sense of itself than 'at play' – at competitive play with friends and neighbours. Those who baulk at the role sport plays in life, who think of it as adolescent and low-brow to invest so much spirit in what is merely physical, miss the point and miss it badly. There is something about the encouragement to individual excellence within a discipline of team loyalty and fair play that speaks strongly to our sense of how a society at large might work."

He is saying this activity, which occurs every day across the nation, has an important place. It is part of the mix of activities and stimulations that frames the lives of the citizens of this country.

Sport is not insignificant and merely the interest of those who are trivial. Sport has beauty in the perfection and rhythm of its actions. The skills required to do it well are developed and honed beautifully over time by those who participate. The search for excellence excites and owns us and we marvel that we might be able, one day, to achieve perfection at this thing.

The manifestation is extrinsic, in that it can be observed, and the introspection and discovery that is that part of the journey is revealing. We reach our limits sometimes, sometimes we are unable to continue, sometimes we fail and sometimes we surprise ourselves.

We are challenged to venture into the unknown and take chances. We make choices, experiment and test ourselves. We seek victory knowing that defeat may be just around the corner. I am told that sometimes we reach a place of 'flow' or altered consciousness. I never got there myself but I certainly was able to totally immerse myself in the contest and so lose myself in the task and release myself from the problems of everyday life.

For me, these things have always been the attraction of sport and its defining strength. These things are very much personal and self-absorbing. They are likely to be different for all of us but when we look at the numbers of people who engage in sporting activities then we must conclude that these people are finding value in their involvement.

However, as Malouf alluded, it is the social engagement and the need for co-operation, which makes the benefit to community so powerful. All over this country probably millions of children and their parents are engaged in these activities every weekend.

Many powerful policy makers at all levels massively underestimate the value of this.

I have not even mentioned the tangible benefit, well understood by the ancients. That benefit remains as relevant today, and comes from *mens sana in corpore sano* (a healthy mind in a healthy body). In Australia, the sport portfolio now resides in the Health Department so the Health Minister has carriage of sport.

While this may be recognition of sport's place it also leaves one of the government's busiest ministers conflicted between priorities. Sport is lost in this huge bureaucracy and the details can rarely find a voice lost in this behemoth.

If the portfolio was about health that would be fine but essentially it is about 'sickness' expenditure and so the preventative aspects of the portfolio continue to be given little attention. Sport, the 'common glue', with a role as fitness and activity promoter, which can be pivotal for personal growth and community fulfilment, is largely ignored. In a portfolio with a bent to promote health sport would be in the vanguard of the preventative approach. It is one of the abject failures of our public administration that prevention is not front and centre.

However, there are circumstances where sport gets some political attention. Sports, which are watched by many and have saturation media attention, can get you seats at the grand final or on television next to sporting heroes. For these sports our politicians are ever present and ever attentive.

For the mass media gladiatorial sports there are huge public resources made available, and seemingly an open door to political access. In Western Australia at the moment the State Government, already carrying massive debt, has embarked on building a $1.5 billion stadium so these big sports can do even better. I read recently, this stadium will cost $50 million per year to run. It will be a huge sinkhole for public monies well into the future. The building of associated infrastructure for pedestrian, road and rail access is an additional public cost.

Premier Colin Barnett has undertaken the whole project on the basis of a captain's pick and the expenditure is obscene. The option of remodelling of Subiaco Oval was overlooked even as Adelaide very successfully transformed the Adelaide Oval for about a third of the cost. The flow-on effects for sport in general is also clear.

Because of the parlous state of the budget the State Government has cut two-thirds of annual funding for community recreational sporting facilities. The irony here is that clubs around the state cannot get assistance to build locally utilised and supported facilities while Crown Casino will have football crowds carried to its front door with a big sports stadium right in the midst of its gambling precinct at Burswood.

All of the nation's stadia lose money. Yet the case for the MCG and Sydney Olympic Park can be understood given the events and populations they serve. Stadia are not profitable businesses yet I understand only Etihad Stadium in Melbourne makes a profit and this is on the basis of 900 events per year utilising all its rooms and facilities. Even this is not enough. Without revenue from parking due to its unique position it would also be sinking in debt. Unfortunately for West Australian taxpayers no such redeeming features will help the Burswood white elephant.

This is public policy that is misdirected and out of touch, but government proceeds wide-eyed into the abyss. The sports that use our network of stadia Australia-wide are, of course, 'professional'. That means they pay their players big salaries and every weekend spectators roll up to watch live or are watching on television.

It is a great pity that there is no recognition of the cost of building such facilities. Government expects a fair return on its expenditure in building them and providing supporting infrastructure like transport and roads. Security is now also a salient question.

However these big sports, and as a consequence the salaries of every athlete, are subsidised by the taxpayer.

In the United Kingdom big sports clubs build their own stadiums and often gain assistance from foreign oligarchs and the like. This is the only way that the crazy salaries make some degree of sense; it is someone else's money. It shouldn't be coming from taxpayers.

The question of support for the struggling 'amateurs' who participate in Olympic sports always comes up for discussion. Indeed just prior to the Rio Olympics it was widely reported that each gold medal won by an Australian swimmer would have cost the taxpayers $4.75 million! $38 million spent on the Australian swim team in four years! Collingwood Football club would spend twice that amount every year.

This support is a pittance compared with public money that goes to the big end of the sporting town. Very seldom is it sufficient for anything beyond subsistence for such athletes who seek to realise their potential.

The small sports must fight for a niche and space in a crowded market. They must endeavour to find their point of difference and utilise all the resources available to allow them to find a place in the sun. Too often they are pushed aside by the big 'media performers'.

What is especially disappointing is the capacity of the well-heeled and well connected to be able to obtain resources from government as a result of their privileged position. Over a short time Frank Lowy (president of the FFA) was able to obtain $105 million for his sport. No other substantial sport would have a snowball's chance in hell of getting that money. The FFA controversially received at least $45 million for their flawed and failed bid to host the soccer World Cup.

That the money was squandered pointlessly (perhaps some distributed to corrupt officials to secure non-existent votes!) only made the allocation worse. That the allocation was the result of a billionaire sidling up to the then PM Kevin Rudd is a real cause for concern. In a country where we believe cronyism and corruption are not part of the way in which government should operate, this behaviour bears close scrutiny. However, the trend continues.

Lowy was able to secure $60 million for the running of the Asia Cup in 2015. Any number of sporting bodies make claims on sums for event support yet again the billionaire was able to secure the funds…this time from a different prime minister – Tony Abbott! Reports were that the competition was a great success. If so, one should speculate whether a profit was made and the government contribution at least partially recompensed!

There has never been an adequate or satisfactory explanation of the way the $45 million was spent but what I find extraordinary is the way a billionaire cannot contribute his own money to such a cause yet politicians are happy to stump up public money. This sort of unsystematic and unaccountable resourcing of mates' projects ought to be called out and sanctioned.

So where is sport now? That sport is now a business is the accepted wisdom. The business is entertainment. It is popular and matched by huge numbers and interest – and therefore a vehicle to sell products and subscriptions. Those who have the rights can enrich themselves, the participants and the administrators.

There is another way…

There is another way. In Ireland the Gaelic Athletic Association (GAA) is very successful in filling Croke Park and run stunningly successful All-Ireland Hurling and All-Ireland Football competitions. These are the most popular sports in the Republic of Ireland in terms of attendance.

Throughout the country competitions occur in villages and towns in facilities that are built, supported and maintained by local and GAA funding. It is central to the national goal of promoting physical fitness and engagement of local communities. This hugely successful sports network is one in which players remain 'amateurs' and the vast profits are utilised to grow and support the sports and communities which are part of the fabric of the nation.

The profits of the GAA are utilised to build community involvement and support for their games and not to enrich the high profile athletes and sponsors. The community out-reach of the GAA goes far beyond anything that high profile professional sports the world around are doing. There is another way for sports to engage with its participants and the community. It goes to the values expressed by David Malouf and it may appear anachronistic in this modern world but it is much, better than the direction that sport has taken over the last decades.

Unfortunately, prevailing wisdom is that business acumen ought to be the base criterion for filling a board. The work of such people will maximise profits and assist sports to grow and thrive. While at first inspection this makes sense, at closer scrutiny a better balanced board, which also reflects the less tangible benefits of sport, may well produce better overall results. Any business of the sporting type should embrace the integrity of sport and balance the profit motive with public good, the integrity of the sport and its place in our culture and way of life.

Not only is this the right thing to do it is also, I would argue, best for all concerned. The emergence of CTE (Chronic Traumatic Encephalopathy) in American football eventually led to a settlement for over $1 billion with the players union. The National Football League, had it been more attuned to its players needs and the way the game was played and trained, would have not been so adversarial in their approach; a player's perspective was needed.

This brutal yet sometimes beautiful and fascinating game of course has history. Extraordinarily in the early part of the twentieth century, the brutality was of monumental proportions. It is hard to understand how the game grew and thrived. 1905, the so called 'crisis' year, saw 18 deaths and 159 serious injuries yet in 1909 there were 26 deaths and 69 serious injuries. The majority of those killed were college athletes!!

This is a violent game even now and it has only been through rule and equipment changes that the injury and death toll has fallen. Since the mid-1970s there has been a sharp decrease in the number of catastrophic cervical spine injuries. This was achieved through rule changes to modify tackling and blocking. In Australian football codes the issue of repeated concussions is finally slipping into our consciousness. It is a 'watch this space' issue!

The recent resurgence in cage fighting and like activities certainly seems to suggest there is public interest in violence. Perhaps it is a proxy for violence elsewhere and thus might serve a purpose. Unfortunately, I suspect violence itself sells tickets and subscriptions. This activity, which sells itself as the Ultimate Fighting Championship (UFC), is in reality a fight promotion business and presents its athletes as the "best in the world".

Rhonda Rousey was supposed to be the best woman athlete on the planet until Holly Holm, who has subsequently forfeited the title to another, brought her down. Rousey won a bronze medal in judo at the Beijing Olympics. She is far from the best female athlete on the planet! Violence and hyperbole together make an intriguing mix.

I suppose it is my hope that sport in and of itself as an expression of skill, speed, challenge, risk-taking and teamwork is a project worth selling. We can do without gratuitous violence. Perhaps I am dreaming?

The danger is that as business runs sport it changes its essence and associations and thereby sullies the product. It can do so in order to increase its attractiveness but too often it seems to occur without too much thought.

Associations with tobacco, alcohol, gambling, violence and drug use all have the potential to harm sport's image and the battles with these issues will always continue. Tobacco has largely been defeated but not by sporting administrators. Alcohol, gambling and drugs are works in progress and violence is perhaps on the rise. Only vigilant and caring sporting administrators will make progress.

But what is happening to sporting competitions? They are changing and being constantly reinvented for the media. One wonders if this is ultimately for the good of our society.

In January 2016, I watched India play Australia in a T20 cricket match in Adelaide. Australia, chasing a hefty total, started well and Aaron Finch and Steve Smith were at the crease when Smith, wearing a microphone at the time, engaged in banter with the commentators in the commentary box. This is what television wants – live insights into the players' thoughts and actions. Smith seemed a little uncomfortable but no doubt as team captain there was a premium on hearing what he had to say and this was important to the broadcaster. And of course what the broadcaster wants the broadcaster gets!

Smith famously went 'off-air' after he was dismissed in a mundane fashion while seemingly reluctant to be part of the theatre. This activity (on-air commentary by players) happens in the Big Bash domestic competition, so why not international games? I presume that is the logic. We are stretching the envelope, trying new things, and seeing how far we can go to provide the best entertainment.

The value of the entertainment is of course questionable as sweaty players and stressed coaches are unlikely to share anything of importance with the world out there! Generally, the analysis is glib at best and often so banal as to be completely uninteresting. So why do the broadcasters want it? Perhaps it makes sense because these days this is seen as another version of reality TV. Mind you, watching the inmates of the Big Bother house sleep and clean their teeth was exceptionally boring and soon lost its audience.

Next, I imagine the player lining up for a penalty will be telling us where he will shoot or the goalkeeper will share his plan with the television audience. I think this is where it is logically heading. Television seemingly has this 'right to know' mentality. When asked about the Smith dismissal scenario the next day, David Warner was supportive. He didn't find it was a problem for him.

Perhaps this is just part of the mythology around 'multi-tasking' that seems to be the justification for doing homework in front of TV or with music in the background. We ought to understand that 'multi-tasking' is possible but this does not mean there is not a cost. We can do more than one thing at a time but we do not do any of the tasks as well as we might if we were totally focussed on one thing!

Surely elite athletes ought to understand that. This is, of course, especially the case when doing something like batting against the new ball! What it does do is give us a glimpse of where sport might be blindly heading.

Last season we had players moving from the commentary box to the game and the line between the participant and reporter was very blurred. Andrew Flintoff famously gave an 'Elvis rendition' while on the field, trying to move with his former athleticism. Perhaps, as his aging frame wasn't able to play at its previous level his vocal projection was supposed to make up the difference!

Another boundary that seems to have been crossed in cricket is that of selection. One of the Australian selectors Mark Waugh appears on television as an expert commentator and gives opinions on form and performance nightly during the competition...this appears an extraordinary conflict of interest unless, of course he has two sets of opinions for different circumstances!

Many of the traditional boundaries are being crossed and there is increasing pressure for coaches and players to 'come out' of the game during the contest, and sponsors, broadcasters and producers drive this behaviour. Athletes acquiesce because they know they must, and in my view the essence of the sporting contest, its uncompromising struggle to dominate the opponent, is diminished.

I always wonder if sporting bodies and administrators are really interested in viewing a competitive struggle. If it was a central theme then we would see closer matches and not the dilution of quality that results from the expansion of the league to more teams, venues and matches. The AFL would be intensely competitive with 14 teams but the talent is stretched filling 18 teams. The extra teams and players are partly the reason that about one third of the weekly matches are grossly uncompetitive, often being won by more than 40 points.

The extra teams in the AFL mean the draw, and therefore the competition, is uneven and unfair but nobody seems to care as extra money is generated. Some teams travel a lot and some hardly ever but again the justification is monetary maximisation. The premise of an even playing field for sporting contests inherent in the draft and salary cap only goes so far for the AFL.

One can understand the Grand Final is always played on the MCG, which is a traditional home of the game and has the greatest capacity. However, if this is to be so then interstate teams ought to be afforded the chance to play on the venue during the season if they are to be able to properly prepare for the big game. Of course here the problem is that these facilities are hugely expensive to open and adequately staff. Cost intervenes when allocating games. While football may complain about these costs again it is long suffering taxpayers (many with no interest in football) who bear the burden.

The issue of drugs in sport is not new and the ructions occurring before the Rio Olympics are yet a further manifestation of this problem. Would a whole nation of athletes be disqualified? The integrity of competitions is at stake yet the individual sports find themselves wanting special performances and world records. Individual athletes with great ambition and few scruples search for an edge, and nations seek to have their champions succeed. The effect of this cocktail of forces means that without continuous vigilance sport will struggle to remain clean.

Recent experience in Australia with football teams and clubs seduced into seeking a short cut to sporting success for their programs exemplifies the lengths to which individuals and teams will go. Essendon Football Club caused itself tremendous harm in its pursuit of chemical assistance to boost performance. The folly of its approach underpinned the naivety of the coaching staff and subsequently club leadership. For Essendon captain Jobe Watson it will likely lead to the forfeiture of his cherished Brownlow Medal.

While the AFL declares itself vigilant and determined in its stance on this issue it has another self-confessed drug user with a Brownlow Medal. It has a premiership team from 2006 during which a number of players trained and played with performance enhancing help. When questioned about their failure to test positive I merely refer to the situation of Marion Jones a triple gold medallist from Sydney who was stripped of her medals but never returned a positive test!

Fifteen years ago when I was writing *The Coach* my publisher referred me to Lance Armstrong's book, *It's not about the Bike*, and indicated that the book was perhaps in the genre that was appropriate for myself. Armstrong being famous for his Tour de France record built after surviving testicular cancer. I was always sceptical of Armstrong because in 1998 one of our athletes in hockey failed a routine drug test. The failed test probably saved Greg Corbitt's life as it led to the diagnosis of his testicular tumour.

Corbitt, an Olympic silver medallist in Barcelona, tested positive because his tumour was producing alfa fetoprotein (AFP) and HCG (human chorionic gonadotrophin) and these showed up in the test. I always wondered why Armstrong never failed the drug tests when he was tested in the US as a competing athlete through 1996. When eventually diagnosed, Armstrong was in an advanced stage of the disease. One wonders if the testing rigour in the US was thorough enough or did the samples go down the sink?

In his book Armstrong described how he found out about the disease in September, 1996. At the time he was coughing up blood, had an enlarged testicle and was suffering headaches. His tiredness had caused him to pull out of the Tour de France in June and he disappointed finishing 6th and 12th at the Atlanta Olympics in the time trial and the road race in July. In the spring of that year he said he had had sore nipples after one race probably because of the HCG (a hormone produced by pregnant women) that was produced by the growing tumour. My question would be why he did not fall foul of the drug testers in all those competitions throughout the year?

It seems international sport has endless controversy. It appears the commercialisation of sports' properties and the attendant corruption and skulduggery know few boundaries. FIFA's principal office bearers are now discredited and removed from office. The process of allocating competitions is replete with bribes and cronyism. The Olympic movement's autocratic structures defy rationality and the IAAF and its president, Lord Coe, are mired in controversy for their ham-fisted oversight of drug taking throughout the sport. The ICC has carved up the rewards of cricket's media bonanza so that the three big nations (India, England and Australia) thrive while others remain mendicants. This is hardly an approach that will serve the growth of the game worldwide.

International sport has for some time been thus but one cannot help but observe that the introduction of massive sponsorships and billion-dollar rewards seem to have increased the number and degree of examples of malfeasance. Sprinter Justin Gatlin was twice found guilty of illegal drug use but finds Nike still keen to sponsor him. For a decade Lance Armstrong was protected from within the sport. The corporate ethics on display in sport are hardly impressive!

Athletics it seems has one shining light in Usain Bolt whose performances and longevity make him an outstanding outlier. In performance and physique he appears an extraordinary outlier. However it is interesting to observe that Jamaica does not have a reputation for the rigour of it's testing regime. Interestingly, Bolt has run eight of the fifteen fastest times in history. Those who have run the other seven are Justin Gatlin, Tyson Gay, Asafa Powell, Tim Montgomery and Nesta Carter. Those five have all at some time failed drug tests...

The new and emerging threat to the sporting scene in Australia is the rapidly developing relationship between corporate sports and the gambling industry. As major sponsors of the professional codes in Australia, this industry has the capacity to take money off the tables of families around the country in the same way that casinos and poker machines create countless misery. Additionally, they are rapidly becoming an influence in the lives of young men, which promotes this activity as macho and sophisticated. The values portrayed in the associated advertising are of being cool, in control and getting something for nothing. I cannot think of a more unlikely reality. The many tragic outcomes of gambling addiction and it's consequences bear consideration beyond the short term fix of a fistful of dollars.

Sport works as a vehicle for broadcast because most still believe the contests are fair and real. Sport is a fresh contest and has real drama as long as this is believed. Too many scandals and too much interference and this quality will be diluted. When at New Zealand cricket I well remember Lou Vincent as an aspiring young player. He clearly lost his way when the inducement to fix matches intervened.

In the end we should be very much aware that corporations that seek an association with sports do so for their own interests and in order to attach themselves to a vehicle to assist their purposes. Whether selling cigarettes in a bygone era or alcohol, junk food, sugary drinks or online betting, these addictions rely on a sport's good name to help flog their wares. The mere fact they are in the businesses they are in should ring alarm bells. Get too close and allow the sponsor or media mogul to make your choices and you may find this good name and goodwill dissipated. "Sport needs to own sport," and this was never so important as in a time of ever increasing corporate interference and influence.

I am hopeful that sport's trajectory will not see it become the coliseum entertainment of the future. Will we see gladiators fighting in struggles that are increasingly manipulated to make them even more spectacular and extreme? To satisfy the sponsors and multimedia interests will there be a need for ever faster change and excess? Sports will be powerless to resist and we will see the decline of the sports of the nineteenth and twentieth centuries.

If I am correct then we will perhaps see the 'Hunger Games' or its equivalent as the new sporting appetite. Certainly, in the near future it is clear that there will be more and more extreme sports to satisfy the appetite of the GoPro generation. I suspect the sports of my youth will be lost.

APPENDIX 1
Kookaburras' Win-Loss Record 2009 – 2014
All games played. Including Olympics and World Cups

	Played	Won	Lost	Draw	For	Against
2009	39	30	6	3	191	72
2010	37	31	3	3	166	53
2011	30	23	4	3	104	56
2012	39	31	3	5	146	44
2013	25	18	2*	5	134	39
2014	23	19	3	1	99	25
Total	193	152	21*	20	840	289
% or average goals per game		78.8	10.9* one game decided in shootout	10.4	4.35	1.50

Hockeyroos
1993-2000

	Played	Won	Lost	Draw	For	Against
Total	252	197**	30	25	814	239
% or average goals per game		78.2** two games decided in shootout	11.9	9.9	3.23	0.95

Kookaburras Olympics Games and World Cups

	Played	Won	Lost	Draw	For	Against
2010	7	6	1	0	27	8
2012	7	4	1	2	28	10
2014	7	7	0	0	30	4
Total	21	17	2	2	85	22
% or average goals per game		81	9.5	9.5	4.05	1.05

Kookaburras Champions Trophies

	Played	Won	Lost	Draw	For	Against
2009	6	5	1	0	29	12
2010	6	6	0	0	28	8
2011	6	6	0	0	20	7
2012	6	5	0	1	12	3
Total	24	22	1	1	79	30
% or average goals per game		91.7%	4.17%	4.17%	3.3	1.25

Hockeyroos and Kookaburras Major Competition Records

(Olympic Games, World Cup and Champions Trophy)

	Played	Won	Lost	Draw	For	Against
Kookaburras Major Competitions 6 years	45	39	3	3	164	52
% or average goals per game		86.67	6.67	6.67	3.64	1.16
Hockeyroos Major Competitions 8 years	60	49**	4	7	187	49
		**Twice won on shootout				
% or average goals per game		81.76	6.67	11.67	3.12	0.82

APPENDIX 2
Kookaburras' Record by Country 2009 – 2014
(Two matches or more)

	Played	Won	Lost	Draw	For	Against
The Netherlands	21	15	4	2	66	40
New Zealand	19	16	1	2	80	29
Malaysia	18	14	1	3	74	26
Korea	17	11	0	6	50	26
Belgium	13	9	2	2	66	26
Germany	13	7	6	0	35	30
Spain	13	11	2	0	48	18
India	13	11	1	1	61	18
Pakistan	13	11	1	1	54	19
England	12	10	2	0	38	17
Argentina	11	9	1	1	43	14
China	5	5	0	0	38	1
Great Britain	5	3	0	2	15	9
France	4	4	0	0	22	8
Canada	4	4	0	0	18	3
Japan	3	3	0	0	13	2
South Africa	3	3	0	0	25	0
Samoa	2	2	0	0	58	0
Egypt	1	1	0	0	4	0
Ireland	1	1	0	0	4	2
Scotland	1	1	0	0	9	0
Papua New Guinea	1	1	0	0	16	0

APPENDIX 3

Kookaburras' Competition Results 2009 – 2014

International Competitions January 2009 – June, 2014

TEST SERIES   WESTERN AUSTRALIA   JANUARY, 2009

20/01/09	Aust v The Netherlands	2-4
21/01/09	Aust v The Netherlands	4-2
23/01/09	Aust v The Netherlands	7-3
25/01/09	Aust v The Netherlands	1-1

TEST SERIES CANBERRA, AUSTRALIA FEBRUARY, 2009

05/02/09	Aust v Belgium	4-4
07/02/09	Aust v Belgium	7-1
08/02/09	Aust v Belgium	10-0

TEST SERIES PARIS, FRANCE MAY, 2009

| 26/05/09 | Aust v France | 5-4 |
| 27/05/09 | Aust v France | 4-1 |

TEST SERIES HAMBURG, GERMANY MAY/JUNE, 2009

| 31/05/09 | Aust v Germany | 3-4 |
| 02/06/09 | Aust v Germany | 1-2 |

HAMBURG MASTERS HAMBURG, GERMANY JUNE, 2009

04/06/09	Aust v The Netherlands	3-2
06/06/09	Aust v England	5-2
07/06/09	Aust v Germany	6-2

TEST SERIES NOTTINGHAM, ENGLAND JUNE, 2009

| 10/06/09 | Aust v England | 5-4 |
| 12/06/09 | Aust v England | 4-1 |

TEST SERIES ADELAIDE, AUSTRALIA JULY, 2009

25/07/09	Aust v Malaysia	8-1
26/07/09	Aust v Malaysia	0-1

THREE NATIONS INVITATION CANBERRA, AUSTRALIA JULY/AUGUST, 2009

29/07/09	Aust v Malaysia	11-3
30/07/09	Aust v Canada	4-0
02/08/09	Aust v Malaysia	1-0
06/08/09	Aust v Canada	2-1
07/08/09	Aust v Canada	6-2

OCEAN CUP VI
INVERCARGILL, NEW ZEALAND AUGUST, 2009

25/08/09	Aust v Somoa	26-0
26/08/09	Aust v New Zealand	5-2
29/08/09	Aust v New Zealand	3-1

TEST SERIES KUALA LUMPUR, MALAYSIA OCTOBER, 2009

19/10/09	Aust v Malaysia	3-1
20/10/09	Aust v Malaysia	5-1
22/10/09	Aust v Malaysia	3-3
24/10/09	Aust v Malaysia	3-1
26/10/09	Aust v Malaysia	2-2

TEST SERIES
PERTH, AUSTRALIA NOVEMBER, 2009

21/11/09	Aust v Spain	8-2
22/11/09	Aust v Spain	1-2

31ˢᵗ CHAMPIONS TROPHY MELBOURNE, AUSTRALIA DECEMBER, 2009

28/11/09	Aust v Korea	4-0
29/11/09	Aust v The Netherlands	7-2
01/12/09	Aust v England	2-1
03/12/09	Aust v Germany	1-3
05/12/09	Aust v Spain	10-3
06/12/09	Aust v Germany	5-3

2009 AUSTRALIA WIN – LOSS RECORD

Played	Won	Loss	Draw	For	Against
39	30	6	3	191	72

TEST SERIES HOBART, AUSTRALIA JANUARY, 2010

28/01/10	Aust v Korea	5-1
30/01/10	Aust v Korea	3-2
31/01/10	Aust v Korea	1-2

TEST SERIES PERTH, AUSTRALIA FEBRUARY, 2010

17/02/10	Aust v New Zealand	7-1
19/02/10	Aust v New Zealand	4-2

WORLD CUP XII NEW DELHI, INDIA MARCH, 2010

28/02/10	Aust v England	2-3
02/03/10	Aust v India	5-2
04/03/10	Aust v South Africa	12-0
06/03/10	Aust v Spain	2-0
08/03/10	Aust v Pakistan	2-1
11/03/10	Aust v The Netherlands	2-1
13/03/10	Aust v Germany	2-1

AZLAN SHAH IPOH, MALAYSIA MAY, 2010

07/05/10	Aust v Egypt	4-0
09/05/10	Aust v Malaysia	2-1
10/05/10	Aust v India	3-4
12/05/10	Aust v Pakistan	5-5
03/05/10	Aust v Korea	2-2
15/05/10	Aust v China	4-0
16/05/10	Aust v Malaysia	5-3

TEST MATCHES BRUSSELS, BELGIUM JULY, 2010

| 24/07/10 | Aust v Belgium | 7-2 |
| 27/07/10 | Aust v Belgium | 10-3 |

32nd CHAMPIONS TROPHY
MONCHENGLADBACH, GERMANY AUGUST, 2010

31/07/10	Aust v New Zealand	9-1
01/08/10	Aust v The Netherlands	6-3
03/08/10	Aust v England	3-2
05/08/10	Aust v Germany	3-1
07/08/10	Aust v Spain	3-1
08/08/10	Aust v England	4-0

TEST SERIES PERTH/SYDNEY, AUSTRALIA SEPTEMBER, 2010

04/09/10	Aust v Argentina	2-2
05/09/10	Aust v Argentina	3-0
11/09/10	Aust v Argentina	3-1
12/09/10	Aust v Argentina	5-2

COMMONWEALTH GAMES XIX NEW DELHI, INDIA OCTOBER, 2010

06/10/10	Aust v Scotland	9-0
07/10/10	Aust v India	5-2
09/10/10	Aust v Pakistan	1-0
10/10/10	Aust v Malaysia	7-0
12/10/10	Aust v New Zealand	6-2
04/10/10	Aust v India	8-0

2010 AUSTRALIA WIN – LOSS RECORD

Played	Won	Lost	Draw	For	Against
37	31	3	3	166	53

AZLAN SHAH KUALA LUMPUR, MALAYSIA MAY, 2011

06/05/11	Aust v Malaysia	2-1
08/05/11	Aust v India	1-1
09/05/11	Aust v Pakistan	5-1
11/05/11	Aust v Korea	4-2
12/05/11	Aust v Great Britain	2-1
14/05/11	Aust v New Zealand	4-2
15/05/11	Aust v Pakistan	3-2

TEST MATCHES BARCELONA, SPAIN JULY, 2011

14/07/11	Aust v Spain	3-2
16/07/11	Aust v Spain	3-0

FOUR NATIONS TOURNAMENT MONCHENGLADBACH, GERMANY   JULY, 2011

21/07/11	Aust v The Netherlands	1-6
23/07/11	Aust v Germany	3-1
24/07/11	Aust v Spain	1-2

FIVE NATIONS TOURNAMENT PARIS, FRANCE JULY, 2011

27/07/11	Aust v Ireland	4-2
28/07/11	Aust v Argentina	2-3
30/07/11	Aust v Korea	4-4
31/07/11	Aust v France	6-2

OCEANIA CUP VII HOBART, AUSTRALIA OCTOBER, 2011

06/10/11	Aust v New Zealand	0-3
08/10/11	Aust v New Zealand	3-3
09/10/11	Aust v New Zealand	6-1

THREE NATIONS SERIES WESTERN AUSTRALIA OCTOBER, 2011

26/10/11	Aust v India	8-3
27/10/11	Aust v Pakistan	3-1
30/10/11	Aust v Pakistan	8-2
31/10/11	Aust v India	5-0
03/11/11	Aust v Pakistan	3-4

33rd CHAMPIONS TROPHY AUCKLAND, NEW ZEALAND DECEMBER, 2011

03/12/11	Aust v Spain	3-2
05/12/11	Aust v Great Britain	4-1
06/12/11	Aust v Pakistan	6-1
08/12/11	Aust v The Netherlands	4-2
10/12/11	Aust v New Zealand	2-1
11/12/11	Aust v Spain	1-0

2011 AUSTRALIA WIN _ LOSS RECORD

Played	Won	Lost	Draw	For	Against
30	23	4	3	104	56

KOOKABURRA CUP PERTH, AUSTRALIA FEBRUARY, 2012

10/02/12	Aust v Argentina	3-1
12/02/12	Aust v The Netherlands	3-1
16/02/12	Aust v The Netherlands	2-1
18/02/12	Aust v The Netherlands	1-0
20/02/12	Aust v Argentina	4-0

TEST SERIES WOOLLONGONG, AUSTRALIA MARCH, 2012

24/03/12	Aust v China	10-1
25/03/12	Aust v China	10-0
27/03/12	Aust v China	7-0

TEST SERIES CANBERRA, AUSTRALIA MARCH/APRIL, 2012

29/03/12	Aust v Japan	3-1
31/03/12	Aust v Japan	3-0
01/04/12	Aust v Japan	7-1

VISA OG TEST EVENT LONDON, ENGLAND MAY, 2012

02/05/12	Aust v India	3-0
03/05/12	Aust v Germany	2-3
05/05/12	Aust v Great Britain	3-3
06/05/12	Aust v Germany	2-5

EUROPEAN TOUR ANTWERP, BELGIUM MAY, 2012

09/05/12	Aust v Belgium	8-2
11/05/12	Aust v Belgium	5-1

EUROPEAN TOUR MANNHEIM, GERMANY MAY, 2012

15/05/12	Aust v Germany	3-0
16/05/12	Aust v Germany	2-1

TEST SERIES PERTH, AUSTRALIA JUNE, 2012

08/06/12	Aust v Korea	2-0
10/06/12	Aust v Korea	2-0
12/06/12	Aust v Korea	5-1
13/06/12	Aust v Korea	2-2

TEST SERIES CAIRNS, AUSTRALIA JUNE, 2012

22/06/12	Aust v New Zealand	6-1
23/06/12	Aust v New Zealand	5-1
25/06/12	Aust v New Zealand	4-1

OLYMPICS LONDON, ENGLAND JULY-AUGUST 2012

30/07/12	Aust v South Africa	6-0
01/08/12	Aust v Spain	5-0
03/08/12	Aust v Argentina	2-2
05/08/12	Aust v Great Britain	3-3
07/08/12	Aust v Pakistan	7-0
09/08/12	Aust v Germany	2-4
11/08/12	Aust v Great Britain	3-1

34th CHAMPIONS TROPHY MELBOURNE, AUSTRALIA DECEMBER, 2012

01/12/12	Aust v Belgium	4-2
02/12/12	Aust v The Netherlands	0-0
04/12/12	Aust v Pakistan	1-0
06/12/12	Aust v England	2-0
08/12/12	Aust v India	3-0
09/12/12	Aust v The Netherlands	2-1

2012 AUSTRALIA WIN – LOSS RECORD

Played	Won	Lost	Draw	For	Against
39	31	3	5	146	44

AZLAN SHAH IPOH, MALAYSIA MARCH, 2013

09/03/13	Aust v India	4-3
10/03/13	Aust v Pakistan	6-0
12/03/13	Aust v Malaysia	1-1
14/03/13	Aust v Korea	3-3
16/03/13	Aust v New Zealand	3-2
17/03/13	Aust v Malaysia	3-2

TEST SERIES PERTH, AUSTRALIA MAY, 2013

03/05/13	Aust v Korea	0-0
05/05/13	Aust v Korea	5-2
07/05/13	Aust v Korea	3-3
09/05/13	Aust v Korea	4-1

TEST MATCHES ROTTERDAM, THE NETHERLANDS JUNE, 2013

05/06/13	Aust v The Netherlands	3-1
08/06/13	Aust v The Netherlands	5-1

TEST ANTWERP, BELGIUM JUNE, 2013

09/06/13	Aust v Belgium	2-2

WORLD LEAGUE SEMI-FINAL ROTTERDAM, THE NETHERLANDS JUNE, 2013

14/06/13	Aust v Belgium	1-3
15/06/13	Aust v Spain	5-2
17/06/13	Aust v France	7-1
20/06/13	Aust v India	5-1
21/06/13	Aust v The Netherlands	4-3
23/06/13	Aust v Belgium	2-2

*(Belgium won in shootout)

TEST MATCHES PERTH, AUSTRALIA OCTOBER, 2013

22/10/13	Aust v Argentina	8-1
24/10/13	Aust v Pakistan	4-2

OCEANIA CUP VIII TARANAKI, NEW ZEALAND OCTOBER, 2013

30/10/13	Aust v Samoa	32-0
21/10/13	Aust v New Zealand	3-1
02/11/13	Aust v Papua New Guinea	16-0
03/11/13	Aust v New Zealand	5-2

2013 AUSTRALIA WIN – LOSS RECORD

Played	Won	Lost	Draw	For	Against
25	18	2*	5	134	39

*(Game decided on penalties)

WORLD LEAGUE FINAL NEW DELHI, INDIA JANUARY, 2014

10/01/14	Aust v Belgium	3-2
11/01/14	Aust v The Netherlands	0-1
13/01/14	Aust v Argentina	6-1
15/01/14	Aust v India	7-2
17/01/14	Aust v The Netherlands	3-4
18/01/14	Aust v England	1-2

AZLAN SHAH CUP IPOH, MALAYSIA MARCH, 2014

13/03/14	Aust v China	7-0
16/03/14	Aust v Canada	6-0
17/03/14	Aust v South Africa	7-0
20/03/14	Aust v Korea	5-1
22/03/14	Aust v Malaysia	6-2
23/03/14	Aust v Malaysia	8-3

TEST MATCHES PERTH, AUSTRALIA APRIL, 2014

17/04/14	Aust v New Zealand	4-1
19/04/14	Aust v New Zealand	1-1

TEST MATCHES MARLOWE, ENGLAND MAY, 2014

24/05/14	Aust v England	2-1
25/05/14	Aust v England	3-1

WORLD CUP XII THE HAGUE, THE NETHERLANDS MAY/JUNE, 2014

31/05/14	Aust v Malaysia	4-0
02/06/14	Aust v Spain	3-0
05/06/14	Aust v Belgium	3-1
07/06/14	Aust v England	5-0
09/06/15	Aust v India	4-0
13/06/14	Aust v Argentina	5-1
15/06/14	Aust v The Netherlands	6-1

2014 AUSTRALIA WIN – LOSS RECORD until June 2014

Played	Won	Lost	Draw	For	Against
23	19	3	1	99	25

APPENDIX 4
KOOKABURRA PLAYERS
2009-2014

Abbott	Des	2009-2012
Bates	Tim	2010, 2013
Bausor	Chris	2011, 2013
Bazeley	George	2009-2014
Beale	Daniel	2013-2014
Begbie	Graeme	2009-2010, 2012
Boyne	Craig	2013-2014
Brown	Kiel	2009-2014
Budgeon	Nick	2013-2014
Burcher	Ian	2009-2011
Burgers	Nathan	2009-2012
Butturini	Matthew	2009-2013
Carroll	Joel	2009-2014
Charlesworth	Jonathon	2009, 2011-2012
Charter	Andrew	2011-2014
Ciriello	Chris	2009-2014
Clemons	Tristan	2011, 2013
Dancer	Brent	2009-2012
Deavin	Tim	2010-2014
De Young	Liam	2009-2014
Doerner	Luke	2009-2012
Dwyer	Jamie	2009-2014
Edwards	Jeremy	2013-2014
Ford	Russell	2009-2014
Gohdes	Matt	2009-2014
Govers	Kieran	2010-2014
Guest	David	2009

Hammond	Rob	2009-2014
Hayward	Jeremy	2014
Kavanagh	Fergus	2009-2014
Kemp	Malcolm	2010
Knowles	Mark	2009-2014
Livermore	Brent	2009-2010
Lovell	Tyler	2013-2014
Matheson	Eli	2009
Meadows	Ross	2009-2010
Miller	Josh	2013
Mirecki	Daniel	2013
Mitton	Trent	2010-2014
Ockenden	Eddie	2009-2014
Orchard	Simon	2009-2014
Paterson	Mark	2009-2012
Philpott	Andrew	2013-2014
Schubert	Grant	2009-2010
Simpson	Glenn	2009-2014
Swann	Matthew	2009-2014
Turner	Glenn	2009-2014
Whetton	Jacob	2011-2014
White	Tristan	2011-2014
Wickham	Tom	2013
Willis	Matthew	2013-2014
Wilson	Jason	2009-2014
Zalewski	Aran	2011, 2013-2014

APPENDIX 5

World Cup Final June 15 2014

My sheet used on the day…GOT and notes for in-game plan.

APPENDIX 6

Kookaburras 'Way of Playing' guidelines for the World Cup developed during the year 2014

PRESSURE	Relentlessness (70 mins). Intercepts. Press tone and Energy (set up)
CALM	Clear... Alert... Looking... Measured (Calculated Risks). Decisive actions Look long - pass well
HELP-SIDE ACTION	With ball attack and defence. Without ball defence and attack
BALL SPEED	Change ownership. Tempo. Tone and energy to create opportunities
TOUGH	Resilient DADD Contest winning (50/50). Desperation.
GIF	Att (Circle Post) Def (IFIT) MF (Post)
FLEXIBILITY	Positioning. Awareness of transition. "Never out of position when we have ball."
CIRCLE EFFICIENCY	PCA/PCD. Attacking outcomes. Perimeter protection. Inside Circle. Tackling and Intercepts
NON NEGOTIABLES	Essential skills RIC, RW, IRB, Run back, H/L Desperation to make a difference

What some of the acronyms mean…

CALM	Clear-Alert-Looking-Measured.
DADD	Down-Alert-Diving-Desperate.
PCA	Penalty corner attack.
PCD	Penalty corner defence.
IFIT	In Front and in Touch.
RIC	Run in Case!
RW	Run With…
IRB	Intelligent Running Back.
H/L	Hot Line (the line between the ball and the goal).

APPENDIX 7

Match sheet for the day. June 15 2014…my last game as coach.

Rabobank Hockey World Cup 2014 (M)
31 May - 15 June 2014
The Hague, Netherlands

Match Report

Match #	Date	Time	Pool / Class	Pitch
38	15 Jun	15:15	Final	K

AUS - Australia

Full Time	6 - 1
Half Time	2 - 1

NED - Netherlands

Minute	Shirt #	Name	Green	Yellow	Red
X	1	DWYER Jamie			
4	2	DE YOUNG Liam			
X	3	ORCHARD Simon		50	
7	4	TURNER Glenn	41		
X	5	CIRIELLO Chris			
8	6	HAMMOND Robert	57		
X	9	KNOWLES Mark (C)			
X	11	OCKENDEN Eddie			
3	12	WHETTON Jacob			
X	16	GOHDES Matt			
X	17	ZALEWSKI Aran			
X	19	DEAVIN Timothy			
4	20	SWANN Matthew			
68	24	LOVELL Tyler (GK)			
X	27	GOVERS Kieran			
X	30	CHARTER Andrew (GK)			
X	31	KAVANAGH Fergus			
5	32	HAYWARD Jeremy			
Coach		CHARLESWORTH Ric			

Minute	Shirt #	Name	Green	Yellow	Red
X	1	STOCKMANN Jaap (GK)			
10	3	van der LINDEN Floris			
7	4	VERMEULEN Klaas			
8	5	BALKESTEIN Marcel			
X	7	JOLIE Wouter			
X	8	BAKKER Billy			
X	10	VERGA Valentin			
5	11	HERTZBERGER Jeroen			
X	12	KEMPERMAN Robbert		50	
X	13	BAART Sander			
8	20	GALEMA Jelle			
X	22	HOFMAN Rogier			
X	23	de WIJN Sander	41		
X	24	van der HORST Robert (C)			
X	25	van ASS Seve			
	26	BLAAK Pirmin (GK)			
8	27	JONKER Constantijn			
X	30	van der WEERDEN Mink			
Coach		van ASS Paul			

REID Graham — Team Manager

van HEESWIJK Maarten — Team Manager

WRIGHT John (RSA) — Umpire

STAGNO Nathan (GIB) — Umpire

NAPIER Helen (NZL) — Judge

STEWART Tony (CAN) — Judge

ISBERG Björn (SWE) — Technical Officer

BLASCH Christian (GER) — Reserve Umpire

Team	Minute	Number	Action	Score		Team	Minute	Number	Action	Score		Team	Minute	Number	Action	Score
NED	14	11	FG	0 - 1												
AUS	20	5	PC	1 - 1												
AUS	24	27	FG	2 - 1												
AUS	37	4	FG	3 - 1												
AUS	47	5	PC	4 - 1												
AUS	53	5	PC	5 - 1												
AUS	64	1	FG	6 - 1												

Official Result

Tournament Director McCRACKEN Jason (NZL)

Page 1 of 1
Generated 15 Jun 2014 14:56

Copyright © 2014 - International Hockey Federation
Altius

ACKNOWLEDGEMENTS

This book was not finalised until about August 2016 after more than a year of contemplation plus a year of writing.

My thanks to my wife Carmen whose word processing and organisational skill brought it to fruition along with long time friend David Hatt who provided valuable advice, support and at times ruthless criticism. David's editorial oversight was pivotal in cleaning the manuscript.

Julie-Ann Harper, at Pickawoowoo, and her team in the South West were central to getting the job done and provided crucial input once our publishing pathway was finalised.

All the players in the teams I coached and assistant coaches and support staff are of course the central characters in this book. Without their effort, passion and contributions our teams would not have been able to do so well and our game would not be so dynamic and engaging.

Dan Carson generously and graciously provided many of the photographs in the book. For over a decade he has been a wonderful supporter of our game and our teams.

Corinne Reid has written with great clarity about her perspective on team sport and her time with our teams. Her chapters contain some of the best writing on the dynamics of team building and coaching. Her contribution has been invaluable.

Alfred Holland and his wife Joy have graciously allowed me to tell the story of the tragic loss of their son in 1977 in my chapter 'Vigilance'. I thank them for that.

Finally, I am grateful for the endorsement I received from Wayne Bennett, our country's most decorated senior coach and Justin Langer, a young emerging tyro who will go far.

Credits for quotes

Page 176, Chad Harbach quoted in *The Art of Fielding*, Little Brown and Company, New York 2011 p257

Page 162, Kerry O'Brien quoted Paul Keating in *Keating*, Allen and Unwin, Sydney, 2015 p341

INDEX OF NAMES